£9.99

ROUTLEDGE ·
GENERAL EDITO

G000152087

D.H. LAWRENCE
Selected Poetry and Non-fictional Prose

ROUTLEDGE · ENGLISH · TEXTS
GENERAL EDITOR · JOHN DRAKAKIS

WILLIAM BLAKE: *Selected Poetry and Prose* ed. David Punter
EMILY BRONTË: *Wuthering Heights* ed. Heather Glen
JOHN CLARE: *Selected Poetry and Prose* ed. Merryn and Raymond Williams
JOSEPH CONRAD: *Selected Literary Criticism and The Shadow-Line* ed.
  Allan Ingram
CHARLES DICKENS: *Hard Times* ed. Terry Eagleton
JOHN DONNE: *Selected Poetry and Prose* ed. T. W. and R. J. Craik
GEORGE ELIOT: *The Mill on The Floss* ed. Sally Shuttleworth
HENRY FIELDING: *Joseph Andrews* ed. Stephen Copley
BEN JONSON: *The Alchemist* ed. Peter Bement
ANDREW MARVELL: *Selected Poetry and Prose* ed. Robert Wilcher
JOHN MILTON: *Selected Poetry and Prose* ed. Tony Davies
WILFRED OWEN: *Selected Poetry and Prose* ed. Jennifer Breen
ALEXANDER POPE: *Selected Poetry and Prose* ed. Robin Sowerby
PERCY BYSSHE SHELLEY: *Selected Poetry and Prose* ed. Alasdair Macrae
WILLIAM WORDSWORTH: *Selected Poetry and Prose* ed. Philip Hobsbaum

Forthcoming

Geoffrey Chaucer   *The Wife of Bath's Prologue and Tale and*
                          The Clerk's Prologue and Tale ed. Marion
                          Wynne-Davies
Gerard Manley Hopkins   *Selected Poetry and Prose* ed. R.J. Watt
James Joyce   *Dubliners* ed. Stan Smith
Christopher Marlowe   *Dr Faustus* ed. John Drakakis
Mary Shelley   *Frankenstein* ed. Patrick Lyons
Edmund Spenser   *The Faerie Queene Book 1 and Selected*
                          Poems ed. Elizabeth Watson
Virginia Woolf   *To the Lighthouse* ed. Sandra Kemp
W. B. Yeats   *Selected Poetry and Prose* ed. Graham
                          Martin

D.H. LAWRENCE

Selected Poetry and Non-fictional Prose

Edited by John Lucas

ROUTLEDGE · LONDON AND NEW YORK

My thanks to Dr Ian Clarke, for helpful suggestions; to Heather Rees, for her criticisms and impeccable typing; and to Pauline, as always.

John Lucas

First published 1990
by Routledge
11 New Fetter Lane,
London EC4P 4EE

Introduction, Critical Commentary and Notes
© 1991 John Lucas

Typeset in 10/12 pt Bem
by Colset Pte. Ltd., Singapore
Printed in Great Britain by
Clays Ltd, St. Ives plc

British Library Cataloguing in
Publication Data

Lawrence, D. H. (David Herbert), 1885–1930
D. H. Lawrence: selected poetry and
   non-fictional prose.
I. Title II. Lucas, John
828'.809

ISBN 0–415–01429–8

Library of Congress Cataloging in
Publication Data also available

Contents

Unless otherwise indicated, all the works listed are by Lawrence.

Introduction

Writing to a friend in February 1914, Lawrence characteristically grumbled that 'In England people have got that loathsome superior knack of refusing to consider me a poet at all: "Your prose is so good," say the kind fools, "that we are obliged to forgive you your poetry." How I hate them.'[1] Lawrence is exaggerating. He knew perfectly well that his *Love Poems and Others* had been favourably received. Edward Thomas called it 'the book of the moment', and for Ezra Pound it was 'the most important book of poems of the season'.[2] Yet it is probably true to say that now, nearly sixty years after his death, Lawrence is best known for his prose fiction. This is not to be wondered at. He is, after all, a great novelist and short-story writer. But the fiction looms so massively that it seems to have dimmed if it hasn't obscured his other achievements: as playwright, social and literary critic, and poet. It is as though so complete a man of letters cannot be allowed to succeed in everything he sets his hand to. And it is of course true that although major novelists have often tried to write in a different literary mode they have seldom succeeded. I think, for example, of Henry James's plays, or of George Eliot's poetry. Yet the rule is by no means absolute. There are Chekhov's stories, Emily Brontë's poems. There are, too, the poems of D.H. Lawrence.

Lawrence's career as a poet divides naturally into four quite distinct phases. The first occupies the years up to 1912, and comes to an end with the publication of *Love Poems and Others* in February 1913. When he put together the body of his poems for a collected edition, Lawrence recalled this early period with wry detachment. 'A young man is afraid of his demon,' he noted, 'and puts his hand over the demon's mouth sometimes and speaks for him. And the things the young man says are very rarely

1

poetry.' Lawrence offers this as a reason for rewriting many of the early poems. 'I have tried to let the demon say his say.'[3] Whether the rewritten poems effectively whip away the restraining hand is not a matter I want to pursue here, although by way of an appendix I print the later version of 'The Wild Common', one of the earliest of Lawrence's poems. But it is at least arguable that this talk of fear of the demon is misleading. The early poems are muffled less by fear than by technical inadequacies.

Inadequacy may not seem to be the right word. Lawrence's early poems are not noticeably inferior to much verse that was appearing in England during the opening decade of the twentieth century. But that is the point. In this early work, Lawrence can look to be little different from a dozen or so of the poets whose reputations, then high, have now sunk below the horizon. This is perhaps inevitable. Any young writer will begin by trying on the styles that seem most available. It takes time to discover, or to have the courage to recognize, that what is available isn't necessarily what is best or, more to the point, appropriate. Auden put the matter succinctly when he remarked of Lawrence's early poems that 'one is continually struck by the originality of the sensibility and the conventionality of the expressive means. . . . [Lawrence] learned quite soon to let his demon speak, but it took him a long time to find the appropriate style for him to speak in.'[4]

Lawrence is at his most conventional – and awkward – when he works within the bonds of rhyme and regular metre. This is so obvious that there is no point in spending time on it. Nor is there much to be gained by complaining that he chafed against these bonds, and then reproving him for his rashness and impatience in breaking free of them. As Auden brilliantly observes:

> The difference between formal and free verse may be likened to the difference between carving and modelling; the formal poet, that is to say, thinks of the poem he is writing as something already latent in the language which he has to reveal, while the free verse poet thinks of language as a plastic passive medium upon which he imposes his artistic conception. One might also say that, in their attitude towards art, the formal verse writer is a catholic, the free verse writer a protestant. And Lawrence was, in every respect, very protestant indeed.[5]

The rashness and impatience, ignorantly and obtusely deplored by such poet critics as R.P. Blackmur and C.H. Sisson, are precisely those qualities which make it possible for Lawrence to snap what for him were the improper constraints of formal verse. Graham Hough's remark on Blackmur's essay is definitive. 'From its own point of view it leaves nothing to be said. Yet at the end the essence of Lawrence's poetry is no more discernible than it was at the beginning.' Sisson claims that 'Lawrence was temperamentally well suited to breaking away from the shackles of post-Victorian poetics, but he lacked the reticence, and the ear, for achieving a satisfactory new form.'[6] To say of the author of 'Sorrow' that he lacked reticence, and that the man who wrote 'Gloire de Dijon' lacked an ear, is so wide of the mark as to be heroic in its perversity. The fact is that Lawrence was dissatisfied with formal properties because they could not help him to produce the poems he sensed were struggling for expression. This is only to be expected of the writer who famously instructed J.B. Pinker to 'tell Arnold Bennett that all rules of construction hold good only for novels which are copies of other novels. A book which is not a copy of other books has its own construction.'[7]

And yet, constrained as many of the poems of Lawrence's first volume undoubtedly are, we have already seen that the more discerning reviewers of *Love Poems and Others* were quick to recognize its strengths. Both Pound and Thomas saluted Lawrence's use of dialect. This is undoubtedly important, in the first place because dialect is a means of redeeming the language from the deadening effects of orthodox or standard English, in the second because it gives utterance and therefore visibility to English people whose manner of speaking is held by orthodoxy not to be 'English' and hence not serious. It is of course true that dialect poetry can be or be made to seem 'quaint'. And it is no accident that 'quaint' became a vogue word of the period. Initially applied to the eclectic manner of contemporary architecture which, in its pastiches of earlier styles – Tudor, Queen Anne – offered to reinstate a vanished past, it then became attached to any cultural artefact which could be regarded as somehow free from the taint of contemporaneity.

Lawrence's dialect poetry is not quaint. It is vivid, eloquent, and it takes its speakers with due seriousness. On the other hand, there is not much of it, and the explanation for *this* can be traced to Lawrence's deep need to break away from home. Here, he is very much part of a wide movement that may be said to have existed on an almost universal scale at the end of the

3

nineteenth century: of the revolt of the sons (and occasionally daughters) against the fathers. In Lawrence's case, however, this is additionally complicated by his complex feelings towards the mother. This is the subject of *Sons and Lovers*. It is also the subject of several of the best poems of *Love Poems and Others*. In his invaluable essay on Lawrence in *The Shaping Spirit*, A. Alvarez singles out 'End of Another Home-Holiday' as perhaps the best of the early poems. As he says, 'the difficulty is in the state of mind: the pull between love and guilt, the tension between man and child'.[8] This is memorably stated in the following lines:

> Love is the great Asker,
> The sun and the rain do not ask the secret
> Of the time when the grain struggles down in the dark.
> The moon walks her lonely way without anguish,
> Because no loved one grieves over her departure.

Vegetative growth is different from human development, and yet the tug towards light is as powerful in the human as in the vegetative. For Lawrence to feel impelled towards such an image indicates that, for all its nourishing warmth, home is an experience which has to be outgrown. So that when, immediately after these lines, he says: 'Forever, ever by my shoulder pitiful Love will linger, / Crouching as little houses crouch under the mist when I turn', it is as though we are to read Love as having rightful claims on him and at the same time expecting rejection, even violent rejection ('linger, / Crouching' – the effect of those two words is to suggest that love is determined to hang on, even though it may be spurned by a blow, rather as an animal is, or, of course, a beaten woman). The 'little houses' implies a further complex of feelings: affection and irritation, loving familiarity and condescension. They have outgrown their usefulness or their capacity to sustain him. This all feels powerfully authentic and imaginatively very intelligent.

The image of the moon is, however, a good deal more conventional. In the act of denying a pathetic fallacy – 'With how sad steps, O Moon' – it virtually reinstates it. As soon as you talk of the moon walking 'her lonely way', with or without anguish, you invite consideration of the plight of the poet himself, and this is surely self-pitying? If so, it is the price one has to pay for what is most original about these early poems, which, as Edward

Thomas noted, has to do with 'matters which cannot be subdued to conventional rhythm and rhyme – chiefly the intense thoughts, emotions, or gropings of self-conscious men or women set on edge by love or fatigue or solitude'. And Thomas adds, with memorable exactness, 'If he trusts to make a general appeal, it is by faithful concentration on the particular.'[9]

Still, the general appeal doesn't often make its appearance in these early poems. In sharp contrast, the concentration on the particular is so often and so remarkably evident as to make it obvious that, whatever their flaws, the poems are the work of a great writer. I think, for example, of the springily playful rhythms of 'A Baby Running Barefoot': 'When the bare feet of the baby beat across the grass / The little white feet nod like white flowers in the wind', which is as far from saccharine coyness as may be, especially in the rippling humour of the stressed assonances, and the tactile alertness of 'her little bare feet in my hands, / Cool like syringa buds, / Firm and silken like pink young peony flowers'. Reading this, you realize why the imagists were so keen to claim Lawrence as one of their own, just as the Georgian poets had been. Whatever their differences, both groups saw themselves as breaking out of the bad habits of much Edwardian poetry, the Georgians in their desire to find their subject-matter in what might be called the dailiness of things, the imagists in their determination to cut away the fat of poetic language and to produce for contemplation the bare-bone thing in itself, whatever that thing happened to be.

The title 'Georgian Poetry' was dreamed up in 1912 by Edward Marsh, at that time secretary to Winston Churchill at the Admiralty. Marsh was a connoisseur of the arts and a friend of Rupert Brooke. Together, they 'conceived the idea of issuing a collection of modern poems aimed at disturbing modern lethargy and bringing to general attention the existence of a body of unrecognised talent'.[10] The first volume, *Georgian Poetry, 1911–1912*, appeared at the end of the latter year, and included one poem by Lawrence, 'Snap-Dragon'. A brief prefatory note famously claimed that the anthology was issued 'in the belief that English poetry is once again putting on new strength and beauty'. Lawrence apart, the volume included poems by W. H. Davies, of whom Lawrence at first approved, James Elroy Flecker, of whom he didn't, Wilfrid Gibson, Ralph Hodgson, and others with whom he had little enough in common. A letter to Edward Marsh, written in October 1913, makes it clear that Lawrence has already moved well beyond the limits of Georgian poetry, even though he allowed Marsh to put more of his work into *Georgian Poetry, 1913–1915*. Davies, he tells Marsh, now makes him furious.

> It isn't as if he were a passionate writer, writing his 'agon'. Oh my God, he's like teaching a bull-finch to talk. I think one ought to be downright cruel to him, and drive him back: say to him 'Davies, your work is getting like Birmingham tinware: Davies, you drop your h's, and everybody is tempering the wind to you, because you are a shorn lamb; Davies, your accent is intolerable in a carpeted room; Davies, you hang on like the mud on a lady's silk petticoat.' Then he might leave his Sevenoaks room, where he is rigged up as rural poet, proud of the gilt mirror and his romantic past: and he might grow his wings again, and chirrup a little sadder song.[11]

For Lawrence, in other words, the Georgians were woefully short of ambition. They were tame linnets.[12]

Like the Georgians, with whom they had precious little else in common, the imagists promoted themselves through a number of anthologies. In a period of anthologies and manifestos, of statements that announced new movements, and where the idea of the manifesto had come to be associated with revolt against the status quo, the imagist anthologies have to be seen as far more radical than those put together by Brooke and Marsh. The term 'imagist' or 'imagiste' seems to have been coined by Ezra Pound in the spring of 1912. Of H.D.'s (Hilda Doolittle's) poems he remarks that they are 'Objective – no slither; direct – no excessive use of adjectives, no metaphors that won't permit exaggeration'. As for her then husband Richard Aldington's poems, they provide 'interesting experiments in *vers libre*'. Pound described an image as 'that which presents an intellectual and emotional complex in an instant of time'. For F. S. Flint, an English poet who worked closely with Pound at this period, imagism was based on three rules:

1 direct treatment of the 'thing', whether subjective or objective
2 to use absolutely no word that did not contribute to presentation
3 as regarding rhythm: to compose in sequence of the musical phrase not in sequence of a metronome.

And Pound, with typically forceful didacticism, laid down some dos and don'ts for his fellow-imagists. 'Use no superfluous word. . . . Go in fear of abstraction. . . . Use no ornament. . . . Don't chop your stuff into separate iambs.'[13]

Both Georgianism and imagism were conceived of as necessary attempts to 'make it new'. Both gave some encouragement to Lawrence. In the first place, they published him.[14] In the second, they helped confirm him in his conviction as to the rightness of the way he wanted to go.

But it is not necessary to make too much of this. Thomas recognized that Lawrence's subject-matter is far more radical than anything to be found in the work of even the best Georgian poets. None of them explores with such troubling precision the kinds of emotion attendant on those relationships between mother and son which form the natural sequence that runs from 'End of Another Home-Holiday' by way of 'The Bride' and 'Sorrow' through to 'Piano'. And the best of the poems about school are unmatched by anything outside *The Rainbow*. As for the imagists, with the exception of Pound none of them has Lawrence's sense of rhythm or the sureness of his ear. Poems, as Mallarmé told Degas, are made with words not ideas, and at his best Lawrence knows this, too. At his worst, which is in many of the *Pansies*, he forgets what he knows and the result is slapdash and cacophonous. The *Pansies* often lack, Auden rightly noted, the conciseness of prose and the jollity of rhymed verse.[15]

One comes back, then, to Lawrence's need to break away from the constraints of formal verse. And in doing so one notices that it coincides with that other break – from home and its limitations. The two almost come together in 'The North Country'.

> Out of the sleep, from the gloom of motion, soundlessly, somnambule,
> Moans and booms the soul of a people imprisoned, asleep in the rule
> Of the strong machine that runs mesmeric, booming the spell of its word
> Upon them and moving them helpless, mechanic, their will to its will
> deferred.

The break isn't complete, as the ineptly managed syntax for the sake of rhyme here makes all too plain. And the large, unfocused claims about people in the North Country is accompanied by a Whitmanesque rhetoric that is almost parodic in effect if not in intention. It would be precisely this insistently vatic side of Whitman that Lawrence would speak out against. But there is no doubt that Whitman meant more to him than to any other poet. Whitman helped him in his breaking away. 'I sound my barbaric yawp over the roofs of the world.' That is Whitman at the end of 'Song of Myself', but it might almost be Lawrence speaking. Lawrence's song of the self involved him in the kinds of exploration, discovery, and assertion out of which much of his poetry comes. As with other young English writers at the end of the nineteenth century and the beginning of the twentieth, so with Lawrence: Whitman mattered supremely to them all, because it was Whitman who seemed most hearteningly to embody Blake's motto: 'Damn braces. Bless relaxes.' Homoerotic, democratic, always making for the open road, Whitman exemplified, positively and redeemingly, the revolt of the sons against the fathers. All this becomes very evident in the poems that Lawrence begins to write after the publication of *Love Poems and Others*.

II

The second phase of Lawrence's career as a poet covers roughly the period 1913–19 and includes the publication of *Look! We Have Come Through!* in December 1917. Bertrand Russell's remark about that volume is well known. 'They may have come through, but why should I look?' A possible answer might be that the poems explore and record with a rare fullness those 'intense thoughts, emotions, or gropings of self-conscious men or women' which Thomas had identified as so radically new in the subject-matter of Lawrence's earlier work. Yet to say this does not dispose of a problem. The poems of *Look! We Have Come Through!* are, as the insistent and slightly hysterical title makes plain, candidly autobiographical. As a result, they often feel more like fragments of life than poems. This is presumably at the back of Auden's confession that 'I find Lawrence's love poems embarrassing because of their lack of reticence; they make me feel like a Peeping Tom.'[16] Besides, there is about the sequence as a whole a lack of balance, a feeling that because these things happened to Lawrence they must be important. Of course, it *was* important to him that he was able to set up a relationship with Frieda Weekley. Frieda was the German-born wife of Ernest Weekley, Professor of German at Nottingham's University College. Lawrence and she met for the first time in April 1912, in Nottingham. The following month they went to Germany. As we shall see, partly at least through her intro-ducing him to liberationist ethics, Lawrence could proclaim his discovery of values beyond the prudential and, as he now saw it, life-denying greyness of England and the English. But with that comes a strident, unlovely insistence that people acknowledge what he has achieved. The title of the volume does not merely solicit our attention, it demands our admiration.

It is significant, then, that in a letter to Henry Savage, Lawrence should say that

> There is something wrong with Whitman, when he addresses American women as his Stalwart brides in whom he is to pour the seed for Stalwart Sons. One doesn't think like that. Imagine yourself addressing English women like that, in the mass. . . . Whitman is like a human document, or a wonderful treatise in human self revelation. It is neither art nor religion nor truth: just a self revelation of a man who could not live, and so had to write himself. But writing should come from a strong root of life: like a battle song after a battle. – And Whitman did this, more or less. But his battle was not a real battle: he never gave his individual self into the fight. . . . He never fought with another person.[17]

Lawrence is right to object to Whitman's abstractions, the unfocused generalizations of his worst writing. But it seems clear that the main inference Savage is to draw from the letter is that Lawrence *has* given his individual self into the fight. *His* self-revelation, *his* human document will, therefore, be of a man who *has* lived. And we have then to note that Lawrence is writing from Italy. The tone of his letter owes much to this. Like many English people before him, and like various of his contemporaries, Lawrence found in Italy a liberation from 'cold Albion'. I think of Byron and Shelley in Venice, of the Brownings in Florence, of Dorothea and Ladislaw in Rome. And in *A Room with a View*, E. M. Forster had allowed his young lovers in Florence to 'come through' to a celebration of the fact that 'love is of the body'. It is not that Lawrence is dependent on this tradition, rather that like other northern discoverers of the Mediterranean he is released into the warmth and light of the south and so discovers a new self. The tradition is well documented by John Pemble, in his *The Mediterranean Passion: Victorians and Edwardians in the South* (Oxford, 1987).

Lawrence's initial breakthrough had, though, occurred in Germany – the Germany to which Frieda had introduced him. It was a *particular* Germany: of free love, the cult of erotic emancipation, the dream of perfect candour made flesh. From that Germany Lawrence had written to his schoolteacher friend, Arthur McLeod: 'I am in love – and, my God, it's the greatest thing that can happen to a man. I tell you, find a woman you can fall in love with. *Do* it. *Let* yourself fall in love, if you haven't already. You are wasting your life. . . . Nowadays, men haven't the courage and the strength to love.' And

9

then, as if this weren't enough, he continues: 'Do you know, I don't think you were fond enough of me. I was very fond of you. But you don't trust yourself, and you don't trust other people. You won't let yourself be really fond, even of a man friend, for fear he will find out your weaknesses.'[18] As with the letter to Savage, this has an unpleasant note of bragging about it. *He* has the courage and strength to love, *he's* unafraid of revealing his weaknesses. In its apparent throwing off of puritan restraint this is very puritan. The stress on individual consciousness, on the authenticity of experience, is also nakedly egotistical. 'Look!'

Yet against this it has to be said that some of the poems in the sequence have about them a rapt attentiveness that isn't at all egotistical. 'Gloire de Dijon' may at first seem merely pictorial, a verbal transcription of a Bonnard painting, for example; but its apparently casual notation is deceptive, its rejoicing in the flesh unashamedly candid, replete with gratified desire.

> In the window full of sunlight
> Concentrates her golden shadow
> Fold on fold, until it glows as
> Mellow as the glory roses.

The unusual use of 'concentrates' as an intransitive verb beautifully suggests how the woman's golden shadow draws all light and energy into itself. (As though it *is* a concentrate: a dense, pure solution.) This sets up the deepening, enriching sounds that echo on from 'golden shadow': 'fold on fold, until it glows as / Mellow as the glory roses'. And the near rhyme of 'glows as / roses' delicately brushes the ear so as to prolong the lovely aural effect of the reversed rhyme 'shadow / glows as'. 'River Roses' is also most delicately composed, a rare example of Lawrence using full rhyme to good effect – in this case, to vivify a sensed wholeness, an emotional amplitude which defies prose analysis but which is undoubtedly there, in the poem.

There is a further point. 'Song of a Man Who Has Come Through' begins: 'Not I, not I, but the wind that blows through me! / A fine wind is blowing the new direction of Time.' There is more than a hint that this is an apocalyptic wind. Lawrence claims for himself a representative achievement. His breakthrough is both keenly registered as that of an individual and as at the same time part of something larger. What that something was can be inferred less from the poems of the period than from the letters and prose fiction and it is not to be pinned down by any formulaic statement. It does, however, have much to do with the entry into new worlds, both inner and outer; and it was undoubtedly prompted by Lawrence's discovery of life beyond the English bounds in which he had previously been confined. But then there is a sense in which his life is one of ceaseless discoveries, of breaking beyond bounds, of transgressing limits. In a beautiful, chirpy late letter, he told the young David Chambers: 'Whatever I forget, I shall never forget the Haggs – I loved it so. I loved to come to you all, it really was a new life began in me there.'[19] What some have condemned as rashness or imprudence is better seen as the evidence of Lawrence's eager desire for testing 'new life'.

In this he was by no means alone. The searching for 'new life' is very much a part of modernism. That is to say, it belongs to that prolonged moment across Europe when impatience with an ageing and perhaps decadent civilization led to a number of very differently expressed desires to overthrow it or at all events to liberate energies which under it had been lost or repressed. *Avant-garde: the vanguard*: these terms indicate the storm-troopers of an advancing army. The vanguard originally meant 'the leading division or units of an army'. Avant-garde came to mean 'those artists, writers, musicians, etc., whose techniques and ideas are markedly experimental or in advance of those generally accepted'. In the late years of the nineteenth century and the early years of the twentieth century the avant-garde included in its ranks cubists, expressionists, psychiatrists and anti-psychiatrists, anarchists, socialists, futurists, exponents of erotic emancipation. For all their differences, they had one thing in common: they were sons in revolt against their fathers. In Lawrence's case much of this revolt centres on his relationship with Frieda. The nature of the revolt rooted in Lawrence's life and work is essentially protestant in spirit. As no serious commentator on him has failed to point out, he was preoccupied with the idea of Apocalypse from the days of his childhood attendance at the Eastwood Congregationalist bethel. Millenarian thought is deep within all types of nonconformity, but it is often tempered to fit the social experiences of suffering and rejection. Nonconformist hymns are remarkable for their imagery of blood and wounds, and these are seen as badges borne as Christian witness. Suffer now and store up future rewards: that is the message implicit in such imagery. It can also, of course, be seen as a crucial aspect of that labourist defeatism which socialist historians argue affects the English working class after 1848. The cultural expression of this defeatism is the culture of consolation.

Lawrence was passionately opposed to such a culture. He hated the religion of humility, of willy wet-legs, of people conspiring in their own degradation. It is notable that in his essay 'Hymns in a Man's Life' he looks back with gratitude to his Congregational upbringing and especially to those hymns he calls 'healthy'. They are 'martial hymns': 'Fight the Good Fight', for example, and 'Sound the Battle-Cry'. The fight is to build a new world, not in heaven, but on earth: its name is variously Canaan, Moab, Jerusalem, and it shines with the promise of the unfamiliar. At the end of his essay he recalls that 'Thirty-six years ago men, even Sunday School teachers, still believed in the fight for life and the fun of it.' At the time he wrote that sentence he was working on his essay, 'Apocalypse'. There, he remarks that 'We ought to dance with rapture that we should be alive and in the flesh, and part of the living, incarnate cosmos.' Lawrence's revolt is always a great kick at misery, a passionate refusal to submit to the way things are. Submission denies the authenticity of individual experience, of how and what a man *feels*. Lawrence's insistence on the authenticity of experience is also very protestant, which is why Auden is right to say that he was 'in every respect, very protestant indeed'. And it is why Frieda was so crucial in his life.

This needs some explanation. I do not mean to imply that she alone liberated him. It is rather that in committing himself to her, Lawrence eagerly accepted exogamy as a means of journeying beyond the familiar. This marks a deep break with 'little houses'. Frieda necessarily opened him up to a new life. It is this which so deeply engages him in the relationship between Tom Brangwen and Lydia Lensky which he explores in the first section of *The Rainbow*. 'He seemed to live thus in contact with her, in contact with the unknown, the unaccountable and incalculable' (Chapter 2). Herself part of the avant-garde, Frieda was a powerful liberating force. Both before her marriage to Ernest Weekley and after it, she had been involved in a number of passionate love affairs. The most important of these was with Otto Gross, for whom she nearly left her husband. Gross was a political and social radical whose detestation for the Austria-Hungary in which he had grown up was total. He had chosen the life of anarchist for himself. He scorned the possession of private property, whether animate or inanimate. His cult of eroticism took for granted the outlawing of possessive jealousy. He set up a kind of anti-psychiatry, in which 'psychoanalysis was called upon to make men capable of freedom, to create a ferment of revolution within the psyche, against the dominant ego'. According to Martin Green, 'Frieda wrote Otto, *Du Bist Erotik*, and it was an ideological statement, with behind it a belief in eroticism as a philosophical and metaphysical value, as, above all, a life-creating value.' Green also notes that Frieda, the favourite among Gross's followers, 'found in D.H. Lawrence the man she was ready to commit herself to, as artist and husband. She told him he was of the same kind as Otto and Frick, and she had plans for Lawrence and Frick to collaborate together.' 'Frick' is Ernest Frick, an anarchist and associate of Gross's, who in 1912 went on trial for a bomb outrage in Zurich,[20] and with whom Frieda had also been erotically involved.

The physical and spiritual centre for this group of utopian anarchists was Ascona, a small Swiss-lake village. Lawrence visited it in September 1913, when he was walking from Bavaria over the Alps to Italy. In the course of that journey he came upon a group of Italian anarchists. Recalling the episode in *Twilight in Italy*, he admits to feeling in their leader 'a new spirit . . . something strange and pure and slightly frightening'.[21] We shall see later that Lawrence tries to confront this complex feeling in 'Hibiscus and Salvia Flowers'. Here, we need to note only that his intense individualism made him distrust the anarchists as conceivably linked together by an abstract programme which denied the very freedom they claimed to champion. Lawrence was with the anarchists in their contempt of prudential values, private ownership, greyness. But: '*noli me tangere*.' For all that Lawrence was occasionally attracted to the dream of an ideal community, he instinctively drew back from the idea of the group, of *any* group, and, beyond this, of those larger communities that made up the old world from which he wanted to escape. As matters turned out, however, he was soon to become inescapably thrown back on the old world.

In August 1914, the Great War began. Lawrence, by now once again in England, suddenly found himself immured in a country whose war mania he would not share, but which took away his freedom and treated his wife and himself as dangerous persons. (Frieda's German name was enough to convince more than one of their neighbours that they must be enemy spies.) The war was a denial of individuality. Lawrence wrote to Lady Cynthia Asquith in November 1915, that 'The spirit of war is, that I am a unit. . . . If I love, then, I am in direct opposition to the principle of war. If war prevails, I do not love.'[22] The war was to prevail for a further three years,

years that have been called Lawrence's 'Nightmare'.[23] During them he wrote comparatively little poetry, and the poems he did manage to write are not among his best work.

Then came the armistice. The Lawrences were free to leave England. In Chapter 12 of *Kangaroo*, written in 1922, but the first part of which is about the war years, Lawrence has his protagonist, Somers, look back at the south coast as he and his wife sail away.

> It was a cold day. There was snow on the Downs like a shroud. And as he looked back from the boat, when they had left Folkestone behind and only England was there, England looked like a grey, a dreary-grey coffin sinking in the sea behind, with her dead grey cliffs and the white, worn-out cloth of snow above.

That this was Lawrence's own feeling, there can be no doubt. In his autobiography, *The Flowers of the Forest*, David Garnett recalls Lawrence haranguing a group of friends who had gathered to celebrate the signing of the armistice. 'Europe is done for: England most of all the countries. This war isn't over. Even if the fighting should stop, the evil will be worse because the hate will be dammed up in men's hearts and will show itself in all sorts of ways which will be worse than war.'[24] Lawrence's detestation was certainly intensified by his deep loathing for those who had treated his wife and himself so badly during the war years. But he had developed an almost crazed hatred of modern society. This was often expressed in a Nietzschean rhetoric of snarling contempt for littleness, for which he may well have been indebted to the Asconans, fuelled by what he called 'perfect androphobia'. He uses the phrase in a letter to his friend S.S. Koteliansky, and proceeds to explain its meaning:

> When I see people in the distance, walking along the path through the fields to Zennor, I want to crouch in the bushes and shoot them silently with invisible arrows of death. I think truly the only righteousness is the destruction of mankind, as in Sodom. Fire and brimstone should fall down.
>
> But I don't want even to hate them. I only want to be in another world than they. Here, it is almost as if one lived on a star, there is a great space of sky and sea in front, in spirit one can circle in space and have the joy of pure motion. But they creep in, the obstructions, the people, like bugs

they creep invidiously in, and they are too many to crush. I see them – fat men in white-flannel trousers – pères de famille – and the familles – passing along the field-path and looking at the scenery. Oh, if one could but have a great box of insect powder, and shake it over them, in the heavens, and exterminate them. Only to clear and cleanse and purify the beautiful earth, and give room for some truth and pure living.[25]

Coming on such letters, and there are plenty of them, it is impossible not to feel appalled by the energy of their hatred. It is, or it seems to be, the quintessence of anti-democratic rage; and as such it can be aligned with that distinctively modernist posture which, however different its modes of expression, is also to be found in the arrogant hauteur of Yeats and the slinky distaste of Eliot.

And yet at this point it is vital to recall that Lawrence always thought of *Leaves of Grass* as one of his 'great books'. How could he do so, one might ask, in view of that letter? But then Whitman, the poet of democratic America, was by no means a simple, unified being. 'Do I contradict myself? / Very well then . . . I contradict myself. / I am large . . . I contain multitudes.' Whitman does not contain in the sense of holding it in. On the contrary, he lets it out.

> I think I could turn and live awhile with the animals . . . they are so
>   placid and self-contained,
> I stand and look at them sometimes half the day long.
>
> They do not sweat and whine about their condition,
> They do not lie awake in the dark and weep for their sins,
> They do not make me sick discussing their duty to God,
> Not one is dissatisfied . . . not one is demented with the mania of
>   owning things,
> Not one kneels to another nor to his kind that lived thousands of years
>   ago,
> Not one is respectable or industrious over the whole earth.[26]

Again, it might almost be Lawrence himself. What Lawrence took from Whitman is sufficiently fully set out in his great essay on him and in a number of letters quoted in the body of this book to need no amplification here.[27] It is, however, important to note that the essay was written at the time when Lawrence felt most cornered by the war. It is as though the very act of working on the essay helped to draw the poison from his system and at the same time allowed him to focus on why Whitman meant so much to him. Above all, it helped to prepare him for the writing of his finest poems. For while these could have been written by nobody but Lawrence, their kinship with the Whitman who thought he could turn awhile and live with the animals is hardly to be denied.

III

The Lawrences finally left England in 1919. They went first to Italy and then on to Taormina, in Sicily. There, Lawrence began to produce some of the poems that would eventually be collected together as *Birds, Beasts and Flowers*. Other of the poems come from his and Frieda's stay in Australia and their time in Mexico and New Mexico. But Sicily reawoke Lawrence's desire to write poetry. Among the poems to have come from that brief period is 'Hibiscus and Salvia Flowers', a characteristically Whitman-like poem in its contemptuous hostility towards the Sicilian socialists and in its contradictory urgent pull towards their primitive force. As Tom Paulin has remarked in an important essay on the poem, 'The socialists with their salvia and hibiscus flowers are outside hotels, outside European civilisation by their association through the flowers with an ancient Polynesian aristocracy.' Paulin goes on to point out that the alignment of prelapsarian Eve with a Polynesian princess 'forces Lawrence to confront the argument deep in his own imagination between the radical idea of human rights and a conservative idea of tradition, duty, hierarchy, art'.[28] While this may be true it may also help to remember that at more or less this same moment Yeats and Eliot were confronting very similar arguments in their own imaginations, and that from these confrontations would come such poems as 'The Second Coming', 'Meditations in Time of Civil War', and 'The Waste Land'. But whatever the differences between these works, and they are very considerable, they are still more different from Lawrence's. For although 'Hibiscus and Salvia Flowers' may confront an argument it doesn't do more than announce apocalypse in purely personal terms.

> I long to be a bolshevist
> And set the stinking rubbish-heap of this foul world

Afire at a myriad scarlet points,
A bolshevist, a salvia-face
To lick the world with flame that licks it clean.
I long to see its chock-full crowdedness
And glutted squirming populousness on fire
Like a field of filthy weeds
Burnt back to ash,
And then to see the new, real souls sprout up.

If this recalls the androphobia of letters which Lawrence was writing in the later years of the war it also recalls his remarks about the American consciousness and under-consciousness, made in the course of his essay on Hawthorne.

The deliberate consciousness of Americans so fair and smooth-spoken, and the under-consciousness so devilish. *Destroy! destroy! destroy!* hums the under-consciousness. *Love and produce! Love and produce!* cackles the upper consciousness. And the world hears only the Love-and produce cackle. Refuses to hear the hum of destruction underneath. Until such time as it will *have* to hear.

The American has got to destroy. It is his destiny. It is his destiny to destroy the whole corpus of the white psyche, the white consciousness.[29]

'Hibiscus and Salvia Flowers' makes clear that Lawrence feels it to be *his* destiny to destroy the white consciousness, where 'white' means everything to do with littleness, meanness, rationality: the world of bungalow culture. It does not, however, amount to anything so portentous as a claim for 'saving civilization', even though his great modernist contemporaries have been seen as committing their poetry to that grand aim.[30] Lawrence's poetry is one of moods, it is not 'philosophical' in the sense that it is possible to call Eliot's poetry 'philosophical', or even Yeats's. Lawrence, it is true, would see this as an essentially meaningless distinction. In one of his most famous 'Pansies' he insists that he loves thought:

But not the juggling and twisting of already existent ideas
I despise that self-important game.
Thought is the welling up of unknown life into consciousness,

> Thought is the testing of statements on the touchstone of the
>   conscience,
> Thought is gazing on to the face of life, and reading what can be read,
> Thought is pondering over experience, and coming to a conclusion.
> Thought is not a trick, or an exercise, or a set of dodges,
> Thought is a man in his wholeness wholly attending.

Apply this test to 'Hibiscus and Salvia Flowers' and it is, perhaps, a thinking poem, at least in the sense that there is in it a welling up of unknown life into consciousness. I'm not sure, though, that it can be said to test statements on the touchstone of conscience. Too much of it seems journalese, that quarrel with others out of which, Yeats said, we make rhetoric, and not the quarrel with ourselves out of which we make poetry. It is not that I expect Lawrence to come to a conclusion. It is rather that, as so often with his later prose, the enemy is so abstract, so unfocused, that it is difficult to feel that what we have here is a man in his wholeness wholly attending. 'I long to see its chock-full crowdedness / And glutted squirming populousness on fire / Like a field of filthy weeds / Burnt back to ash.' That is slovenly language and I would expect Lawrence in a different mood to realize as much.

The different mood, or moods, is what we find in *Birds, Beasts and Flowers*. These really do reveal a man in his wholeness wholly attending and I can therefore understand why Auden should say that in them 'Lawrence's writing is so transparent that one forgets him entirely and simply sees what he saw'.[31] Certainly no later poet makes one see so intensely the lords and lesser beings of life which Lawrence writes about in these magical poems. I do not think, however, that we can ever forget his presence. He is so palpably involved in the seeing, or, as we should more properly say, in the attending. Alvarez is nearer the mark than Auden when he says of these poems that they are

> quite as personal as any of his others. In them he doesn't merely describe, nor does he go at his subjects with a preconceived idea and try to twist them into meanings they would not naturally take. They are neither all subject nor all poet. It is a matter of a vital and complex relationship between the two, difficult, fluent, inward and wholly unabstract. He even avoids the final abstraction of formal perfection. For that gives to experience a kind of ghostly Platonic idealness: in the end, everything

is so perfectly accounted for that the poetic world is complete and isolated. In the relationship Lawrence tries to catch, everything is in flux; it is a flow between two creatures, with nothing fixed. The artist has constantly to improvise at the full pitch of his intelligence.[32]

That is excellently said and it serves to indicate a difference between Lawrence and poets who have been much indebted to him, such as Theodore Roethke and Ted Hughes. For both of these, no matter how hard they try wholly to attend, there is always the risk of designed meanings, the procrustean tug that distorts the recognition of true otherness. Their birds, plants, and fish, that is, threaten to turn into metaphor. Not the thing in itself, but the thing as something else. With Lawrence this never happens. The result is that when he says to the mosquito 'How you sail like a heron, or a dull clot of air', the words are visually unimprovable while carrying no hidden or freighted significance. Such language is *absolutely* about what it sees, is wholly attentive. John Clare apart, there is no English poet who can match Lawrence's entire responsiveness to, his complete absorption in, the otherness of life to which he attends in these poems. This is emphatically not the poetry of 'nature'. As Lawrence himself said, 'we must always beware of romance: of people who love nature, or flowers, or dogs, or babies, or pure adventure. It means they are getting into a love-swing where everything is easy and nothing opposes their egoism.'[33] The man who wrote that is recognizably the same man who complained at the manner of Keats's writing about the nightingale. '"Adieu! adieu! thy plaintive anthem fades. . . ." It never was a plaintive anthem – it was Caruso at his jauntiest.'[34]

Birds, Beasts and Flowers takes opposition not so much for granted as the grounds of being. That is why Alvarez is right to remark on the 'flow between two creatures, with nothing fixed', and why the poems cannot allow themselves any formal perfection. Although it is impossible to see how they could be improved on, they are in no sense 'closed' forms, they come to no conclusions. Their apparent informality is the sign of Lawrence's resistance to thought as 'a trick, or an exercise, or a set of dodges'. It is also an expression of the shifts in contingence that necessarily occur between perceiver and perceived. You can break off such shifts. You cannot bring them to a conclusion.

There is, however, some evidence that in the poems written in New Mexico Lawrence was moving towards conclusion. I think in particular of 'Mountain Lion' and the much more disturbing 'Eagle in New Mexico'. The closing lines of this poem have about them what he himself might have called 'the blood drowse'. They are heavy with the drugged, dangerous excitement of forbidden thoughts: blood sacrifice, ritual slaughter. It is as though the move from Sicily to the new-old world of Australia and then the Americas urged on Lawrence a commitment to the pre-modern, anti-rational, which he had already confronted and which would find ultimate expression in the doctrinal and terrible *Plumed Serpent*, for which 'Eagle in New Mexico' is in some sense a preparation. For all its intense, vivid perception, the poem is by no means as open as most in the sequence. The current of feeling that sustains it flows, slowly and thickly, in one direction only, towards the closing lines:

> Even the sun in heaven can be curbed and chastened at last
> By the life in the hearts of men.
> And you, great bird, sun-starer, heavy black beak
> Can be put out of office as sacrifice bringer.

The life Lawrence has in mind presumably fits men to be sacrifice bringers. Not so much lords of life as lords of death.

IV

To praise the best poems of *Birds, Beasts and Flowers* for their openness is not to mistake them for bits of life. They are art, right enough. That much becomes clear when we come across Lawrence's odd and unsatisfactory explanation for the poems – if that is the word for them – of his last years.

> I offer a bunch of pansies, not a wreath of immortelles. I don't want everlasting flowers and I don't want to offer them to anybody else. A flower passes, and that perhaps is the best of it. . . . Don't nail the pansy down. You won't keep it any better if you do.

Of this, Auden rightly remarks that 'Lawrence draws a false analogy between the process of artistic creation and the organic growth of living creatures'. Lawrence may hope to produce 'something which will seem as natural as a flower, but the qualities of the natural are exactly what his product will lack'.[35] Many of the *Pansies* are marred by crude writing and by what D.J. Enright has called a 'rasping sterility'. As Enright notes, Lawrence didn't inevitably, as he hoped, 'exclude a "repellent, slightly bullying" effect by putting his thoughts into verse'.[36] Whether you can call *Pansies* and *More Pansies* verse is, I would think, very doubtful. Yet neither are they particularly satisfactory as prose epigrams. More often they are neither one thing nor the other. But then it should be noted that by the time Lawrence came to write them he was very ill, frail, and all but exhausted. And for all that many of them are at best trivial, at worst nasty, there are some *Pansies* which one wouldn't be without.

There are also, from this last period, some more considerable poems, among them 'Bavarian Gentians' and 'The Ship of Death', both of which exist in different versions. This suggests that Lawrence set some store by them. It is understandable. They were composed under the shadow of death and they are a way of coming to terms with oblivion. They seek to find a language of acceptance, of lapsing out. 'Bavarian Gentians' in particular has an incantatory depth which hints at a meaning, an understanding of 'the dark', which is beyond rational comprehension yet not to be written off as delusion. Having said that, however, I have to add that with the exception of 'Bavarian Gentians' none of the last poems seems to me to be among Lawrence's best. And I do not think that anything in them can compare with the ending of Wallace Stevens's great poem 'Sunday Morning', which had already been written, and which images the lapsing out into oblivion more memorably than any of Lawrence's late poems.

> And, in the isolation of the sky,
> At evening, casual flocks of pigeons make
> Ambiguous undulations as they sink
> Downward to darkness, on extended wings.

Other commentators feel more enthusiastic about the late poems than I can. It is to the Lawrence of *Birds, Beasts and Flowers* that I want to return, again and again.

A NOTE ON THE TEXT

For the poems I have gone to the relevant first editions. They are:

Love Poems and Others, London, Duckworth, 1913
Amores, London, Duckworth, 1916
Look! We Have Come Through!, London, Chatto & Windus, 1917
New Poems, London, Secker, 1918
Birds, Beasts and Flowers, London, Secker, 1923
Collected Poems, London, Secker, 1928
Last Poems, London, Secker, 1933.

For prose I have also gone to the relevant first editions:

Twilight in Italy, London, Duckworth, 1916
Fantasia of the Unconscious, New York, Seltzer, 1922
Sea and Sardinia, London, Secker, 1923
Studies in Classic American Literature, New York, Seltzer, 1923
Mornings in Mexico, London, Secker, 1927.

For the letters I have used *The Letters of D.H. Lawrence*, edited, with an introduction, by Aldous Huxley, London, Heinemann, 1932. However, the letter to Henry Savage, of 22 December 1913, is quoted by kind permission of Cambridge University Press.

NOTES

1 *The Cambridge Edition of the Letters of D.H. Lawrence*, Volume II, 1913–16, ed. George J. Zytaruk and James T. Boulton, Cambridge/London, Cambridge University Press, 1981, p. 146.

2 Thomas's review is reprinted in *A Language Not To Be Betrayed: Selected Prose of Edward Thomas*, ed. Edna Longley, Manchester, Carcanet, 1981, pp. 106–7. For Pound's review see H. Coombes, *D.H. Lawrence: Penguin Critical Anthology*, Harmondsworth, Penguin, 1973, p. 78.

3 D.H. Lawrence, *The Complete Poems of D.H. Lawrence*, 'The Phoenix Edition', ed. Vivian de Sola Pinto and Warren Roberts, 3 vols, London, Heinemann, 1957, Volume I, p. xxxvi.

4 W.H. Auden, 'D.H. Lawrence', in *The Dyer's Hand*, New York, Vintage Books, 1968, p. 285.

5 ibid., p. 287.

6 Sisson's ill-natured and obtuse account of Lawrence may be found in his *English Poetry 1900–1950*, London, Methuen, 1971. Blackmur's essay is included in his *Language as Gesture*, London, Allen & Unwin, 1954. For Hough's remark, see *The Dark Sun: A Study of D.H. Lawrence*, Harmondsworth, Penguin, 1961, p. 224.

7 Quoted by F.R. Leavis in *D.H. Lawrence, Novelist*, Harmondsworth, Penguin, 1964, p. 315.

8 A. Alvarez, *The Shaping Spirit: Studies in Modern English and American Poets*, London, Grey Arrow Books, 1963, p. 147.

9 Thomas, op. cit., p. 107.

10 *Georgian Poetry*, edited and introduced by James Reeves, Harmondsworth, Penguin, 1962, p. xiii.

11 *Letters*, Volume II, p. 92.

12 For a more sympathetic and illuminating account of the Georgian movement, see C.K. Stead, *The New Poetic*, London, Hutchinson, 1964, *passim*.

13 See *Imagist Poetry*, ed. Peter Jones, Harmondsworth, Penguin, 1972, esp. pp. 17–19.

14 Lawrence appeared in the imagist anthologies for 1915 and 1916.

15 Auden, op. cit., p. 288.

16 ibid.

17 *Letters*, Volume II, p. 130.

18 *The Cambridge Edition of the Letters of D.H. Lawrence*, Volume I, 1901–13, ed. James T. Boulton, Cambridge/London, Cambridge University Press, 1979, p. 148.

19 *D.H. Lawrence: Selected Letters*, Harmondsworth, Penguin, 1950, p. 172.

20 For all this and more see Martin Green, *Mountain of Truth: The Counter Culture Begins, Ascona 1900–1920*, New Jersey, University Press of New England, 1986. Green provides a very full account of Frieda's involvement with Ascona and of Lawrence's more tangential relationship with some of its luminaries.

21 D.H. Lawrence, *Twilight in Italy*, Harmondsworth, Penguin, 1960, p. 144.

22 *Letters*, Volume II, p. 424.

23 See Paul Delany, *D.H. Lawrence's Nightmare: The Writer and His Circle in the Years of the Great War*, Hassocks, Harvester Press, 1979.

24 ibid., p. 385.

25 *Letters*, Volume II, p. 650.

26 *Walt Whitman: Leaves of Grass. The Original Edition*, ed. Malcolm Cowley, London, Secker & Warburg, 1959, pp. 55–6.

27 In *D.H. Lawrence and Edward Carpenter: A Study in Edwardian Transition*, London, Heinemann, 1971, Emile Delavenay is able to show that Lawrence's attachment to Whitman was typical of its period. Those whom Delavenay calls the 'Midlands Intelligentsia' were particularly sympathetic to both *Leaves of Grass* and *Democratic Vistas*. But it needs to be said that Lawrence was far less interested in Whitman's political vision than he was in 'The Song of Myself' and all that offered.

28 In *D.H. Lawrence in the Modern World*, ed. Peter Preston and Peter Hoare, London, Macmillan, 1988, p. 186.

29 The essay on Hawthorne, also written during the Nightmare years, was published in *Studies in Classic American Literature*, 1924. I am here quoting it from *D.H. Lawrence: Selected Literary Criticism*, ed. Anthony Beal, London, Mercury Books, 1961, pp. 347–8.

30 Lawrence is absent from Lucy MacDiarmid's study *Saving Civilisation: Yeats, Eliot and Auden Between the Wars*, Cambridge, 1984.

31 Auden, op. cit., p. 292.

32 Alvarez, op. cit., p. 150.

33 Quoted by Charles Davey in *D.H. Lawrence: A Living Poet*, London, Brentham Press, 1985, p. 31. Davey's enthusiastic pamphlet concentrates on *Pansies*, which he feels to be far more successful than I can bring myself to do.

34 Beal, op. cit., p. 101.

35 Auden, op. cit., pp. 283–4.

36 Enright's remark occurs in the course of his review of the *Collected Poems* and is to be found in Coombes's *Critical Anthology*, op. cit., p. 447.

D.H. LAWRENCE
Selected Poetry and Non-fictional Prose

HYMNS IN A MAN'S LIFE

Nothing is more difficult than to determine what a child takes in, and does not take in, of its environment and its teaching. This fact is brought home to me by the hymns which I learned as a child, and never forgot. They mean to me almost more than the finest poetry, and they have for me a more permanent value, somehow or other.

It is almost shameful to confess that the poems which have meant most to me, like Wordsworth's 'Ode to Immortality' and Keats's 'Odes', and pieces of *Macbeth* or *As You Like It* or *Midsummer Night's Dream*, and Goethe's lyrics, such as 'Uber allen Gipfeln ist Ruh', and Verlaine's 'Ayant poussé la porte qui chancelle' – all these lovely poems which after all give the ultimate shape to one's life; all these lovely poems woven deep into a man's consciousness, are still not woven so deep in me as the rather banal Nonconformist hymns that penetrated through and through my childhood.

> Each gentle dove
> And sighing bough
> That makes the eve
> So fair to me
> Has something far
> Diviner now
> To draw me back
> To Galilee.
> O Galilee, sweet Galilee,
> Where Jesus loved so much to be,
> O Galilee, sweet Galilee,
> Come sing thy songs again to me!

To me the word Galilee has a wonderful sound. The Lake of Galilee! I don't want to know where it is. I never want to go to Palestine. Galilee is one of those lovely, glamorous worlds, not places, that exist in the golden haze of a child's half-formed imagination. And in my man's imagination it is just the same. It has been left untouched. With regard to the hymns which had such a profound influence on my childish consciousness, there has been no

*Numbers in square brackets refer to pages on which notes may be found.

crystallising out, no dwindling into actuality, no hardening into the commonplace. They are the same to my man's experience as they were to me nearly forty years ago.

The moon, perhaps, has shrunken a little. One has been forced to learn about orbits, eclipses, relative distances, dead worlds, craters of the moon, and so on. The crescent at evening still startles the soul with its delicate flashing. But the mind works automatically and says: 'Ah, she is in her first quarter. She is all there, in spite of the fact that we see only this slim blade. The earth's shadow is over her.' And, willy-nilly, the intrusion of the mental processes dims the brilliance, the magic of the first apperception.

It is the same with all things. The sheer delight of a child's apperception is based on *wonder*; and deny it as we may, knowledge and wonder counteract one another. So that as knowledge increases wonder decreases. We say again: Familiarity breeds contempt. So that as we grow older, and become more familiar with phenomena, we become more contemptuous of them. But that is only partly true. It has taken some races of men thousands of years to become contemptuous of the moon, and to the Hindu the cow is still wondrous. It is not familiarity that breeds contempt: it is the assumption of knowledge. Anybody who looks at the moon and says, 'I know all about that poor orb,' is, of course, bored by the moon.

Now the great and fatal fruit of our civilisation, which is a civilisation based on knowledge, and hostile to experience, is boredom. All our wonderful education and learning is producing a grand sum-total of boredom. Modern people are inwardly thoroughly bored. Do as they may, they are bored.

They are bored because they experience nothing. And they experience nothing because the wonder has gone out of them. And when the wonder has gone out of a man he is dead. He is henceforth only an insect.

When all comes to all, the most precious element in life is wonder. Love is a great emotion, and power is power. But both love and power are based on wonder. Love without wonder is a sensational affair, and power without wonder is mere force and compulsion. The one universal element in consciousness which is fundamental to life is the element of wonder. You cannot help feeling it in a bean as it starts to grow and pulls itself out of its jacket. You cannot help feeling it in the glisten of the nucleus of the amœba. You recognise it, willy-nilly, in an ant busily tugging at a straw; in a rook, as it walks the frosty grass.

They all have their own obstinate will. But also they all live with a sense of wonder. Plant consciousness, insect consciousness, fish consciousness, animal consciousness, all are related by one permanent element, which we may call the religious element inherent in all life, even in a flea: the sense of wonder. That is our sixth sense. And it is the *natural* religious sense.

Somebody says that mystery is nothing, because mystery is something you don't know, and what you don't know is nothing to you. But there is more than one way of knowing.

Even the real scientist works in the sense of wonder. The pity is, when he comes out of his laboratory he puts aside his wonder along with his apparatus, and tries to make it all perfectly didactic. Science in its true condition of wonder is as religious as any religion. But didactic science is as dead and boring as dogmatic religion. Both are wonderless and productive of boredom, endless boredom.

Now we come back to the hymns. They live and glisten in the depths of the man's consciousness in undimmed wonder, because they have not been subjected to any criticism or analysis. By the time I was sixteen I had criticised and got over the Christian dogma.

It was quite easy for me; my immediate forebears had already done it for me. Salvation, heaven, Virgin birth, miracles, even the Christian dogmas of right and wrong – one soon got them adjusted. I never could really worry about them. Heaven is one of the instinctive dreams. Right and wrong is something you can't dogmatise about; it's not so easy. As for my soul, I simply don't and never did understand how I could 'save' it. One can save one's pennies. But how can one save one's soul? One can only *live* one's soul. The business is to live, really alive. And this needs wonder.

So that the miracle of the loaves and fishes is just as good to me now as when I was a child. I don't care whether it is historically a fact or not. What does it matter? It is part of the genuine wonder. The same with all the religious teaching I had as a child, *apart* from the didacticism and sentimentalism. I am eternally grateful for the wonder with which it filled my childhood.

29

Sun of my soul, thou Saviour dear,
　It is not night if Thou be near –

That was the last hymn at the board school. It did not mean to
me any Christian dogma or any salvation. Just the words, 'Sun of
my soul, thou Saviour dear,' penetrated me with wonder and the
mystery of twilight. At another time the last hymn was:

Fair waved the golden corn
In Canaan's pleasant land –

And again I loved 'Canaan's pleasant land'. The wonder of 'Canaan',　100
which could never be localised.

I think it was good to be brought up a Protestant: and among
Protestants, a Nonconformist, and among Nonconformists, a
Congregationalist. Which sounds pharisaic. But I should have missed
bitterly a direct knowledge of the Bible, and a direct relation to
Galilee and Canaan, Moab and Kedron, those places that never existed
on earth. And in the Church of England one would hardly have
escaped those snobbish hierarchies of class, which spoil so much for
a child. And the Primitive Methodists, when I was a boy, were always
having 'revivals' and being 'saved', and I always had a horror of being　110
saved.

So, altogether, I am grateful to my 'Congregational' upbringing.
The Congregationalists are the oldest Nonconformists, descendants
of the Oliver Cromwell Independents. They still had the Puritan
traditional of no ritual. But they avoided the personal emotionalism
which one found among the Methodists when I was a boy.

I liked our chapel, which was tall and full of light, and yet still;
and colour-washed pale green and blue, with a bit of lotus pattern.
And over the organ-loft, 'O worship the Lord in the beauty of
holiness,' in big letters.　120

That was a favourite hymn, too:

O worship the Lord, in the beauty of holiness,
　Bow down before Him, His glory proclaim;
With gold of obedience and incense of lowliness
　Kneel and adore Him, the Lord is His name.

I don't know what the 'beauty of holiness' is, exactly. It easily

30

becomes cant, or nonsense. But if you don't think about it – and why should you? – it has a magic. The same with the whole verse. It is rather bad, really, 'gold of obedience' and 'incense of lowliness'. But in me, to the music, it still produces a sense of splendour.

I am always glad we had the Bristol hymn-book, not Moody and Sankey. And I am glad our Scotch minister on the whole avoided sentimental messes such as *Lead, Kindly Light*, or even *Abide With Me*. He had a healthy preference for healthy hymns.

130

> At even, ere the sun was set,
>> The sick, O Lord, around Thee lay.
> Oh, in what divers pains they met!
>> Oh, in what joy they went away!

And often we had 'Fight the good fight with all thy might'.

In Sunday School I am eternally grateful to old Mr. Remington, with his round white beard and his ferocity. He made us sing! And he loved the martial hymns:

> Sound the battle-cry,
> See, the foe is nigh.
> Raise the standard high
> For the Lord.

The ghastly sentimentalism that came like a leprosy over religion had not yet got hold of our colliery village. I remember when I was in Class II in the Sunday School, when I was about seven, a woman teacher trying to harrow us about the Crucifixion. And she kept saying: 'And aren't you sorry for Jesus? Aren't you sorry?' And most of the children wept. I believe I shed a crocodile tear or two, but very vivid is my memory of saying to myself: 'I don't *really* care a bit.' And I could never go back on it. I never *cared* about the Crucifixion, one way or another. Yet the *wonder* of it penetrated very deep in me.

140

Thirty-six years ago men, even Sunday School teachers, still believed in the fight for life and the fun of it. 'Hold the fort, for I am coming.' It was far, far from any militarism or gun-fighting. But it was the battle-cry of a stout soul, and a fine thing too.

> Stand up, stand up for Jesus,
> Ye soldiers of the Lord.

Here is the clue to the ordinary Englishman – in the Nonconformist hymns.

THE WILD COMMON

The quick sparks on the gorse bushes are leaping,
Little jets of sunlight-texture imitating flame;
Above them, exultant, the peewits are sweeping:
They are lords of the desolate wastes of sadness their screamings
    proclaim.

Rabbits, handfuls of brown earth, lie
Low-rounded on the mournful grass they have bitten down to the
    quick.
Are they asleep? – Are they alive? – Now see, when I
Move my arms the hill bursts and heaves under their spurting kick.

The common flaunts bravely; but below, from the rushes
Crowds of glittering king-cups surge to challenge the blossoming   10
    bushes;
There the lazy streamlet pushes
Its curious course mildly; here it wakes again, leaps, laughs, and
    gushes

Into a deep pond, an old sheep-dip,
Dark, overgrown with willows, cool, with the brook ebbing
    through so slow;
Naked on the steep, soft lip
Of the bank I stand watching my own white shadow quivering to
    and fro.

What if the gorse flowers shrivelled and kissing were lost?
Without the pulsing waters, where were the marigolds and the songs
    of the brook?
If my veins and my breasts with love embossed
Withered, my insolent soul would be gone like flowers that the hot   20
    wind took.

So my soul like a passionate woman turns,
Filled with remorseful terror to the man she scorned, and her love

32

For myself in my own eyes' laughter burns,
Runs ecstatic over the pliant folds rippling down to my belly from
   the breast-lights above.

Over my sunlit skin the warm, clinging air,
Rich with the songs of seven larks singing at once, goes kissing me
   glad.
And the soul of the wind and my blood compare
Their wandering happiness, and the wind, wasted in liberty, drifts
   on and is sad.

Oh but the water loves me and folds me,
Plays with me, sways me, lifts me and sinks me as though it were   30
   living blood,
Blood of a heaving woman who holds me,
Owning my supple body a rare glad thing, supremely good.

DISCORD IN CHILDHOOD

Outside the house an ash-tree hung its terrible whips,
And at night when the wind arose, the lash of the tree
Shrieked and slashed the wind, as a ship's
Weird rigging in a storm shrieks hideously.

Within the house two voices rose in anger, a slender lash
Whistling delirious rage, and the dreadful sound
Of a thick lash booming and bruising, until it drowned
The other voice in a silence of blood, 'neath the noise of the ash.

DOG-TIRED

If she would come to me here,
   Now the sunken swaths
   Are glittering paths
To the sun, and the swallows cut clear
Into the low sun – if she came to me here!

If she would come to me now,
Before the last mown harebells are dead,

While that vetch clump yet burns red;
Before all the bats have dropped from the bough
Into the cool of night – if she came to me now!   10

The horses are untackled, the chattering machine
Is still at last. If she would come,
I would gather up the warm hay from
The hill-brow, and lie in her lap till the green
Sky ceased to quiver, and lost its tired sheen.

I should like to drop
On the hay, with my head on her knee
And lie stone still, while she
Breathed quiet above me – we could stop
Till the stars came out to see.   20

I should like to lie still
As if I was dead – but feeling
Her hand go stealing
Over my face and my hair until
This ache was shed.

CHERRY ROBBERS

Under the long, dark boughs, like jewels red
    In the hair of an Eastern girl
Shine strings of crimson cherries, as if had bled
    Blood-drops beneath each curl.

Under the glistening cherries, with folded wings
    Three dead birds lie:
Pale-breasted throstles and a blackbird, robberlings
    Stained with red dye.

Under the haystack a girl stands laughing at me,
    With cherries hung round her ears –   10
Offering me her scarlet fruit: I will see
    If she has any tears.

34

CRUELTY AND LOVE

What large, dark hands are those at the window
Lifted, grasping the golden light
Which weaves its way through the creeper leaves
    To my heart's delight?

Ah, only the leaves! But in the west,
In the west I see a redness come
Over the evening's burning breast –
    – 'Tis the wound of love goes home!

The woodbine creeps abroad
Calling low to her lover: 10
  The sun-lit flirt who all the day
  Has poised above her lips in play
  And stolen kisses, shallow and gay
  Of pollen, now has gone away
  – She woos the moth with her sweet, low word,
And when above her his broad wings hover
Then her bright breast she will uncover
And yield her honey-drop to her lover.

Into the yellow, evening glow
Saunters a man from the farm below,   20
Leans, and looks in at the low-built shed
Where hangs the swallow's marriage bed.
  The bird lies warm against the wall.
  She glances quick her startled eyes
  Towards him, then she turns away
  Her small head, making warm display
  Of red upon the throat. His terrors sway
  Her out of the nest's warm, busy ball,
  Whose plaintive cry is heard as she flies
  In one blue stoop from out the sties   30
Into the evening's empty hall.

Oh, water-hen, beside the rushes
Hide your quaint, unfading blushes,

35

Still your quick tail, and lie as dead,
Till the distance folds over his ominous tread.

The rabbit presses back her ears,
Turns back her liquid, anguished eyes
And crouches low: then with wild spring
Spurts from the terror of *his* oncoming
To be choked back, the wire ring   40
Her frantic effort throttling:
  Piteous brown ball of quivering fears!

Ah soon in his large, hard hands she dies,
And swings all loose to the swing of his walk.
Yet calm and kindly are his eyes
And ready to open in brown surprise
Should I not answer to his talk
Or should he my tears surmise.

I hear his hand on the latch, and rise from my chair
Watching the door open: he flashes bare   50
His strong teeth in a smile, and flashes his eyes
In a smile like triumph upon me; then careless-wise
He flings the rabbit soft on the table board
And comes towards me; ah, the uplifted sword
Of his hand against my bosom, and oh, the broad
Blade of his hand that raises my face to applaud
His coming: he raises up my face to him
And caresses my mouth with his fingers, which still smell grim
Of the rabbit's fur! God, I am caught in a snare!
I know not what fine wire is round my throat,   60
I only know I let him finger there
My pulse of life, letting him nose like a stoat
Who sniffs with joy before he drinks the blood:
And down his mouth comes to my mouth, and down
His dark bright eyes descend like a fiery hood
Upon my mind: his mouth meets mine, and a flood
Of sweet fire sweeps across me, so I drown
Within him, die, and find death good.

SNAP-DRAGON

She bade me follow to her garden, where
The mellow sunlight stood as in a cup
Between the old grey walls; I did not dare
To raise my face, I did not dare look up,
Lest her bright eyes like sparrows should fly in
My windows of discovery, and shrill 'Sin.'

So with a downcast mien and laughing voice
I followed, followed the swing of her white dress
That rocked in a lilt along: I watched the poise
Of her feet as they flew for a space, then paused to press   10
The grass deep down with the royal burden of her:
And gladly I'd offered my breast to the tread of her.

'I like to see,' she said, and she crouched her down,
She sunk into my sight like a settling bird;
And her bosom couched in the confines of her gown
Like heavy birds at rest there, softly stirred
By her measured breaths: 'I like to see,' said she,
'The snap-dragon put out his tongue at me.'

She laughed, she reached her hand out to the flower,
Closing its crimson throat. My own throat in her power   20
Strangled, my heart swelled up so full
As if it would burst its wine-skin in my throat,
Choke me in my own crimson. I watched her pull
The gorge of the gaping flower, till the blood did float

Over my eyes, and I was blind –
Her large brown hand stretched over
The windows of my mind;
And there in the dark I did discover
Things I was out to find:
My Grail, a brown bowl twined   30
With swollen veins that met in the wrist,
Under whose brown the amethyst
I longed to taste. I longed to turn
My heart's red measure in her cup,

I longed to feel my hot blood burn
With the amethyst in her cup.

Then suddenly she looked up,
And I was blind in a tawny-gold day,
Till she took her eyes away.

So she came down from above   40
And emptied my heart of love.
So I held my heart aloft
To the cuckoo that hung like a dove,
And she settled soft.

It seemed that I and the morning world
Were pressed cup-shape to take this reiver
Bird who was weary to have furled
Her wings in us,
As we were weary to receive her.

   This bird, this rich,   50
   Sumptuous central grain,
   This mutable witch,
   This one refrain,
   This laugh in the fight,
   This clot of night,
   This field of delight.

She spoke, and I closed my eyes
To shut hallucinations out.
I echoed with surprise
Hearing my mere lips shout   60
The answer they did devise.

Again I saw a brown bird hover
Over the flowers at my feet;
I felt a brown bird hover
Over my heart, and sweet
Its shadow lay on my heart.
I thought I saw on the clover
A brown bee pulling apart

The closed flesh of the clover
And burrowing in its heart.   70

> She moved her hand, and again
> I felt the brown bird cover
> My heart; and then
> The bird came down on my heart,
> As on a nest the rover
> Cuckoo comes, and shoves over
> The brim each careful part
> Of love, takes possession, and settles her down,
> With her wings and her feathers to drown
> The nest in a heat of love.   80

She turned her flushed face to me for the glint
Of a moment, 'See,' she laughed, 'if you also
Can make them yawn.' I put my hand to the dint
In the flower's throat, and the flower gaped wide with woe.
She watched, she went of a sudden intensely still,
She watched my hand, to see what it would fulfil.

I pressed the wretched, throttled flower between
My fingers, till its head lay back, its fangs
Poised at her. Like a weapon my hand was white and keen,
And I held the choked flower-serpent in its pangs   90
Of mordant anguish, till she ceased to laugh,
Until her pride's flag, smitten, cleaved down to the staff.

She hid her face, she murmured between her lips
The low word 'Don't.' I let the flower fall,
But held my hand afloat towards the slips
Of blossom she fingered, and my fingers all
Put forth to her: she did not move, nor I,
For my hand like a snake watched hers, that could not fly.

Then I laughed in the dark of my heart, I did exult
Like a sudden chuckling of music. I bade her eyes   100
Meet mine, I opened her helpless eyes to consult
Their fear, their shame, their joy that underlies

Defeat in such a battle. In the dark of her eyes
My heart was fierce to make her laughter rise.

Till her dark deeps shook with convulsive thrills, and the dark
Of her spirit wavered like water thrilled with light;
And my heart leaped up in longing to plunge its stark
Fervour within the pool of her twilight,
Within her spacious soul, to find delight.

And I do not care, though the large hands of revenge   110
Shall get my throat at last, shall get it soon,
If the joy that they are lifted to avenge
Have risen red on my night as a harvest moon,
Which even death can only put out for me;
And death, I know, is better than not-to-be.

A COLLIER'S WIFE

Somebody's knocking at the door
    Mother, come down and see,
– I's think it's nobbut a beggar,
    Say, I'm busy.

It's not a beggar, mother, – hark
    How hard he knocks . . .
– Eh, tha'rt a mard-'arsed kid,
    'E'll gi'e thee socks!

Shout an' ax what 'e wants,
    I canna come down.   10
– 'E says 'Is it Arthur Holliday's?'
    Say 'Yes,' tha clown.

'E says, 'Tell your mother as 'er mester's
    Got hurt i' th' pit.'
What – oh my sirs, 'e never says that,
    That's niver it.

Come out o' the way an' let me see,
    Eh, there's no peace!

40

An' stop thy scraightin', childt,
  Do shut thy face.
20

'Your mester's 'ad an accident,
  An' they're ta'ein 'im i' th' ambulance
To Nottingham,' – Eh dear o' me
  If 'e's not a man for mischance!

Wheers he hurt this time, lad?
  – I dunna know,
They on'y towd me it wor bad –
  It would be so!

Eh, what a man! – an' that cobbly road,
  They'll jolt him a'most to death,
I'm sure he's in for some trouble
  Nigh every time he takes breath.
30

Out o' my way, childt – dear o' me, wheer
  Have I put his clean stockings and shirt;
Goodness knows if they'll be able
  To take off his pit dirt.

An' what a moan he'll make – there niver
  Was such a man for a fuss
If anything ailed him – at any rate
  I shan't have him to nuss.
40

I do hope it's not very bad!
  Eh, what a shame it seems
As some should ha'e hardly a smite o'trouble
  An' others has reams.

It's a shame as 'e should be knocked about
  Like this, I'm sure it is!
He's had twenty accidents, if he's had one;
  Owt bad, an' it's his.

There's one thing, we'll have peace for a bit,
  Thank Heaven for a peaceful house;
50

An' there's compensation, sin' it's accident,
  An' club money – I nedn't grouse.

An' a fork an' a spoon he'll want, an' what else;
  I s'll never catch that train –
What a traipse it is if a man gets hurt –
  I s'd think he'll get right again.

VIOLETS

Sister, tha knows while we was on the planks
  Aside o' th' grave, while th' coffin wor lyin' yet
On th' yaller clay, an' th' white flowers top of it
  Tryin' to keep off 'n him a bit o' th' wet,

An' parson makin' haste, an' a' the black
  Huddlin' close together a cause o' th' rain,
Did t' 'appen ter notice a bit of a lass away back
  By a head-stun, sobbin' an' sobbin' again?

  – How should I be lookin' round
    An' me standin' on the plank
  Beside the open ground,
    Where our Ted 'ud soon be sank?

  Yi, an' 'im that young,
    Snapped sudden out of all
  His wickedness, among
    Pals worse n'r ony name as you could call.

Let be that; there's some o' th' bad as we
  Like better nor all your good, an' 'e was one.
– An' cos I liked him best, yi, bett'r nor thee,
  I canna bide to think where he is gone.

Ah know tha liked 'im bett'r nor me. But let
  Me tell thee about this lass. When you had gone
Ah stopped behind on t' pad i' th' drippin' wet
  An' watched what 'er 'ad on.

Tha should ha' seed 'er slive up when we'd gone,
  Tha should ha' seed her kneel an' look in

10

20

At th' sloppy wet grave – an' 'er little neck shone
　　That white, an' 'er shook that much, I'd like to begin

Scraightin' mysen as well. 'Er undid 'er black
　　Jacket at th' bosom, an' took from out of it　　　　　　30
Over a double 'andful of violets, all in a pack
　　Ravelled blue and white – warm, for a bit

O' th' smell come waftin' to me. 'Er put 'er face
　　Right intil 'em and scraighted out again,
Then after a bit 'er dropped 'em down that place,
　　An' I come away, because o' the teemin' rain.

THE BEST OF SCHOOL

The blinds are drawn because of the sun,
And the boys and the room in a colourless gloom
Of under-water float: bright ripples run
Across the walls as the blinds are blown
To let the sunlight in; and I,
As I sit on the beach of the class alone,
Watch the boys in their summer blouses,
As they write, their round heads busily bowed:
And one after another rouses
And lifts his face and looks at me,　　　　　　　　　　10
And my eyes meet his very quietly,
Then he turns again to his work, with glee.

With glee he turns, with a little glad
Ecstasy of work he turns from me,
An ecstasy surely sweet to be had.

And very sweet while the sunlight waves
In the fresh of the morning, it is to be
A teacher of these young boys, my slaves
Only as swallows are slaves to the eaves
They build upon, as mice are slaves　　　　　　　　　20
To the man who threshes and sows the sheaves.

　　　　　Oh, sweet it is
To feel the lads' looks light on me,

Then back in a swift, bright flutter to work,
As birds who are stealing turn and flee.

Touch after touch I feel on me
As their eyes glance at me for the grain
Of rigour they taste delightedly.

       And all the class,
As tendrils reached out yearningly   30
Slowly rotate till they touch the tree
That they cleave unto, that they leap along
Up to their lives – so they to me.

So do they cleave and cling to me,
So I lead them up, so do they twine
Me up, caress and clothe with free
Fine foliage of lives this life of mine;
The lowest stem of this life of mine,
The old hard stem of my life
That bears aloft towards rarer skies   40
My top of life, that buds on high
Amid the high wind's enterprise.

They all do clothe my ungrowing life
With a rich, a thrilled young clasp of life;
A clutch of attachment, like parenthood,
Mounts up to my heart, and I find it good.

And I lift my head upon the troubled tangled world, and though the
    pain
Of living my life were doubled, I still have this to comfort and
    sustain,
I have such swarming sense of lives at the base of me, such sense of
    lives
Clustering upon me, reaching up, as each after the other strives   50
To follow my life aloft to the fine wild air of life and the storm of
    thought,
And though I scarcely see the boys, or know that they are there,
    distraught

As I am with living my life in earnestness, still progressively and
  alone,
Though they cling, forgotten the most part, not companions,
  scarcely known
To me – yet still because of the sense of their closeness clinging
  densely to me,
And slowly fingering up my stem and following all tinily
The way that I have gone and now am leading, they are dear to me.

They keep me assured, and when my soul feels lonely,
All mistrustful of thrusting its shoots where only
I alone am living, then it keeps   60
Me comforted to feel the warmth that creeps
Up dimly from their striving; it heartens my strife:
And when my heart is chill with loneliness,
Then comforts it the creeping tenderness
Of all the strays of life that climb my life.

A BABY RUNNING BAREFOOT

When the bare feet of the baby beat across the grass
The little white feet nod like white flowers in the wind,
They poise and run like ripples lapping across the water;
And the sight of their white play among the grass
Is like a little robin's song, winsome,
Or as two butterflies settle in the cup of one flower
For a moment, then away with a flutter of wings.

I long for the baby to wander hither to me
Like a wind-shadow wandering over the water,
So that she can stand on my knee   10
With her little bare feet in my hands,
Cool like syringa buds,
Firm and silken like pink young peony flowers.

END OF ANOTHER HOME-HOLIDAY

1

When shall I see the half moon sink again
Behind the black sycamore at the end of the garden?

45

When will the scent of the dim, white phlox
Creep up the wall to me, and in at my open window?

Why is it, the long slow stroke of the midnight bell,
  (Will it never finish the twelve?)
Falls again and again on my heart with a heavy reproach?

The moon-mist is over the village, out of the mist speaks the bell,
And all the little roofs of the village bow low, pitiful, beseeching,
   resigned:
    Oh, little home, what is it I have not done well?   10

Ah home, suddenly I love you,
As I hear the sharp clean trot of a pony down the road,
Succeeding sharp little sounds dropping into the silence,
Clear upon the long-drawn hoarseness of a train across the valley.

The light has gone out from under my mother's door.
    That she should love me so,
    She, so lonely, greying now,
    And I leaving her,
    Bent on my pursuits!

Love is the great Asker,   20
The sun and the rain do not ask the secret
Of the time when the grain struggles down in the dark.
The moon walks her lonely way without anguish,
Because no loved one grieves over her departure.

2

Forever, ever by my shoulder pitiful Love will linger,
Crouching as little houses crouch under the mist when I turn.
Forever, out of the mist the church lifts up her reproachful finger,
Pointing my eyes in wretched defiance where love hides her face to mourn.

    Oh but the rain creeps down to wet the grain
      That struggles alone in the dark,   30
    And asking nothing, cheerfully steals back again!
      The moon sets forth o' nights
      To walk the lonely, dusky heights
      Serenely, with steps unswerving;

Pursued by no sigh of bereavement,
No tears of love unnerving
Her constant tread:
While ever at my side,
Frail and sad, with grey bowed head,
The beggar-woman, the yearning-eyed   40
Inexorable love goes lagging.

The wild young heifer, glancing distraught,
With a strange new knocking of life at her side
    Runs seeking a loneliness.
The little grain draws down the earth to hide.
Nay, even the slumberous egg, as it labours under the shell,
    Patiently to divide, and self-divide,
Asks to be hidden, and wishes nothing to tell.

But when I draw the scanty cloak of silence over my eyes,
Piteous Love comes peering under the hood.   50
Touches the clasp with trembling fingers, and tries
To put her ear to the painful sob of my blood,
While her tears soak through to my breast,
        Where they burn and cauterise.

3

The moon lies back and reddens.
In the valley, a corncrake calls
        Monotonously,
With a piteous, unalterable plaint, that deadens
        My confident activity:
With a hoarse, insistent request that falls   60
        Unweariedly, unweariedly,
        Asking something more of me,
            Yet more of me!

THE BRIDE

My love looks like a girl to-night,
    But she is old.

The plaits that lie along her pillow
  Are not gold,

But threaded with filigree silver,
  And uncanny cold.

She looks like a young maiden, since her brow
  Is smooth and fair,
Her cheeks are very smooth, her eyes are closed.
  She sleeps a rare   10
Still winsome sleep, so still, and so composed.

Nay, but she sleeps like a bride, and dreams her dreams
  Of perfect things.
She lies at last, the darling, in the shape of her dream,
  And her dead mouth sings
By its shape, like the thrushes in clear evenings.

SORROW

Why does the thin grey strand
Floating up from the forgotten
Cigarette between my fingers,
Why does it trouble me?

Ah, you will understand;
When I carried my mother downstairs,
A few times only, at the beginning
Of her soft-foot malady,

I should find, for a reprimand
To my gaiety, a few long grey hairs   10
On the breast of my coat; and one by one
I watched them float up the dark chimney.

PIANO

Softly, in the dusk, a woman is singing to me;
Taking me back down the vista of years, till I see
A child sitting under the piano, in the boom of the tingling strings

And pressing the small, poised feet of a mother who smiles as she
    sings.

In spite of myself, the insidious mastery of song
Betrays me back, till the heart of me weeps to belong
To the old Sunday evenings at home, with winter outside
And hymns in the cosy parlour, the tinkling piano our guide.

So now it is vain for the singer to burst into clamour
With the great black piano appassionato. The glamour   10
Of childish days is upon me, my manhood is cast
Down in the flood of remembrance, I weep like a child for the past.

PARLIAMENT HILL IN THE EVENING

The houses fade in a melt of mist
   Blotching the thick, soiled air
With reddish places that still resist
   The Night's slow care.

The hopeless, wintry twilight fades,
   The city corrodes out of sight
As the body corrodes when death invades
   That citadel of delight.

Now verdigris smoulderings softly spread
   Through the shroud of the town, as slow   10
Night-lights hither and thither shed
   Their ghastly glow.

THE NORTH COUNTRY

In another country, black poplars shake themselves over a pond,
And rooks and the rising smoke-waves scatter and wheel from the
   works beyond;
The air is dark with north and with sulphur, the grass is a darker
   green,
And people darkly invested with purple move palpable through the
   scene.

Soundlessly down across the counties, out of the resonant gloom
That wraps the north in stupor and purple travels the deep, slow boom
Of the man-life north-imprisoned, shut in the hum of the purpled steel
As it spins to sleep on its motion, drugged dense in the sleep of the wheel.

Out of the sleep, from the gloom of motion, soundlessly, somnambule
Moans and booms the soul of a people imprisoned, asleep in the rule   10
Of the strong machine that runs mesmeric, booming the spell of its word
Upon them and moving them helpless, mechanic, their will to its will deferred.

Yet all the while comes the droning inaudible, out of the violet air,
The moaning of sleep-bound beings in travail that toil and are will-less there
In the spell-bound north, convulsive now with a dream near morning, strong
With violent achings heaving to burst the sleep that is now not long.

GIORNO DEI MORTI

Along the avenues of cypresses
All in their scarlet cloaks and surplices
Of linen go the chanting choristers,
The priests in gold and black, the villagers . . .

And all along the path to the cemetery
The round dark heads of men crowd silently,
And black-scarved faces of women-folk, wistfully
Watch at the banner of death, and the mystery.

And at the foot of a grave a father stands
With sunken head, and forgotten, folded hands;   10
And at the foot of a grave a mother kneels
With pale shut face, nor either hears nor feels

The coming of the chanting choristers
Between the avenues of cypresses,
The silence of the many villagers,
The candle-flames beside the surplices.

EDWARD THOMAS: REVIEW OF *LOVE POEMS AND OTHERS*

The book of the moment in verse is Mr D.H. Lawrence's. He is
remarkable for what he does not do and for what he does. Thus, he
does not write smoothly, sweetly and with dignity, nor does he
choose subjects, such as blackbirds at sunset, which ask to be so
treated. For some time past it has been understood that verse is not
best written in jerks of a line in length. Mr Lawrence goes further,
and at times seems bent on insulting rhyme, as in this stanza from
'Dog-tired':

> The horses are untackled, the chattering machine
> Is still at last. If she would come,
> I would gather up the warm hay from
> The hill-brow, and lie in her lap till the green
> Sky ceased to quiver and lost its tired sheen.

Correspondingly, he writes of matters which cannot be subdued to
conventional rhythm and rhyme – chiefly the intense thoughts,   10
emotions, or gropings of self-conscious men or women set on edge
by love or fatigue or solitude. If he trusts to make a general appeal,
it is by faithful concentration on the particular – a woman receiving
a lover straight from bloodshed, a man repulsed, standing like an
'insect small in the fur of this hill' in the night when

> The night's flood-winds have lifted my last desire from me,
> And my hollow flesh stands up in the night abandonedly

and saying to the woman:

> And I in the fur of the world, and you a pale fleck from
>   the sky,
> How we hate each other to-night, hate, you and I,
> As the world of activity hates the dream that goes on high,
> As a man hates the dreaming woman he loves, but who
>   will not reply.
> ('Repulsed')

The last comparison would be a flaw were it not that Mr Lawrence
sacrifices everything to intensity, particularly in amorousness. His
triumph is, by image and hint and direct statement, to bring before
us some mood which overpowers all of a sick, complex man save his   20
self-consciousness. Mr Lawrence is fearless in treatment as in choice
of subject. He will be exact in defining an intuition, a physical state,
or an appearance due to the pathetic fallacy – herein resembling the
man in 'We have bit no forbidden apple'. He will give us in dialect
the plainest of a working-class tragedy, and in careful abstract
monologue a schoolmaster's moment of satisfaction when it is sweet
in the morning to teach boys who are his slaves:

> Only as swallows are slaves to the eaves
> They build upon, as mice are slaves
> To the man who threshes and sows the sheaves.
> ('The Best of School')

Such moods he will sometimes follow with a painful curiosity that
makes us rather sharers in a process than witnesses of a result. He
does not refuse external things, a gang of labourers at work on   30
timber, a picture by Corot, the Moon. A surprising number of his
poems are tributary to the moon, but a moon of his own world,
'divesting herself of her golden shift', or bringing him a pang of
reminiscence, or reddening:

> The moon lies back and reddens.
> In the valley a corncrake calls
>   Monotonously,
> With a plaintive, unalterable voice, that deadens
>   My confident activity;
> With hoarse, insistent request that falls
>   Unweariedly, unweariedly,
>   Asking something more of me,
>   Yet more of me.
> ('End of Another Home-Holiday')

I doubt if much of his effect is due to rhythm. Verse aids him chiefly
by allowing him to use a staccato shorthand which would be more
uncomfortable in prose. But, whether the verse is always relevant or

not, Mr Lawrence writes in a concentration so absolute that the poetry is less questionable than the verse.

GEORGIAN POETRY, 1911–1912

Georgian Poetry is an anthology of verse which has been published during the reign of our present king, George V. It contains one poem of my own, but this fact will not, I hope, preclude my reviewing the book.

This collection is like a big breath taken when we are waking up after a night of oppressive dreams. The nihilists, the intellectual, hopeless people – Ibsen, Flaubert, Thomas Hardy – represent the dream we are waking from. It was a dream of demolition. Nothing was, but was nothing. Everything was taken from us. And now our lungs are full of new air, and our eyes see it is morning, but we have not forgotten the terror of the night. We dreamed we were falling through space into nothingness, and the anguish of it leaves us rather eager.

But we are awake again, our lungs are full of new air, our eyes of morning. The first song is nearly a cry, fear and the pain of remembrance sharpening away the pure music. And that is this book.

The last years have been years of demolition. Because faith and belief were getting pot-bound, and the Temple was made a place to barter sacrifices, therefore faith and belief and the Temple must be broken. This time art fought the battle, rather than science or any new religious faction. And art has been demolishing for us: Nietzsche, the Christian religion as it stood; Hardy, our faith in our own endeavour; Flaubert, our belief in love. Now, for us, it is all smashed, we can see the whole again. We were in prison, peeping at the sky through loop-holes. The great prisoners smashed at the loop-holes, for lying to us. And behold, out of the ruins leaps the whole sky.

It is we who see it and breathe in it for joy. God is there, faith, belief, love, everything. We are drunk with the joy of it, having got away from the fear. In almost every poem in the book comes this note of exultation after fear, the exultation in the vast freedom, the illimitable wealth that we have suddenly got.

> But send desire often forth to scan
> The immense night that is thy greater soul,

says Mr. Abercrombie. His deadly sin is Prudence, that will not risk to avail itself of the new freedom. Mr. Bottomley exults to find men for ever building religions which yet can never compass all.

> Yet the yielding sky
> Invincible vacancy was there discovered.

Mr. Rupert Brooke sees

> every glint
> Posture and jest and thought and tint
> Freed from the mask of transiency
> Triumphant in eternity,
> Immote, immortal

and this at Afternoon Tea. Mr. John Drinkwater sings:

> We cherish every hour that strays
> Adown the cataract of days:
> We see the clear, untroubled skies,
> We see the glory of the rose –

Mr. Wilfrid Wilson Gibson hears the 'terror turned to tenderness,' then

> I watched the mother sing to rest
> The baby snuggling on her breast.

And to Mr. Masefield:

40

> When men count
> Those hours of life that were a bursting fount
> Sparkling the dusty heart with living springs,
> There seems a world, beyond our earthly things,
> Gated by golden moments.

It is all the same – hope, and religious joy. Nothing is really wrong. Every new religion is a waste-product from the last, and every religion stands for us for ever. We love Christianity for what it has brought us, now that we are no longer upon the cross.

The great liberation gives us an overwhelming sense of joy, *joie d'être, joie de vivre*. This sense of exceeding keen relish and appreciation of life makes romance. I think I could say every poem in the book is romantic, tinged with a love of the marvellous, a joy of natural things, as if the poet were a child for the first time on the seashore, finding treasures. 'Best trust the happy moments,' says Mr. 50 Masefield, who seems nearest to the black dream behind us. There is Mr. W.H. Davies's lovely joy, Mr. De La Mare's perfect appreciation of life at still moments, Mr. Rupert Brooke's brightness, when he 'lived from laugh to laugh', Mr. Edmund Beale Sargant's pure, excited happiness in the woodland – it is all the same, keen zest in life found wonderful. In Mr. Gordon Bottomley it is the zest of activity, of hurrying, labouring men, or the zest of the utter stillness of long snows. It is a bookful of Romance that has not quite got clear of the terror of realism.

There is no *carpe diem* touch. The joy is sure and fast. It is not the 60 falling rose, but the rose for ever rising to bud and falling to fruit that gives us joy. We have faith in the vastness of life's wealth. We are always rich: rich in buds and in shed blossoms. There is no winter that we fear. Life is like an orange tree, always in leaf and bud, in blossom and fruit.

And we ourselves, in each of us, have everything. Somebody said: 'The Georgian poets are not love poets. The influence of Swinburne has gone.' But I should say the Georgian poets are just ripening to be love poets. Swinburne was no love poet. What are the Georgian poets, nearly all, but just bursting into a thick blaze of being? They 70 are not poets of passion, perhaps, but they are essentially passionate poets. The time to be impersonal has gone. We start from the joy we have in being ourselves, and everything must take colour from that joy. It is the return of the blood, that has been held back, as when the heart's action is arrested by fear. Now the warmth of blood is in everything, quick, healthy, passionate blood. I look at my hands as I write and know they are mine, with red blood running its way, sleuthing out Truth and pursuing it to eternity, and I am full of awe for this flesh and blood that holds this pen. Everything that ever was thought and ever will be thought, lies in this body of mine. This 80 flesh and blood sitting here writing, the great impersonal flesh and blood, greater than me, which I am proud to belong to, contains all the future. What is it but the quick of all growth, the seed of all harvest, this body of mine? And grapes and corn and birds and rocks and visions, all are in my fingers. I am so full of wonder at my own miracle of flesh and blood that I could not contain myself, if I did not remember we are all alive, have all of us living bodies. And that is a joy greater than any dream of immortality in the spirit, to me. It reminds me of Rupert Brooke's moment triumphant in its eternality; and of Michelangelo, who is also the moment triumphant   90 in its eternality; just the opposite from Corot, who is the eternal triumphing over the moment, at the moment, at the very point of sweeping it into the flow.

Of all love poets, we are the love poets. For our religion is loving. To love passionately, but completely, is our one desire.

What is 'The Hare' but a complete love poem, with none of the hackneyed 'But a bitter blossom was born' about it, nor yet the Yeats, 'Never give all the heart.' Love is the greatest of all things, no 'bitter blossom' nor suchlike. It is sex-passion, so separated, in which we do not believe. The *Carmen* and *Tosca* sort of passion is not interesting   100 any longer, because it can't progress. Its goal and aim is possession, whereas possession in love is only a means to love. And because passion cannot go beyond possession, the passionate heroes and heroines – Tristans and what-not – must die. We believe in the love that is happy ever after, progressive as life itself.

I worship Christ, I worship Jehovah, I worship Pan, I worship Aphrodite. But I do not worship hands nailed and running with blood upon a cross, nor licentiousness, nor lust. I want them all, all the gods. They are all God. But I must serve in real love. If I take my whole, passionate, spiritual and physical love to the woman who   110 in return loves me, that is how I serve God. And my hymn and my game of joy is my work. All of which I read in the anthology of *Georgian Poetry*.

EXTRACT FROM A LETTER TO EDWARD MARSH,
FROM ITALY, 28 OCTOBER 1913

Poor Davies – he makes me so furious, and so sorry. He's really like a linnet that's got just a wee little sweet song, but it only sings when it's wild. And he's made himself a tame bird – poor little devil. He makes me furious. 'I shall be all right now the winter is coming', he writes, 'now I can sit by the fire and work'. As if he could sing when he's been straining his heart to make a sound of music, for months. It isn't as if he were a passionate writer, writing his 'agon'. Oh my God, he's like teaching a bull-finch to talk. I think one ought to be downright cruel to him, and drive him back: say to him 'Davies, your work is getting like Birmingham tinware; Davies, you drop your h's,   10
and everybody is tempering the wind to you, because you are a shorn lamb; Davies, your accent is intolerable in a carpeted room; Davies, you hang on like the mud on a lady's silk petticoat.' Then he might leave his Sevenoaks room, where he is rigged up as rural poet, proud of the gilt mirror and his romantic past: and he might grow his wings again, and chirrup a little sadder song.

And now I've got to quarrel with you about the Ralph Hodgson poem because I think it is banal in utterance. The feeling is there, right enough – but not in itself, only represented. It's like 'I asked for bread, and he gave me a penny'. Only here and there is the least   20
touch of personality in the poem: it is the currency of poetry, not poetry itself. Every single line of it is poetic currency – and a good deal of emotion handling it about. But it isn't really poetry. I hope to God you won't hate me and think me carping, for this. But look

'the ruby's and the rainbow's song
the nightingale's – all three'

There's the emotion in the rhythm, but it's loose emotion, inarticulate, common – the words are mere currency. It is exactly like a man who feels very strongly for a beggar, and gives him a sovereign. The feeling is at either end, for the moment, but the sovereign is a dead bit of metal. And this poem is the sovereign. 'Oh, I do want to give you this emotion', cries Hodgson, 'I do'. And so he takes out   30
his poetic purse, and gives you a handful of cash, and feels very strongly, even a bit sentimentally over it.

'. . . the sky was lit
The sky was stars all over it,
I stood, I knew not why'

No one should say 'I knew not why' any more. It is as meaningless as 'yours truly' at the end of a letter.

EXTRACT FROM A LETTER TO EDWARD MARSH,
18 NOVEMBER 1913

Lerici, per Fiascherino, Golfo della Spezia, Italy
Tuesday

Dear Marsh,

You *are* wrong. It makes me open my eyes. I think I read my poetry more by length than by stress – as a matter of movements in space than footsteps hitting the earth.

Just a few of the roses we gathered by the Isar
Are fallen, and their blood-red petals on the cloth,
Float like boats on a river, waiting
For a fairy wind to wake them from their sloth.

I think more of a bird with broad wings flying and lapsing through the air, than anything, when I think of metre. – So I read

I wonder if that is quite unintelligible. I am sure I am right. There is a double method of scanning verse – if you'll notice it.

Ì have / forgòt / much/, Cỳnara! / goǹe with the / wiǹd
Flung ròses/, ròses / riòtously / with the / thròng /

Daǹcing / to pùt / thy pàle, / lost lìl/ies oùt / of miǹd;
But Ì / was dès/olàte/, and sìck / of an ol̀d / pàssion/,
 Yea, all the time because the dance was long:
I have been faithful to thee Cynara, in my fashion.

Would you scan like that? I hate an on-foot method of reading. I should go

υ υ υ υ _   ‿υυ   _υυ_
υ   ‿υ ‿υ   ‿υυ   υυ _
‿‿υ υυυ __   υ   ‿υ   _
υυυ ‿υυ υ   _υυ_   ‿υ

It all depends on the *pause* – the natural pause, the natural *lingering*   10
of the voice according to the feeling – it is the hidden *emotional*
pattern that makes poetry, not the obvious form.

υ υ   υυ   ——   ——υυ   ——   υ   υ ——
I have forgot much, Cynara, gone with the wind

It is the lapse of the feeling, something as indefinite as expression in
the voice, carrying emotion. It doesn't depend on the ear,
particularly, but on the sensitive soul. And the ear gets a habit, and
becomes master, when the ebbing and lifting emotion should be
master, and the ear the transmitter. If your ear has got stiff and a bit
mechanical, *don't* blame my poetry. That's why you like *Golden
Journey to Samarkand* – it fits your habituated ear, and your feeling
crouches subservient and a bit pathetic. 'It satisfies my ear' you say.   20
Well, I don't write for your ear. This is the constant war, I reckon,
between new expression and the habituated, mechanical transmitters
and receivers of the human constitution.

 I can't tell you what *pattern* I see in any poetry, save one complete
thing. But surely you don't class poetry among the decorative or
conventional arts. I always wonder if the Greeks and Romans really
did scan, or if scansion wasn't a thing invented afterwards by the
schoolmaster. – Yet I seem to find about the same number of long,
lingering notes in each line. – I know nothing about it. I only know
you aren't right.   30

 You are wrong, I think, about the two rhymes – why need you
notice they are rhymes? – you are a bit of a policeman in poetry. I

never put them in because they are rhymes.

'Drearisome' I am guilty of – peccavo.

'Sloth' I feel a *bit* guilty about – not quite so guilty as you would have me. I'm not sure about 'Purity' – I always felt suspicious of it, and yet I am inclined to think it is good.

'The land of her glad surmise' is a penny, not a sovereign. I always knew it was shocking bad. – I must think about that ballad.

I rather suspect you of being a young Philistine with the poetry   40
of youth on you, and the –

But I *am* being a David that throws stones.

Don't mind me. I find it frightfully easy to theorise and say all the things I don't mean, and frightfully difficult to find out even for myself, what I do mean.

I only *know* that the verse you quote against me is right, and you are wrong. And I am a poor, maligned, misunderstood, patronised and misread poet, and soon I shall burst into tears.

But thanks be to God above, my poetry doesn't stick to me. My wife has a beastly habit of comparing poetry – all literature in   50
fact – to the droppings of the goats among the rocks – mere excreta that fertilises the ground it falls on.

I think I came a *real* cropper in my belief in metre, over Shelley. I tried all roads to scan him, but could never *read* him as he could be scanned. And I thought what bit of Latin scansion I did was a *horrible* fake: I never believed for an instant in the Sapphic form – and Horace is already a bit of a mellow varsity man who never quite forgot Oxford.

EXTRACT FROM A LETTER TO HENRY SAVAGE,
22 DECEMBER 1913

> *Lerici*, per Fiascherino, Golfo della Spezia, Italy
> 22 Dec 1913

Dear Savage,

What a rum chap you are. Now you're discovering Whitman and humanity. But don't you see, he says all men are my brothers, and straightway goes into the wilderness to love them. Don't let yourself

in for a terrific chagrin. But I'm glad you've discovered Humanity: it is fearfully nice to feel it round one. If you read my poetry – especially the earlier rough stuff which was published in the *English Review*, and isn't in the book of poems, you would see how much it has meant to me. Only, the bitterness of it is, that while one is brother to all men, and wrote *Macbeth* with Shakespeare and the Bible with James the First's doctors, one still remains Henry Savage or   10
D.H. Lawrence, with one's own little life to live, and one's own handful of thoughts to write. And it is so hard to combine the two, and not to lose oneself in the generalisation, and not to lose the big joy of the whole in being narrowly oneself. Which is a preach. But perhaps you, like Whitman or Christ, can take the Church to bride, and give yourself, bodily and spiritually, to the abstract. The fault about Whitman is, strictly, that he is too self-conscious to be what he says he is: he's not Walt Whitman, I, the joyous American, he is Walt Whitman, the Cosmos, trying to fit a cosmos inside his own skin: a man rongé with unsatisfiedness not at all pouring his seed into   20
American brides to make Stalwart American Sons, but pouring his seed into the space, into the idea of humanity. Poor man, it is pathetic when he makes even an idea of his own flesh and blood. He was a martyr like Christ, in a slightly different sort. – I don't mind people being martyrs in themselves, but to make an idea of the flesh and blood is wrong. The flesh and blood must go its own road. There is something wrong with Whitman, when he addresses American women as his Stalwart brides in whom he is to pour the seed for Stalwart Sons. One doesn't think like that. Imagine yourself addressing English women like that, in the mass. One *doesn't* feel like   30
that – except in the moments of wide, gnawing desire when everything has gone wrong. – Whitman is like a human document, or a wonderful treatise in human self revelation. It is neither art nor religion nor truth: Just a self revelation of a man who could not live, and so had to write himself. But writing should come from a strong root of life: like a battle song after a battle. – And Whitman did this, more or less. But his battle was not a real battle: he never gave his individual self into the fight: he was too much aware of it. He never fought with another person – he was like a wrestler who only wrestles with his own shadow – he never came to grips. He chucked   40

his body into the fight, and stood apart saying 'Look how I am living'. He is really false as hell. – But he is fine too. Only, I am sure, the generalisations are *no good* to the individual: the individual comes first, then the generalisation is a kind of game, not a reality: just a surplus, an excess, not a whole.

About spiritual pride, I think you are right. I can't understand you when you think so much of books and genius. They are great too – but they are the cake and wine of life – there is the bread and butter first, the ordinary human contact, the exchange with individuals of a bit of our individual selves, like beggars might exchange   50
bits of crust on the road side. But Whitman did not take a person: he took that generalised thing, a Woman, an Athlete, a Youth. And this is wrong, wrong, wrong. He should take Gretchen, or one Henry Wilton. It *is* no use blanking the person out to have a sort of representative.

A harangue, all for Christmas. I wish I could send you some little thing, you have been so good for me – we are [. . .] very grateful. Soon my play will come, and then I shall send you a copy. – At any rate, whatever Whitman is, I hope he's really let you loose from some bondage – he can do. I am glad you will rejoice in humanity. There   60
is something a bit Greek, and a bit Christian in it: it has produced Greek art, and Michael Angelo – but not Rembrandt. – And it is largely wrong: too much intellect, too much generalisation in it. You *should* read Gilbert Murray's Euripides translations – I wish I'd got some to give you.

Yrs D. H. Lawrence

LETTER TO HARRIET MONROE, 17 NOVEMBER 1914

Bellingdon Lane, Chesham, Bucks.
17 Nov. 1914

Dear Harriet Monroe:

Yesterday came your cheque for £8. Thank you very much.

Today came the War Number of *Poetry,* for which also I thank you. It put me into such a rage – how dare Amy talk about bohemian glass and stalks of flame? – that in a real fury I had to write my war poem, because it breaks my heart, this war.

I hate, and hate, and hate the glib irreverence of some of your contributors – Aldington with his 'do you know what it's all about, brother Jonathan, we don't?' It is obvious he doesn't. And your nasty, obscene, vulgar in the last degree – 'Hero' – John Russell McCarthy – may God tread him out – why did you put him in? You shouldn't.

At least I like the woman who wrote 'Metal Checks' – her idea, her attitude – but her poetry is pretty bad. I rather like the suggestion of Marian Ramie's 'Face I shall never see – man I shall never see'. And 'Unser Gott' isn't bad – but unbeautifully ugly. Your people have such little pressure: their safety valve goes off at the high scream when the pressure is still so low. Have you no people with any force in them. Aldington almost shows most – if he weren't so lamentably imitating Hueffer.

I don't care what you do with my war poem. I don't particularly care if I don't hear of it any more. The war is dreadful. It is the business of the artist to follow it home to the heart of the individual fighters – not to talk in armies and nations and numbers – but to track it home – home – their war – and it's at the bottom of almost every Englishman's heart – the war – the desire of war – the *will* to war – and at the bottom of every German's.

Don't put common things in like the 'Campfollower' – why do you? They are only ugly ugly – 'putrid lips' – it is something for the nasty people of this world to batten on.

I typed my poem on a typewriter Amy Lowell gave me. I think I did it quite well – and it was thrilling. I like it when you send me *Poetry*, even if it makes me rage.

Vale. D.H. Lawrence

Take care how you regard my war poem – it is good.

POEM AND LETTER TO LADY CYNTHIA ASQUITH,
2 NOVEMBER 1915

THE TURNING BACK

There has been so much noise
So much bleeding and shouting and dying
So much clamour of death.

There are so many dead
So many ghosts among us:
Between me and thee, so many ghosts of the slain.

Be still then, and let be.
How long shall we strike through the immutable ghosts of the slain?
How long shall we shriek and shout across the silence of ghosts?

Hush, let the silence be   10
For a moment over us,
Perfect and utter stillness within and without

Oh listen to the stillness of the ghosts
That press noiselessly about us, for a place
Wherein to rest, wherein to lie at peace.

II

But I have enemies, and something they want,
Houses and land and having, chattels and goods!
Say they may have it all, I give it them

They must be lords and masters over me
Bidding my outgoing and my incoming?   20
Say they may have it so, I yield it them.

They want my life, they want me to be dead?
Tell them they are mistaken, it is not true,
They do not want my life, me to be dead.

Yes, still they want my life, me to be dead.
Tell them to come and see that they are mistaken.
But if in the end they want it, let them take it.

For as for me, I have no enemies.
I am older than they, so I can understand
That they do evil, seeing I have done so ill.   30

III

We have gone too far, oh very much too far;
Only attend to the noiseless multitudes
Of ghosts that throng about our muffled hearts.

Only behold the ghosts, the ghosts of the slain,
Behold them homeless and houseless, without complaint
Of their patient waiting upon us, the throng of the ghosts.

And say, what matters any more, what matters
Save the cold ghosts that homeless flock about
Our serried hearts, drifting without a place?

What matters any more, but only love?   40
There's only love that matters any more.
There's only love, the rest is all outspent.

Let us receive our ghosts, and give them place,
Open the ranks, and let them in our hearts,
And lay them deep in love, lay them to sleep.

The foe can take our goods, and homes and land,
Also the lives that still he may require,
But leave us still to love, still leave us love.

Leave us to take our ghosts into our hearts,
To lap them round with love, and lay them by   50
To sleep at last in immemorial love.

We let the weapons slip from out our hands,
We loose our grip, and we unstrain our eyes,
We let our souls be pure and vulnerable.

We cover the houseless dead, so they sleep in peace,
We yield the enemy his last demands
So he too may be healed, be soothed to peace.

For now the hosts of homeless ghosts do throng
Too many about us, so we wander about
Blind with the gossamer of prevalent death.   60

But let us free our eyes, and look beyond
This serried ecstasy of prevalent death,
And pass beyond, with the foe and the homeless ghosts.

Let us rise up, and go from out this grey
Last twilight of the gods, to find again
The lost Hesperides where love is pure.

For we have gone too far, oh much too far
Towards the darkness and the shadow of death;
Let us turn back, lest we should all be lost

Let us go back now, though we give up all   70
The treasure and the vaunt we ever had,
Let us go back, the only way is love.

                                        Hampstead.
                                        2 Nov. 1915.

My dear Lady Cynthia,

   I will answer you straight away about the 'downing tools'. First
of all I send you the poem, which might help to convince you. You
say that the war does not prevent *personal* life from going on, that
the individual can still love and be complete. It isn't true. The one
quality of love is that it universalises the individual. If I love, then
I am extended over all people, but particularly over my own nation.
It is an extending in concentric waves over all people. This is the
process of love. And if I love, I, the individual, then necessarily the
love extends from me to my nearest neighbour, and outwards, and
outwards, till it loses itself in vast distance. This *is* love, there is no   10
love but this. So that if I love, the love must beat upon my
neighbours, till they too live in the spirit of the love, and so on,
further and further. And how can this be, in war, when the spirit
is against love.

   The spirit of war is, that I am a unit, a single entity that has no

66

intrinsic reference to the rest: the reference is extrinsic, a question of living, not of *being*. In war, in my *being* I am a detached entity, and every one of my actions is an act of further detaching my own single entity from all the rest.

If I love, then, I am in direct opposition to the principle of war. If war prevails, I do not love. If love prevails, there is no war. War is a great and necessary disintegrating autumnal process. Love is the great creative process, like Spring, the making an integral unity out of many disintegrated factors. We have had enough of the disintegrating process. If it goes on any further, we shall so thoroughly have destroyed the unifying force from among us, we shall have become each one of us so completely a separate entity, that the whole will be an amorphous heap, like sand, sterile, hopeless, useless, like a dead tree. This is true, and it is so great a danger, that one almost goes mad, facing it.

That is why I almost went away, out of the country: I may still have to go: because in myself I can never agree to the complete disintegration, never stand witness to it, never.

Then the Prussian rule. The Prussian rule would be an external evil. The disintegrating process of the war has become an internal evil, so vast as to be almost unthinkable, so nearly overwhelming us, that we stand on the very brink of oblivion. Better *anything* than the utter disintegration. And it is *England* who is the determining factor for Europe: if England goes, then Europe goes: for we are at this time the vital core of the whole organism. Let the leaves perish, but let the tree stand, living and bare. For the tree, the living organism of the soul of Europe is good, only the external forms and growths are bad. Let all the leaves fall, and many branches. But the quick of the tree must not perish. There are unrevealed buds which can come forward into another epoch of civilisation, if only we can shed this dead form and be strong in the spirit of love and creation.

Besides, Germany, Prussia, is not evil through and through. Her mood is now *evil*. But we reap what we have sowed. It is as with a child: if with a sullen, evil soul one provokes an evil mood in the child, there is destruction. But no child is all evil. And Germany is the child of Europe: and senile Europe, with her conventions and arbitrary rules of conduct and life and very being, has provoked

Germany into a purely destructive mood. If a mother does this to a child – and it often happens – is she to go on till the child is killed or broken, so that the mother have her way? – Is she not rather, at a certain point, to yield to the paroxysm of the child, which passes away *swiftly* when the opposition is removed? And if Prussia for a time imposes her rule on us, let us bear it, as a mother temporarily bears the ugly tyranny of the child, trusting in the ultimate good. The good will not be long in coming, all over Europe, if we can but   60 trust it within ourselves. (This is not yielding to the child – this is knowing beyond the child's knowledge.)

I very much want you to tell me what you think, because it is a question for the *women* of the land now to decide: the men will never see it. I don't know one single man who would give the faintest response to this. But I still have some hope of the women: they should *know* that only love matters, now; that further destruction only means death, universal death, disintegration.

THE SEA

You, you are all unloving, loveless, you;
Restless and lonely, shaken by your own moods,
You are celibate and single, scorning a comrade even,
Threshing your own passions with no woman for the threshing-
    floor,
Finishing your dreams for your own sake only,
Playing your great game around the world, alone,
Without playmate, or helpmate, having no one to cherish,
No one to comfort, and refusing any comforter.

Not like the earth, the spouse all full of increase,
Moiled over with the rearing of her many-mouthed young;   10
You are single, you are fruitless, phosphorescent, cold and callous,
Naked of worship, of love or of adornment,
Scorning the panacea even of labour,
Sworn to a high and splendid purposelessness
Of brooding and delighting in the secret of life's goings,
Sea, only you are free, sophisticated.

You who toil not, you who spin not,
Surely but for you and your like, toiling
Were not worth while, nor spinning worth the effort!

You who take the moon as in a sieve, and sift   20
Her flake by flake and spread her meaning out;
You who roll the stars like jewels in your palm,
So that they seem to utter themselves aloud;
You who steep from out the days their colour,
Reveal the universal tint that dyes
Their web; who shadow the sun's great gestures and expressions
So that he seems a stranger in his passing;
Who voice the dumb night fittingly;
Sea, you shadow of all things, now mock us to death with your
    shadowing.

Bournemouth

GREEN

The dawn was apple-green,
    The sky was green wine held up in the sun,
The moon was a golden petal between.

She opened her eyes, and green
    They shone, clear like flowers undone
For the first time, now for the first time seen.

Icking

RIVER ROSES

By the Isar, in the twilight
We were wandering and singing,
By the Isar, in the evening
We climbed the huntsman's ladder and sat swinging
In the fir-tree overlooking the marshes,
While river met with river, and the ringing
Of their pale-green glacier-water filled the evening.

By the Isar, in the twilight
We found the dark wild roses
Hanging red at the river; and simmering   10
Frogs were singing, and over the river closes
Was savour of ice and roses; and glimmering
Fear was abroad. We whispered: 'No one knows us.
Let it be as the snake disposes
Here in this simmering marsh.'

Kloster Schaeftlarn

GLOIRE DE DIJON

When she rises in the morning
I linger to watch her;
She spreads the bath-cloth underneath the window
And the sunbeams catch her
Glistening white on the shoulders,
While down her sides the mellow
Golden shadow glows as
She stoops to the sponge, and her swung breasts
Sway like full-blown yellow
Gloire de Dijon roses.   10

She drips herself with water, and her shoulders
Glisten as silver, they crumple up
Like wet and falling roses, and I listen
For the sluicing of their rain-dishevelled petals.
In the window full of sunlight
Concentrates her golden shadow
Fold on fold, until it glows as
Mellow as the glory roses.

Icking

A DOE AT EVENING

As I went through the marshes
a doe sprang out of the corn
and flashed up the hill-side
leaving her fawn.

On the sky-line
she moved round to watch,
she pricked a fine black blotch
on the sky.

I looked at her
and felt her watching;   10
I became a strange being.
Still, I had my right to be there with her.

Her nimble shadow trotting
along the sky-line, she
put back her fine, level-balanced head.
And I knew her.

Ah yes, being male, is not my head hard-balanced, antlered?
Are not my haunches light?
Has she not fled on the same wind with me?
Does not my fear cover her fear?   20

Irschenhausen

CRAVING FOR SPRING

I wish it were spring in the world.

Let it be spring!
Come, bubbling, surging tide of sap!
Come, rush of creation!
Come, life! surge through this mass of mortification!
Come, sweep away these exquisite, ghastly first-flowers,
which are rather last-flowers!
Come, thaw down their cool portentousness, dissolve them;

snowdrops, straight, death-veined exhalations of white and purple
     crocuses,
flowers of the penumbra, issue of corruption, nourished in
     mortification,   10
jets of exquisite finality;
Come, spring, make havoc of them!

I trample on the snowdrops, it gives me pleasure to tread down the
     jonquils,
to destroy the chill Lent lilies;
for I am sick of them, their faint-bloodedness,
slow-blooded, icy-fleshed, portentous.

I want the fine, kindling wine-sap of spring,
gold, and of inconceivably fine, quintessential brightness,
rare almost as beams, yet overwhelmingly potent,
strong like the greatest force of world-balancing.   20

This is the same that picks up the harvest of wheat
and rocks it, tons of grain, on the ripening wind;
the same that dangles the globe-shaped pleiads of fruit
temptingly in mid-air, between a playful thumb and finger;
oh, and suddenly, from out of nowhere, whirls the pear-bloom,
upon us, and apple- and almond- and apricot- and quince-blossom,
storms and cumulus clouds of all imaginable blossom
about our bewildered faces,
though we do not worship.

I wish it were spring   30
cunningly blowing on the fallen sparks, odds and ends of the old,
     scattered fire,
and kindling shapely little conflagrations
curious long-legged foals, and wide-eared calves, and naked
     sparrow-bubs.

I wish that spring
would start the thundering traffic of feet
new feet on the earth, beating with impatience.

I wish it were spring, thundering
delicate, tender spring.
I wish these brittle, frost-lovely flowers of passionate, mysterious
   corruption
were not yet to come still more from the still-flickering discontent.   40

Oh, in the spring, the bluebell bows him down for very exuberance,
exulting with secret warm excess,
bowed down with his inner magnificence!

Oh, yes, the gush of spring is strong enough
to toss the globe of earth like a ball on a water-jet
dancing sportfully;
as you see a tiny celluloid ball tossing on a squirt of water
for men to shoot at, penny-a-time, in a booth at a fair.

The gush of spring is strong enough
to play with the globe of earth like a ball on a fountain;   50
At the same time it opens the tiny hands of the hazel
with such infinite patience.

The power of the rising, golden, all-creative sap could take the earth
and heave it off among the stars, into the invisible;
the same sets the throstle at sunset on a bough
singing against the blackbird;
comes out in the hesitating tremor of the primrose,
and betrays its candour in the round white strawberry flower,
is dignified in the foxglove, like a Red-Indian brave.

Ah come, come quickly, spring!   60
Come and lift us towards our culmination, we myriads;
we who have never flowered, like patient cactuses.
Come and lift us to our end, to blossom, bring us to our summer
we who are winter-weary in the winter of the world.
Come making the chaffinch nests hollow and cosy,
come and soften the willow buds till they are puffed and furred,
then blow them over with gold.
Come and cajole the gawky colt's-foot flowers.

Come quickly, and vindicate us
against too much death.   70

Come quickly, and stir the rotten globe of the world from within,
burst it with germination, with world anew.
Come now, to us, your adherents, who cannot flower from the ice.
All the world gleams with the lilies of Death the Unconquerable,
but come, give us our turn.
Enough of the virgins and lilies, of passionate, suffocating perfume
    of corruption,
no more narcissus perfume, lily harlots, the blades of sensation
piercing the flesh to blossom of death.
Have done, have done with this shuddering, delicious business
of thrilling ruin in the flesh, of pungent passion, of rare,   80
    death-edged ecstasy.
Give us our turn, give us a chance, let our hour strike,
O soon, soon!

Let the darkness turn violet with rich dawn.
Let the darkness be warmed, warmed through to a ruddy violet,
incipient purpling towards summer in the world of the heart of man.

Are the violets already here!
Show me! I tremble so much to hear it, that even now
on the threshold of spring, I fear I shall die.
Show me the violets that are out.

Oh, if it be true, and the living darkness of the blood of man is
    purpling with violets,   90
if the violets are coming out from under the rack of men, winter-
    rotten and fallen
we shall have spring.
Pray not to die on this Pisgah blossoming with violets.
Pray to live through.

If you catch a whiff of violets from the darkness of the shadow of
    man
it will be spring in the world,
it will be spring in the world of the living;
wonderment organising itself, heralding itself with the violets,
stirring of new seasons.

Ah, do not let me die on the brink of such anticipation!   100
Worse, let me not deceive myself.

Zennor

AFTER THE OPERA

Down the stone stairs
Girls with their large eyes wide with tragedy
Lift looks of shocked and momentous emotions up at me.
And I smile.

Ladies
Stepping like birds with their bright and pointed feet
Peer anxiously forth, as if for a boat to carry them out of the
    wreckage,
And among the wreck of the theatre crowd
I stand and smile.

They take tragedy so becomingly.   10
Which pleases me.

But when I meet the weary eyes
The reddened aching eyes of the bar-man with thin arms,
I am glad to go back where I came from.

JOHN GOULD FLETCHER: FROM A REVIEW OF *LOOK! WE HAVE COME THROUGH!*

D. H. Lawrence has recently published a third volume of poetry
[*Look! We Have Come Through!*] to stand beside his *Love Poems* and
Amores. This event has, so far as I am aware, passed almost without
notice in the English press. The reviewers of the English press know
perfectly well that Mr Lawrence is supposed to be a dangerous man,
writing too frankly on certain subjects which are politely considered
taboo in good society, and therefore they do their best to prevent Mr
Lawrence from writing at all, by tacitly ignoring him. If they are
driven to the admission, these selfsame reviewers are obliged grud-
gingly to acknowledge that Mr Lawrence is one of the most   10

interesting of modern writers. Such are the conditions which a modern writer with something new to say is obliged to accept in England today. The Press can make a great to-do about the innocuous, blameless and essentially minor poetry of Edward Thomas (to take but one example); they politely refuse to discuss the questionable, but essentially major effort of a D.H. Lawrence. Is it any wonder that such an attitude drives a man to sheer fanaticism? . . .

Poetry is at once highly objective and highly subjective. It is objective in so far as it deals with words, which are in a strong sense objects, as with the external world in its objective aspects. It is subjective, because it also states the poet's subjective reactions to words and to all external phenomena. Lawrence is one of the few poets in England today who keeps this dual role of poetry well in mind; and that is why his poetry, though it may often be badly written, is never without energy and a sense of power.

The reason for his failings as a poet must be sought elsewhere than in his attitude to life. We can only understand why he fails if we understand the conditions under which he is forced to write. With a reasonable degree of independence, a public neither openly hostile nor totally indifferent, an intellectual *milieu* capable of finer life and better understanding, Lawrence would become nothing but an artist. He has none of these things; and so he is forced, by destiny itself, to become the thing he probably began by loathing, a propagandist, a preacher, an evangelist.

This brings him into close connection with Walt Whitman, who similarly spent his life in preaching with puritanical fervour a most unpuritan gospel. Indeed, if one examines closely Lawrence's latest technique as shown here in such poems as 'Manifesto' and 'New Heaven and Earth', one is surprised to see how close this comes in many respects to that of the earlier Whitman, the Whitman of 'The Song of Myself'. For example, note the selfsame use of long, rolling, orchestral rhythm in the two following passages:

> When I gathered flowers, I knew it was myself plucking my
> own flowering,
> When I went in a train, I knew it was myself travelling by my
> own invention,

> When I heard the cannon of war, I listened with my own ears
>   to my own destruction.
> When I saw the torn dead, I knew it was my own torn dead body.
> It was all me, I had done it all in my own flesh.
> ('New Heaven and Earth')

> Every kind for itself and its own, for me, mine, male and female,
> For me those that have been boys and that love women,
> For me the man that is proud and feels how it stings to be slighted,
> For me the sweet-heart and the old maid, for me mothers and
>   the mothers of mothers,
> For me lips that have smiled, eyes that have shed tears,
> For me children and the begetters of children.
> ('The Song of Myself')

The difference is (and this too is curiously brought out in the technique) that Lawrence is more delicate, more sensitive, more personal. He deliberately narrows his range, to embrace only life and his own life in particular. Unlike Whitman, he has a horror of the infinite, and I am sure that he could never bring himself to 'utter the word Democracy, the word *en-masse*'. He is an aristocrat, an individualist, and indeed, he has only a horror of the collective mass of mankind, which he sees (and in this case, he sees more clearly than Whitman) to have been always conservative, conventional, timid, and persecutors of genius. In fact, the only similarity is, that both he and Whitman are preachers of new gospels, and therefore are obliged to adopt a similar tone of oratory in their work.

For this reason, Lawrence in his best poetry is unquotable, as is the case with all poets who depend rather on the extension of emotion, than on its minute concentration. But now and again he produces something that seems to transform all the poetry now written in English into mere prettiness and feebleness, so strong is the power with which his imagination pierces its subject. Such a poem, for example, is the one called 'The Sea'. I have space for only its last magnificent stanza:

> You who take the moon as in a sieve, and sift
> Her flake by flake and spread her meaning out;
> You who roll the stars like jewels in your palm,
> So that they seem to utter themselves aloud;

You who steep from out the days their colour,
Reveal the universal tint that dyes
Their web; who shadow the sun's great gestures and
    expressions
So that he seems a stranger in his passing;
Who voice the dumb night fittingly;
Sea, you shadow of all things, now mock us to death with your
    shadowing.

The man who wrote this, and many other passages in this volume, has at last arrived at his maturity – the maturity of the creative artist who is able to grasp a subject through its external aspect and internal meaning simultaneously, and to express both aspects in conjunction, before the subject is laid aside.

INTRODUCTION TO *NEW POEMS*

It seems when we hear a skylark singing as if sound were running into the future, running so fast and utterly without consideration, straight on into futurity. And when we hear a nightingale, we hear the pause and the rich, piercing rhythm of recollection, the perfected past. The lark may sound sad, but with the lovely lapsing sadness that is almost a swoon of hope. The nightingale's triumph is a pæan, but a death-pæan.

So it is with poetry. Poetry is, as a rule, either the voice of the far future, exquisite and ethereal, or it is the voice of the past, rich, magnificent. When the Greeks heard the *Iliad* and the *Odyssey*, they heard their own past calling in their hearts, as men far inland sometimes hear the sea and fall weak with powerful, wonderful regret, nostalgia; or else their own future rippled its time-beats through their blood, as they followed the painful, glamorous progress of the Ithacan. This was Homer to the Greeks: their Past, splendid with battles won and death achieved, and their Future, the magic wandering of Ulysses through the unknown.

With us it is the same. Our birds sing on the horizons. They sing out of the blue, beyond us, or out of the quenched night. They sing at dawn and sunset. Only the poor, shrill, tame canaries whistle while we talk. The wild birds begin before we are awake, or as we drop into dimness, out of waking. Our poets sit by the gateways, some by the east, some by the west. As we arrive and as we go out our hearts surge with response. But whilst we are in the midst of life, we do not hear them.

The poetry of the beginning and the poetry of the end must have that exquisite finality, perfection which belongs to all that is far off. It is in the realm of all that is perfect. It is of the nature of all that is complete and consummate. This completeness, this consummateness, the finality and the perfection are conveyed in exquisite form: the perfect symmetry, the rhythm which returns upon itself like a dance where the hands link and loosen and link for the supreme moment of the end. Perfected bygone moments, perfected moments in the glimmering futurity, these are the treasured gem-like lyrics of Shelley and Keats.

But there is another kind of poetry: the poetry of that which is at hand: the immediate present. In the immediate present there is no perfection, no consummation, nothing finished. The strands are all flying, quivering, intermingling into the web, the waters are shaking the moon. There is no round, consummate moon on the face of running water, nor on the face of the unfinished tide. There are no gems of the living plasm. The living plasm vibrates unspeakably, it inhales the future, it exhales the past, it is the quick of both, and yet it is neither. There is no plasmic finality, nothing crystal, permanent. If we try to fix the living tissue, as the biologists fix it with formation, we have only a hardened bit of the past, the bygone life under our observation.

Life, the ever-present, knows no finality, no finished crystallisation. The perfect rose is only a running flame, emerging and flowing off, and never in any sense at rest, static, finished. Herein lies its transcendent loveliness. The whole tide of all life and all time suddenly heaves, and appears before us as an apparition, a revelation. We look at the very white quick of nascent creation. A water-lily heaves herself from the flood, looks around, gleams, and is gone. We have seen the incarnation, the quick of the ever-swirling flood. We have seen the invisible. We have seen, we have touched, we have partaken of the very substance of creative change, creative mutation. If you tell me about the lotus, tell me of nothing changeless or eternal.

Tell me of the mystery of the inexhaustible, forever-unfolding creative spark. Tell me of the incarnate disclosure of the flux, muta-   60
tion in blossom, laughter and decay perfectly open in their transit, nude in their movement before us.

Let me feel the mud and the heavens in my lotus. Let me feel the heavy, silting, sucking mud, the spinning of sky winds. Let me feel them both in purest contact, the nakedness of sucking weight, nakedly passing radiance. Give me nothing fixed, set, static. Don't give me the infinite or the eternal: nothing of infinity, nothing of eternity. Give me the still, white seething, the incandescence and the coldness of the incarnate moment: the moment, the quick of all change and haste and opposition: the moment, the immediate   70
present, the Now. The immediate moment is not a drop of water running downstream. It is the source and issue, the bubbling up of the stream. Here, in this very instant moment, up bubbles the stream of time, out of the wells of futurity, flowing on to the oceans of the past. The source, the issue, the creative quick.

There is poetry of this immediate present, instant poetry, as well as poetry of the infinite past and the infinite future. The seething poetry of the incarnate Now is supreme, beyond even the everlasting gems of the before and after. In its quivering momentaneity it surpasses the crystalline, pearl-hard jewels, the poems of the eter-   80
nities. Do not ask for the qualities of the unfading timeless gems. Ask for the whiteness which is the seethe of mud, ask for that incipient putrescence which is the skies falling, ask for the never-pausing, never-ceasing life itself. There must be mutation, swifter than iridescence, haste, not rest, come-and-go, not fixity, inconclusive-ness, immediacy, the quality of life itself, without denouement or close. There must be the rapid momentaneous association of things which meet and pass on the for ever incalculable journey of creation: everything left in its own rapid, fluid relationship with the rest of things.   90

This is the unrestful, ungraspable poetry of the sheer present, poetry whose very permanency lies in its wind-like transit. Whitman's is the best poetry of this kind. Without beginning and without end, without any base and pediment, it sweeps past for ever, like a wind that is for ever in passage, and unchainable. Whitman truly looked before and after. But he did not sigh for what is not. The clue to all his utterance lies in the sheer appreciation of the instant moment, life surging itself into utterance at its very well-head. Eternity is only an abstraction from the actual present. Infinity is only a great reservoir of recollection, or a reservoir of aspiration: man-   100 made. The quivering nimble hour of the present, this is the quick of Time. This is the immanence. The quick of the universe is the *pulsating, carnal self,* mysterious and palpable. So it is always.

Because Whitman put this into his poetry, we fear him and respect him so profoundly. We should not fear him if he sang only of the 'old unhappy far-off things', or of the 'wings of the morning'. It is because his heart beats with the urgent, insurgent Now, which is even upon us all, that we dread him. He is so near the quick.

From the foregoing it is obvious that the poetry of the instant present cannot have the same body or the same motion as the poetry   110 of the before and after. It can never submit to the same conditions. It is never finished. There is no rhythm which returns upon itself, no serpent of eternity with its tail in its own mouth. There is no static perfection, none of that finality which we find so satisfying because we are so frightened.

Much has been written about free verse. But all that can be said, first and last, is that free verse is, or should be, direct utterance from the instant, whole man. It is the soul and the mind and body surging at once, nothing left out. They speak all together. There is some confusion, some discord. But the confusion and the discord only   120 belong to the reality, as noise belongs to the plunge of water. It is no use inventing fancy laws for free verse, no use drawing a melodic line which all the feet must toe. Free verse toes no melodic line, no matter what drill-sergeant. Whitman pruned away his clichés – perhaps his clichés of rhythm as well as of phrase. And this is about all we can do, deliberately, with free verse. We can get rid of the stereotyped movements and the old hackneyed associations of sound or sense. We can break down those artificial conduits and canals through which we do so love to force our utterance. We can break the stiff neck of habit. We can be in ourselves spontaneous and   130 flexible as flame, we can see that utterance rushes out without arti-ficial form or artificial smoothness. But we cannot positively prescribe any motion, any rhythm. All the laws we invent or discover – it amounts to pretty much the same – will fail to apply to free verse. They will only apply to some form of restricted, limited unfree verse.

All we can say is that free verse does *not* have the same nature as restricted verse. Is it not of the nature of reminiscence. It is not the past which we treasure in its perfection between our hands. Neither is it the crystal of the perfect future, into which we gaze. Its tide is neither the full, yearning flow of aspiration, nor the sweet, poignant ebb of remembrance and regret. The past and the future are the two great bournes of human emotion, the two great homes of the human days, the two eternities. They are both conclusive, final. Their beauty is the beauty of the goal, finished, perfected. Finished beauty and measured symmetry belong to the stable, unchanging eternities.

But in free verse we look for the insurgent naked throb of the instant moment. To break the lovely form of metrical verse, and to dish up the fragments as a new substance, called *vers libre*, this is what most of the free-versifiers accomplish. They do not know that free verse has its own *nature*, that it is neither star nor pearl, but instantaneous like plasm. It has no goal in either eternity. It has no finish. It has no satisfying stability, satisfying to those who like the immutable. None of this. It is the instant; the quick; the very jetting source of all will-be and has-been. The utterance is like a spasm, naked contact with all influences at once. It does not want to get anywhere. It just takes place.

For such utterance any externally applied law would be mere shackles and death. The law must come new each time from within. The bird is on the wing in the winds, flexible to every breath, a living spark in the storm, its very flickering depending upon its supreme mutability and power of change. Whence such a bird came: whither it goes: from what solid earth it rose up, and upon what solid earth it will close its wings and settle, this is not the question. This is a question of before and after. Now, *now*, the bird is on the wing in the winds.

Such is the rare new poetry. One realm we have never conquered: the pure present. One great mystery of time is *terra incognita* to us: the instant. The most superb mystery we have hardly recognised: the immediate, instant self. The quick of all time is the instant. The quick

140

150

160

of all the universe, of all creation, is the incarnate, carnal self. Poetry   170
gave us the clue: free verse: Whitman. Now we know.

The ideal – what is the ideal? A figment. An abstraction. A static
abstraction, abstracted from life. It is a fragment of the before or the
after. It is a crystallised aspiration, or a crystallised remembrance:
crystallised, set, finished. It is a thing set apart, in the great storehouse
of eternity, the storehouse of finished things.

We do not speak of things crystallised and set apart. We speak of
the instant, the immediate self, the very plasm of the self. We speak
also of free verse.

All this should have come as a preface to *Look! We Have Come*   180
Through! But is it not better to publish a preface long after the book
it belongs to has appeared? For then the reader will have had his fair
chance with the book, alone.

HUMAN RELATIONS AND THE UNCONSCIOUS, FROM *PSYCHOANALYSIS AND THE UNCONSCIOUS*

The aim of this little book is merely to establish the smallest foothold
in the swamp of vagueness which now goes by the name of the
unconscious. At last we form some sort of notion what the unconscious actually is. It is that active spontaneity which rouses in each
individual organism at the moment of fusion of the parent nuclei, and
which, in polarized connection with the external universe, gradually
evolves or elaborates its own individual psyche and corpus, bringing
both mind and body forth from itself. Thus it would seem that the
term *unconscious* is only another word for life. But life is a general
force, whereas the unconscious is essentially single and unique in each   10
individual organism; it is the active, self-evolving soul bringing forth
its own incarnation and self-manifestation. Which incarnation and
self-manifestation seems to be the whole goal of the *unconscious* soul:
the whole goal of life. Thus it is that the unconscious brings forth
not only consciousness, but tissue and organs also. And all the time
the working of each organ depends on the primary spontaneous-
conscious centre of which it is the issue – if you like, the soul-centre.
And consciousness is like a web woven finally in the mind from the

various silken strands spun forth from the primal centre of the
unconscious.   20

But the unconscious is never an abstraction, *never to be abstracted*.
It is never an ideal entity. It is always concrete. In the very first
instance, it is the glinting nucleus of the ovule. And proceeding from
this, it is the chain or constellation of nuclei which derive directly
from this first spark. And further still it is the great nerve-centres of
the human body, in which the primal and pristine nuclei still act
direct. The nuclei are centres of spontaneous consciousness. It seems
as if their bright grain were germ-consciousness, consciousness
germinating forever. If that is a mystery, it is not my fault. Certainly
it is not mysticism. It is obvious, demonstrable scientific fact, to be   30
verified under the microscope and within the human psyche,
subjectively and objectively, both. Of course, the subjective veri-
fication is what men kick at. Thin-minded idealists cannot bear any
appeal to their bowels of comprehension.

We can quite tangibly deal with the human unconscious. We trace
its source and centres in the great ganglia and nodes of the nervous
system. We establish the nature of the spontaneous consciousness at
each of these centres; we determine the polarity and the direction of
the polarized flow. And from this we know the motion and individual manifestation of the psyche itself; we also know the motion   40
and rhythm of the great organs of the body. For at every point psyche
and functions are so nearly identified that only by holding our breath
can we realize their *duality* in identification – a polarized duality once
more. But here is no place to enter the great investigation of the duality and polarization of the vital-creative activity and the mechanico-
material activity. The two are two in one, a polarized quality. They
are unthinkably different.

On the first field of human consciousness – the first plane of the
unconscious – we locate four great spontaneous centres, two below
the diaphragm, two above. These four centres control the four   50
greatest organs. And they give rise to the whole basis of human
consciousness. Functional and psychic at once, this is their first polar
duality.

But the polarity is further. The horizontal division of the
diaphragm divides man forever into his individual duality, the duality

84

of the upper and lower man, the two great bodies of upper and lower consciousness and function. This is the horizontal line.

The vertical division between the voluntary and the sympathetic systems, the line of division between the spinal system and the great plexus-system of the front of the human body, forms the second 60 distinction into duality. It is the great difference between the soft, recipient front of the body and the wall of the back. The front of the body is the live end of the magnet. The back is the closed opposition. And again there are two parallel streams of function and consciousness, vertically separate now. This is the vertical line of division. And the horizontal line and the vertical line form the cross of all existence and being. And even this is not mysticism – no more than the ancient symbols used in botany or biology.

On the first field of human consciousness, which is the basis of life and consciousness, are the four first poles of spontaneity. These have 70 their fourfold polarity within the individual, again figured by the cross. But the individual is never purely a thing-by-himself. He cannot exist save in polarized relation to the external universe, a relation both functional and psychic-dynamic. Development takes place only from the polarized circuits of the dynamic unconscious, and these circuits must be both individual and extra-individual. There must be the circuit of which the complementary pole is external to the individual.

That is, in the first place there must be the *other individual*. There must be a polarized connection with the other individual – or even 80 other individuals. On the first field there are four poles in each individual. So that the first, the basic field of extra-individual consciousness contains eight poles – an eightfold polarity, a fourfold circuit. It may be that between two individuals, even mother and child, the polarity may be established only fourfold, a dual circuit. It may be that one circuit of spontaneous consciousness may never be fully established. This means, for a child, a certain deficiency in development, a psychic inadequacy.

So we are again face to face with the basic problem of human conduct. No human being can develop save through the polarized 90 connection with other beings. This circuit of polarized unison precedes all mind and all knowing. It is anterior to and ascendant over the human will. And yet the mind and the will can both interfere with the dynamic circuit, an idea, like a stone wedged in a delicate machine, can arrest one whole process of psychic interaction and spontaneous growth.

How then? Man doth not live by bread alone. It is time we made haste to settle the bread question, which after all is only the ABC of social economies, and proceeded to devote our attention to this much more profound and vital question: how to establish and maintain the circuit of vital polarity from which the psyche actually develops, as the body develops from the circuit of alimentation and respiration. We have reached the stage where we can settle the alimentation and respiration problems almost off-hand. But woe betide us, the unspeakable agony we suffer from the failure to establish and maintain the vital circuits between ourselves and the effectual correspondent, the other human being, other human beings, and all the extraneous universe. The tortures of psychic starvation which civilized people proceed to suffer, once they have solved for themselves the bread-and-butter problem of alimentation, will not bear thought. Delicate, creative desire, sending forth its fine vibrations in search of the true pole of magnetic rest in another human being or beings, how it is thwarted, insulated by a whole set of india-rubber ideas and ideals and conventions, till every form of perversion and death-desire sets in! How can we *escape* neuroses? Psychoanalysis won't tell us. But a mere shadow of understanding of the true unconscious will give us the hint.

The amazingly difficult and vital business of human relationship has been almost laughably underestimated in our epoch. All this nonsense about love and unselfishness, more crude and repugnant than savage fetish-worship. Love is a thing to be *learned,* through centuries of patient effort. It is a difficult, complex maintenance of individual integrity throughout the incalculable processes of interhuman-polarity. Even on the first great plane of consciousness, four prime poles in each individual, four powerful circuits possible between two individuals, and each of the four circuits to be established to perfection and yet maintained in pure equilibrium with all the others. Who can do it? Nobody. Yet we have all got to do it, or else suffer ascetic tortures of starvation and privation or of

distortion and overstrain and slow collapse into corruption. The   130
whole of life is one long, blind effort at an established polarity with
the outer universe, human and non-human; and the whole of modern
life is a shrieking failure. It is our own fault.

The actual evolution of the individual psyche is a result of the
interaction between the individual and the outer universe. Which
means that just as a child in the womb grows as a result of the parental
blood-stream which nourishes the vital quick of the foetus, so does
every man and woman grow and develop as a result of the polarized
flux between the spontaneous self and some other self or selves. It
is the circuit of vital flux between itself and another being or beings   140
which brings about the development and evolution of every individual psyche and physique. This is a law of life and creation, from
which we cannot escape. Ascetics and voluptuaries both try to dodge
this main condition, and both succeed perhaps for a generation. But
after two generations all collapses. Man doth not live by bread alone.
He lives even more essentially from the nourishing creative flow
between himself and another or others.

This is the reality of the extra-individual circuits of polarity, those
established between two or more individuals. But a corresponding
reality is that of the internal, purely individual polarity – the polarity   150
within a man himself of his upper and lower consciousness, and his
own voluntary and sympathetic modes. Here is a fourfold interaction
within the self. And from this fourfold reaction within the self results
that final manifestation which we know as *mind*, mental consciousness.

The brain is, if we may use the word, the terminal instrument of
the dynamic consciousness. It transmutes what is a creative flux into
a certain fixed cipher. It prints off, like a telegraph instrument, the
glyphs and graphic representations which we call percepts, concepts,
ideas. It produces a new reality – the ideal. The idea is another static
entity, another unit of the mechanical-active and materio-static   160
universe. It is thrown off from life, as leaves are shed from a tree,
or as feathers fall from a bird. Ideas are the dry, unliving, insentient
plumage which intervenes between us and the circumambient universe, forming at once an insulator and an instrument for the
subduing of the universe. The mind is the instrument of instruments;
it is not a creative reality.

Once the mind is awake, being in itself a finality, it feels very assured. 'The word became flesh, and began to put on airs,' says Norman Douglas wittily. It is exactly what happens. Mentality, being automatic in its principle like the machine, begins to assume life. It begins to affect life, to pretend to make and unmake life. 'In the beginning was the Word.' This is the presumptuous masquerading of the mind. The Word cannot be the beginning of life. It is the *end* of life, that which falls shed. The mind is the dead end of life. But it has all the mechanical force of the non-vital universe. It is a great dynamo of super-mechanical force. Given the *will* as accomplice, it can even arrogate its machine-motions and automatizations over the whole of life, till every tree becomes a clipped teapot and every man a useful mechanism. So we see the brain, like a great dynamo and accumulator, accumulating *mechanical* force and presuming to apply this mechanical force-control to the living unconscious, subjecting everything spontaneous to certain machine-principles called ideals or ideas.

And the human will assists in this humiliating and sterilizing process. We don't know what the human will is. But we do know that it is a certain faculty belonging to every living organism, the faculty for self-determination. It is a strange faculty of the soul itself, for its own direction. The will is indeed the faculty which every individual possesses from the very moment of conception, for exerting a certain control over the vital and automatic processes of his own evolution. It does not depend originally on mind. Originally it is a purely spontaneous control-factor of the living unconscious. It seems as if, primarily, the will and the conscience were identical, in the premental state. It seems as if the will were given as a great balancing faculty, the faculty whereby automatization is *prevented* in the evolving psyche. The *spontaneous* will reacts at once against the exaggeration of any one particular circuit of polarity. Any vital circuit – a fact known to psychoanalysis. And against this automatism, this degradation from the spontaneous-vital reality into the mechanic-material reality, the human soul must always struggle. And the will is the power which the unique self possesses to right itself from automatism.

Sometimes, however, the free psyche really collapses, and the will *identifies* itself with an automatic circuit. Then a complex is set up, a paranoia. Then incipient madness sets in. If the identification continues, the derangement becomes serious. There may come sudden jolts of dislocation of the whole psychic flow, like epilepsy. Or there may come any of the known forms of primary madness.

The second danger is that the will shall identify itself with the mind and become an instrument of the mind. The same process of auto- 210 matism sets up, only now it is slower. The mind proceeds to assume control over every organic-psychic circuit. The spontaneous flux is destroyed, and a certain automatic circuit substituted. Now an automatic establishment of the psyche must, like the building of a machine, proceed according to some definite fixed scheme, based upon certain fixed principles. And it is here that ideals and ideas enter. They are the machine-plan and the machine-principles of an auto- matized psyche.

So, humanity proceeds to derange itself, to automatize itself from the mental consciousness. It is a process of derangement, just as the 220 fixing of the will upon any other primary process is a derangement. It is a long, slow development in madness. Quite justly do the advanced Russian and French writers acclaim madness as a great goal. It is the genuine goal of self-automatism, mental-conscious supremacy.

True, we must all develop into mental consciousness. But mental-consciousness is not a goal; it is a cul-de-sac. It provides us only with endless *appliances* which we can use for the all-too-difficult business of coming to our spontaneous-creative fullness of being. It provides us with means to adjust ourselves to the external universe. It gives 230 us further means for subduing the external, materio-mechanical universe to our great end of creative life. And it gives us plain indications of how to avoid falling into automatism, hints for the *applying* of the will, the loosening of false, automatic fixations, the brave adherence to a profound soul-impulse. This is the use of the mind – a great indicator and instrument. The mind as author and director of life is anathema.

So, the few things we have to say about the unconscious end for the moment. There is almost nothing said. Yet it is a beginning. Still remain to be revealed the other great centres of the unconscious. We 240 know four: two pairs. In all there are seven planes. That is, there are six dual centres of spontaneous polarity, and then the final one. That is, the great upper and lower consciousness is only just broached – the further heights and depths are not even hinted at. Nay, in public it would hardly be allowed us to hint at them. There is so much to know, and every step of the progress in knowledge is a death to the human idealism which governs us now so ruthlessly and vilely. It must die, and we *will* break free. But what tyranny is so hideous as that of an automatically ideal humanity?

WHITMAN

Post-mortem effects?

But what of Walt Whitman?

The 'good grey poet'.

Was he a ghost, with all his physicality?

The good grey poet.

Post-mortem effects. Ghosts.

A certain ghoulish insistency. A certain horrible pottage of human parts. A certain stridency and portentousness. A luridness about his beatitudes.

DEMOCRACY! THESE STATES! EIDOLONS! LOVERS, ENDLESS   10
LOVERS!

ONE IDENTITY!

ONE IDENTITY!

I AM HE THAT ACHES WITH AMOROUS LOVE.

Do you believe me, when I say post-mortem effects?

When the *Pequod* went down, she left many a rank and dirty steamboat still fussing in the seas. The *Pequod* sinks with all her souls, but their bodies rise again to man innumerable tramp steamers, and ocean-crossing liners. Corpses.

What we mean is that people may go on, keep on, and rush on,   20
without souls. They have their ego and their will; that is enough to keep them going.

So that you see, the sinking of the *Pequod* was only a metaphysical tragedy after all. The world goes on just the same. The ship of the *soul* is sunk. But the machine-manipulating body works just the same:

digests, chews gum, admires Botticelli and aches with amorous love.

I AM HE THAT ACHES WITH AMOROUS LOVE.

What do you make of that? I AM HE THAT ACHES. First gene-
ralisation. First uncomfortable universalisation. WITH AMOROUS
LOVE! Oh, God! Better a bellyache. A bellyache is at least specific.   30
But the ACHE OF AMOROUS LOVE!

Think of having that under your skin. All that!

I AM HE THAT ACHES WITH AMOROUS LOVE.

Walter, leave off. You are not HE. You are just a limited Walter.
And your ache doesn't include all Amorous Love, by any means. If
you ache you only ache with a small bit of amorous love, and there's
so much more stays outside the cover of your ache, that you might
be a bit milder about it.

I AM HE THAT ACHES WITH AMOROUS LOVE.

CHUFF! CHUFF! CHUFF!   40

CHU-CHU-CHU-CHU-CHUFF!

Reminds one of a steam-engine. A locomotive. They're the only
things that seem to me to ache with amorous love. All that steam
inside them. Forty million foot-pounds pressure. The ache of
AMOROUS LOVE. Steam-pressure. CHUFF!

An ordinary man aches with love for Belinda, or his Native Land,
or the Ocean, or the Stars, or the Oversoul: if he feels that an ache
is in the fashion.

It takes a steam-engine to ache with AMOROUS LOVE. All of it.

Walt was really too superhuman. The danger of the superman is   50
that he is mechanical.

They talk of his 'splendid animality'. Well, he'd got it on the
brain, if that's the place for animality.

> I am he that aches with amorous love:
> Does the earth gravitate, does not all matter, aching, attract all
>   matter?
> So the body of me to all I meet or know.

What can be more mechanical? The difference between life and
matter is that life, living things, living creatures, have the instinct
of turning right away from *some* matter, and of blissfully ignoring
the bulk of most matter, and of turning towards only some certain

bits of specially selected matter. As for living creatures all helplessly hurtling together into one great snowball, why, most very living creatures spend the greater part of their time getting out of the sight, smell or sound of the rest of living creatures. Even bees only cluster on their own queen. And that is sickening enough. Fancy all white humanity clustering on one another like a lump of bees.

No, Walt, you give yourself away. Matter *does* gravitate, helplessly. But men are tricky-tricksy, and they shy all sorts of ways.

Matter gravitates because it *is* helpless and mechanical.

And if you gravitate the same, if the body of you gravitates to all you meet or know, why, something must have gone seriously wrong with you. You must have broken your mainspring.

You must have fallen also into mechanisation.

Your Moby Dick must be really dead. That lonely phallic monster of the individual you. Dead mentalised.

I only know that my body doesn't by any means gravitate to all I meet or know. I find I can shake hands with a few people. But most I wouldn't touch with a long prop.

Your mainspring is broken, Walt Whitman. The mainspring of your own individuality. And so you run down with a great whirr, merging with everything.

You have killed your isolate Moby Dick. You have mentalised your deep sensual body, and that's the death of it.

I am everything and everything is me and so we're all One in One Identity, like the Mundane Egg, which has been addled quite a while.

Whoever you are, to endless announcements—
And of these one and all I weave the song of myself.

Do you? Well then, it just shows you haven't *got* any self. It's a mush, not a woven thing. A hotch-potch, not a tissue. Your self.

Oh, Walter, Walter, what have you done with it? What have you done with yourself? With your own individual self? For it sounds as if it had all leaked out of you, leaked into the universe.

Post-mortem effects. The individuality had leaked out of him.

No, no, don't lay this down to poetry. These are post-mortem effects. And Walt's great poems are really huge fat tomb-plants, great rank graveyard growths.

All that false exuberance. All those lists of things boiled in one pudding-cloth! No, no!

I don't want all those things inside me, thank you.

'I reject nothing,' says Walt.

If that is so, one must be a pipe open at both ends, so everything runs through.

Post-mortem effects.

'I embrace ALL,' says Whitman. 'I weave all things into myself.'

Do you really! There can't be much left of *you* when you've done. 100 When you've cooked the awful pudding of One Identity.

'And whoever walks a furlong without sympathy walks to his own funeral dressed in his own shroud.'

Take off your hat then, my funeral procession of one is passing.

This awful Whitman. This post-mortem poet. This poet with the private soul leaking out of him all the time. All his privacy leaking out in a sort of dribble, oozing into the universe.

Walt becomes in his own person the whole world, the whole universe, the whole eternity of time, as far as his rather sketchy knowledge of history will carry him, that is. Because to *be* a thing 110 he had to know it. In order to assume the identity of a thing he had to know that thing. He was not able to assume one identity with Charlie Chaplin, for example, because Walt didn't know Charlie. What a pity! He'd have done poems, pæans and what not, Chants, Songs of Cinematernity.

Oh, Charlie, my Charlie, another film is done —

As soon as Walt *knew* a thing, he assumed a One Identity with it. If he knew that an Eskimo sat in a kyak, immediately there was Walt being little and yellow and greasy, sitting in a kyak.

Now will you tell me exactly what a kyak is?

Who is he that demands petty definition? Let him behold me *sitting* 120 *in a kyak*.

I behold no such thing. I behold a rather fat old man full of a rather senile, self-conscious sensuosity.

DEMOCRACY. EN MASSE. ONE IDENTITY.

The universe in short, adds up to ONE.

ONE.

I.

Which is Walt.

His poems, *Democracy, En Masse, One Identity*, they are long sums
in addition and multiplication, of which the answer is invariably   130
MYSELF.

He reaches the state of ALLNESS.

And what then? It's all empty. Just an empty Allness. An addled
egg.

Walt wasn't an Eskimo. A little, yellow, sly, cunning, greasy little
Eskimo. And when Walt blandly assumed Allness, including
Eskimoness, unto himself, he was just sucking the wind out of a
blown egg-shell, no more. Eskimos are not minor little Walts. They
are something that I am not, I know that. Outside the egg of my
Allness chuckles the greasy little Eskimo. Outside the egg of   140
Whitman's Allness too.

But Walt wouldn't have it. He was everything and everything
was in him. He drove an automobile with a very fierce headlight,
along the track of a fixed idea, through the darkness of this world.
And he saw everything that way. Just as a motorist does in the
night.

I, who happen to be asleep under the bushes in the dark, hoping
a snake won't crawl into my neck; I, seeing Walt go by in his great
fierce poetic machine, think to myself: What a funny world that
fellow sees!   150

ONE DIRECTION! toots Walt in the car, whizzing along it.

Whereas there are myriads of ways in the dark, not to mention
trackless wildernesses, as anyone will know who cares to come off
the road – even the Open Road.

ONE DIRECTION whoops America, and sets off also in an
automobile.

ALLNESS! shrieks Walt at a cross-road, going whizz over an
unwary Red Indian.

ONE IDENTITY! chants democratic En Masse, pelting behind in
motor-cars, oblivious of the corpses under the wheels.   160

God save me, I feel like creeping down a rabbit-hole, to get away
from all these automobiles rushing down the ONE IDENTITY track
to the goal of ALLNESS.

A woman waits for me —

He might as well have said: 'The femaleness waits for my maleness.' Oh, beautiful generalisation and abstraction! Oh, biological function.

'Athletic mothers of these States—' Muscles and wombs. They needn't have had faces at all.

As I see myself reflected in Nature,
As I see through a mist, One with inexpressible completeness, sanity, beauty,
See the bent head, and arms folded over the breast, the Female I see.

Everything was female to him: even himself. Nature just one great function.   170

This is the nucleus – after the child is born of woman, man is born of woman,
This is the bath of birth, the merge of small and large, and the outlet again—

'The Female I see—'

If I'd been one of his women, I'd have given him Female, with a flea in his ear.

Always wanting to merge himself into the womb of something or other.

'The Female I see—'

Anything, so long as he could merge himself.

Just a horror. A sort of white flux.

Post-mortem effects.

He found, as all men find, that you can't really merge in a woman,   180
though you may go a long way. You can't manage the last bit. So you have to give it up, and try elsewhere if you *insist* on merging.

In *Calamus* he changes his tune. He doesn't shout and thump and exult any more. He begins to hesitate, reluctant, wistful.

The strange calamus has its pink-tinged root by the pond, and it sends up its leaves of comradeship, comrades from one root, without the intervention of woman, the female.

So he sings of the mystery of manly love, the love of comrades. Over and over he says the same thing: the new world will be built

on the love of comrades, the new great dynamic of life will be manly 190
love. Out of this manly love will come the inspiration for the
future.

Will it though? Will it?

Comradeship! Comrades! This is to be the new Democracy of
Comrades. This is the new cohering principle in the world:
Comradeship.

Is it? Are you sure?

It is the cohering principle of true soldiery, we are told in *Drum
Taps*. It is the cohering principle in the new unison for creative
activity. And it is extreme and alone, touching the confines of death. 200
Something terrible to bear, terrible to be responsible for. Even Walt
Whitman felt it. The soul's last and most poignant responsibility, the
responsibility of comradeship, of manly love.

> Yet you are beautiful to me, you faint-tinged roots, you make
>   me think of death.
> Death is beautiful from you (what indeed is finally beautiful
>   except death and love?)
> I think it is not for life I am chanting here my chant of lovers,
>   I think it must be for death,
> For how calm, how solemn it grows to ascend to the
>   atmosphere of lovers,
> Death or life, I am then indifferent, my soul declines to prefer,
> (I am not sure but the high soul of lovers welcomes death most)
> Indeed, O death, I think now these leaves mean precisely the
>   same as you mean—

This is strange, from the exultant Walt.
Death!
Death is now his chant! Death!
Merging! And Death! Which is the final merge.
The great merge into the womb. Woman.
And after that, the merge of comrades: man-for-man love.
And almost immediately with this, death, the final merge of death. 210

There you have the progression of merging. For the great mergers,
woman at last becomes inadequate. For those who love to extremes.
Woman is inadequate for the last merging. So the next step is the

merging of man-for-man love. And this is on the brink of death. It slides over into death.

David and Jonathan. And the death of Jonathan.

It always slides into death.

The love of comrades.

Merging.

So that if the new Democracy is to be based on the love of comrades, it will be based on death too. It will slip so soon into death.   220

The last merging. The last Democracy. The last love. The love of comrades.

Fatality. And fatality.

Whitman would not have been the great poet he is if he had not taken the last steps and looked over into death. Death, the last merging, that was the goal of his manhood.

To the mergers, there remains the brief love of comrades, and then Death.

> Whereto answering, the sea
> Delaying not, hurrying not,
> Whispered me through the night, and very plainly before
>   daybreak,
> Lisp'd to me the low and delicious word death,
> And again death, death, death, death.
> Hissing melodious, neither like the bird nor like my arous'd
>   child's heart,
> But edging near as privately for me rustling at my feet,
> Creeping thence steadily up to my ears and laving me softly all
>   over,
> Death, death, death, death, death—

Whitman is a very great poet, of the end of life. A very great post-   230
mortem poet, of the transitions of the soul as it loses its integrity.
The poet of the soul's last shout and shriek, on the confines of death.
Après moi le déluge.

But we have all got to die, and disintegrate.

We have got to die in life, too, and disintegrate while we live.

But even then the goal is not death.

Something else will come.

Out of the cradle endlessly rocking.

We've got to die first, anyhow. And disintegrate while we still live.

Only we know this much: Death is not the *goal*. And Love, and   240
merging, are now only part of the death-process. Comradeship – part of the death-process. Democracy – part of the death-process. The new Democracy – the brink of death. One Identity – death itself.

We have died, and we are still disintegrating.

But IT IS FINISHED.

Consummatum est.

Whitman, the great poet, has meant so much to me. Whitman, the one man breaking a way ahead. Whitman, the one pioneer. And only Whitman. No English pioneers, no French. No European pioneer-poets. In Europe the would-be pioneers are mere innovators.   250
The same in America. Ahead of Whitman, nothing. Ahead of all poets, pioneering into the wilderness of unopened life, Whitman. Beyond him, none. His wide, strange camp at the end of the great high-road. And lots of new little poets camping on Whitman's camping-ground now. But none going really beyond. Because Whitman's camp is at the end of the road, and on the edge of a great precipice. Over the precipice, blue distances, and the blue hollow of the future. But there is no way down. It is a dead end.

Pisgah. Pisgah sights. And Death. Whitman like a strange, modern, American Moses. Fearfully mistaken. And yet the great   260
leader.

The essential function of art is moral. Not æsthetic, not decorative, not pastime and recreation. But moral. The essential function of art is moral.

But a passionate, implicit morality, not didactic. A morality which changes the blood, rather than the mind. Changes the blood first. The mind follows later, in the wake.

Now Whitman was a great moralist. He was a great leader. He was a great changer of the blood in the veins of men.

Surely it is especially true of American art, that it is all essentially   270
moral. Hawthorne, Poe, Longfellow, Emerson, Melville: it is the

moral issue which engages them. They all feel uneasy about the old morality. Sensuously, passionally, they all attack the old morality. But they know nothing better, mentally. Therefore they give tight mental allegiance to a morality which all their passion goes to destroy. Hence the duplicity which is the fatal flaw in them: most fatal in the most perfect American work of art, *The Scarlet Letter*. Tight mental allegiance given to a morality which the passional self repudiates.

Whitman was the first to break the mental allegiance. He was the 280 first to smash the old moral conception that the soul of man is something 'superior' and 'above' the flesh. Even Emerson still maintained this tiresome 'superiority' of the soul. Even Melville could not get over it. Whitman was the first heroic seer to seize the soul by the scruff of her neck and plant her down among the potsherds.

'There!' he said to the soul. 'Stay there!'

Stay there. Stay in the flesh. Stay in the limbs and lips and in the belly. Stay in the breast and womb. Stay there, O Soul, where you belong.

Stay in the dark limbs of negroes. Stay in the body of the prostitute. 290 Stay in the sick flesh of the syphilitic. Stay in the marsh where the calamus grows. Stay there, Soul, where you belong.

The Open Road. The great home of the Soul is the open road. Not heaven, not paradise. Not 'above'. Not even 'within'. The soul is neither 'above' nor 'within'. It is a wayfarer down the open road.

Not by meditating. Not by fasting. Not by exploring heaven after heaven, inwardly, in the manner of the great mystics. Not by exaltation. Not by ecstasy. Not by any of these ways does the soul come into her own.

Only by taking the open road. 300

Not through charity. Not through sacrifice. Not even through love. Not through good works. Not through these does the soul accomplish herself.

Only through the journey down the open road.

The journey itself, down the open road. Exposed to full contact. On two slow feet. Meeting whatever comes down the open road. In company with those that drift in the same measure along the same way. Towards no goal. Always the open road.

Having no known direction even. Only the soul remaining true to herself in her going.   310

Meeting all the other wayfarers along the road. And how? How meet them, and how pass? With sympathy, says Whitman. Sympathy. He does not say love. He says sympathy. Feeling with. Feel with them as they feel with themselves. Catching the vibration of their soul and flesh as we pass.

It is a new great doctrine. A doctrine of life. A new great morality. A morality of actual living, not of salvation. Europe has never got beyond the morality of salvation. America to this day is deathly sick with saviourism. But Whitman, the greatest and the first and the only American teacher, was no Saviour. His morality was no morality   320 of salvation. His was a morality of the soul living her life, not saving herself. Accepting the contact with other souls along the open way, as they lived their lives. Never trying to save them. As leave try to arrest them and throw them in gaol. The soul living her life along the incarnate mystery of the open road.

This was Whitman. And the true rhythm of the American continent speaking out in him. He is the first white aboriginal.

'In my Father's house are many mansions.'

'No,' said Whitman. 'Keep out of mansions. A mansion may be heaven on earth, but you might as well be dead. Strictly avoid   330 mansions. The soul is herself when she is going on foot down the open road.'

It is the American heroic message. The soul is not to pile up defences round herself. She is not to withdraw and seek her heavens inwardly, in mystical ecstasies. She is not to cry to some God beyond, for salvation. She is to go down the open road, as the road opens, into the unknown, keeping company with those whose soul draws them near to her, accomplishing nothing save the journey, and the works incident to the journey, in the long life-travel into the unknown, the soul in her subtle sympathies accomplishing herself by   340 the way.

This is Whitman's essential message. The heroic message of the American future. It is the inspiration of thousands of Americans to-day, the best souls of to-day, men and women. And it is a message that only in America can be fully understood, finally accepted.

Then Whitman's mistake. The mistake of his interpretation of his
watchword: Sympathy. The mystery of SYMPATHY. He still con-
founded it with Jesus's LOVE, and with Paul's CHARITY. Whitman,
like all the rest of us, was at the end of the great emotional highway
of Love. And because he couldn't help himself, he carried on his Open   350
Road as a prolongation of the emotional highway of Love, beyond
Calvary. The highway of Love ends at the foot of the Cross. There
is no beyond. It was a hopeless attempt to prolong the highway of
Love.

He didn't follow his Sympathy. Try as he might, he kept on
automatically interpreting it as Love, as Charity. Merging!

This merging, *en masse*, One Identity, Myself monomania was a
carry-over from the old Love idea. It was carrying the idea of Love
to its logical physical conclusion. Like Flaubert and the leper. The
decree of unqualified Charity, as the soul's one means of salvation,   360
still in force.

Now Whitman wanted his soul to save itself; *he* didn't want to
save it. Therefore he did not need the great Christian receipt for
saving the soul. He needed to supersede the Christian Charity, the
Christian Love, within himself, in order to give his Soul her last
freedom. The highroad of Love is no Open Road. It is a narrow, tight
way, where the soul walks hemmed in between compulsions.

Whitman wanted to take his Soul down the open road. And he
failed in so far as he failed to get out of the old rut of Salvation. He
forced his Soul to the edge of a cliff, and he looked down into death.   370
And there he camped, powerless. He had carried out his Sympathy
as an extension of Love and Charity. And it had brought him almost
to madness and soul-death. It gave him his forced, unhealthy, post-
mortem quality.

His message was really the opposite of Henley's rant:

> I am the master of my fate,
> I am the captain of my soul.

Whitman's essential message was the Open Road. The leaving of the
soul free unto herself, the leaving of his fate to her and to the loom
of the open road. Which is the bravest doctrine man has ever
proposed to himself.

Alas, he didn't quite carry it out. He couldn't quite break the old 380
maddening bond of the love-compulsion; he couldn't quite get out
of the rut of the charity habit – for Love and Charity have
degenerated now into habit: a bad habit.

Whitman said Sympathy. If only he had stuck to it! Because
Sympathy means feeling with, not feeling for. He kept on having a
passionate feeling *for* the negro slave, or the prostitute, or the
syphilitic – which is merging. A sinking of Walt Whitman's soul in
the souls of these others.

He wasn't keeping to his open road. He was forcing his soul down
an old rut. He wasn't leaving her free. He was forcing her into other 390
people's circumstances.

Supposing he had felt true sympathy with the negro slave? He
would have felt *with* the negro slave. Sympathy – compassion –
which is partaking of the passion which was in the soul of the negro
slave.

What was the feeling in the negro's soul?

'Ah, I am a slave! Ah, it is bad to be a slave! I must free myself.
My soul will die unless she frees herself. My soul says I must free
myself.'

Whitman came along, and saw the slave, and said to himself: 'That 400
negro slave is a man like myself. We share the same identity. And
he is bleeding with wounds. Oh, oh, is it not myself who am also
bleeding with wounds?'

This was not *sympathy*. It was merging and self-sacrifice. 'Bear ye
one another's burdens': 'Love thy neighbour as thyself': 'Whatsoever
ye do unto him, ye do unto me.'

If Whitman had truly *sympathised*, he would have said: 'That negro
slave suffers from slavery. He wants to free himself. His soul wants
to free him. He has wounds, but they are the price of freedom. The
soul has a long journey from slavery to freedom. If I can help him 410
I will: I will not take [over] his wounds and his slavery to myself.
But I will help him fight the power that enslaves him when he wants
to be free, if he wants my help, since I see in his face that he needs
to be free. But even when he is free, his soul has many journeys down
the open road, before it is a free soul.'

And of the prostitute Whitman would have said:

'Look at that prostitute! Her nature has turned evil under her mental lust for prostitution. She has lost her soul. She knows it herself. She likes to make men lose their souls. If she tried to make me lose my soul, I would kill her. I wish she may die.'   420

But of another prostitute he would have said:

'Look! She is fascinated by the Priapic mysteries. Look, she will soon be worn to death by the Priapic usage. It is the way of her soul. She wishes it so.'

Of the syphilitic he would say:

'Look! She wants to infect all men with syphilis. We ought to kill her.'

And of still another syphilitic:

'Look! She has a horror of her syphilis. If she looks my way I will help her to get cured.'   430

This is sympathy. The soul judging for herself, and preserving her own integrity.

But when, in Flaubert, the man takes the leper to his naked body; when Bubu de Montparnasse takes the girl because he knows she's got syphilis; when Whitman embraces an evil prostitute: that is not sympathy. The evil prostitute has no desire to be embraced with love; so if you sympathise with her, you won't try to embrace her with love. The leper loathes his leprosy, so if you sympathise with him, you'll loathe it too. The evil woman who wishes to infect all men with her syphilis hates you if you haven't got syphilis. If you   440 sympathise, you'll feel her hatred, and you'll hate too, you'll hate her. Her feeling is hate, and you'll share it. Only your soul will choose the direction of its own hatred.

The soul is a very perfect judge of her own motions, if your mind doesn't dictate to her. Because the mind says Charity! Charity! you don't have to force your soul into kissing lepers or embracing syphilitics. Your lips are the lips of your soul, your body is the body of your soul; your own single, individual soul. That is Whitman's message. And your soul hates syphilis and leprosy. Because it *is* a soul, it hates these things, which are against the soul.   450 And therefore to force the body of your soul into contact with uncleanness is a great violation of your soul. The soul wishes to keep clean and whole. The soul's deepest will is to preserve its own integrity, against the mind and the whole mass of disintegrating forces.

Soul sympathises with soul. And that which tries to kill my soul, my soul hates. My soul and my body are one. Soul and body wish to keep clean and whole. Only the mind is capable of great perversion. Only the mind tries to drive my soul and body into uncleanness and unwholesomeness. 460

What my soul loves, I love.

What my soul hates, I hate.

When my soul is stirred with compassion, I am compassionate.

What my soul turns away from, I turn away from.

That is the *true* interpretation of Whitman's creed: the true revelation of his Sympathy.

And my soul takes the open road. She meets the souls that are passing, she goes along with the souls that are going her way. And for one and all, she has sympathy. The sympathy of love, the sympathy of hate, the sympathy of simple proximity; all the subtle 470 sympathisings of the incalculable soul, from the bitterest hate to passionate love.

It is not I who guide my soul to heaven. It is I who am guided by my own soul along the open road, where all men tread. Therefore, I must accept her deep motions of love, or hate, or compassion, or dislike, or indifference. And I must go where she takes me, for my feet and my lips and my body are my soul. It is I who must submit to her.

This is Whitman's message of American democracy.

The true democracy, where soul meets soul, in the open road. 480 Democracy. American democracy where all journey down the open road, and where a soul is known at once in its going. Not by its clothes or appearance. Whitman did away with that. Not by its family name. Not even by its reputation. Whitman and Melville both discounted that. Not by a progression of piety, or by works of Charity. Not by works at all. Not by anything, but just itself. The soul passing unenhanced, passing on foot and being no more than itself. And recognised, and passed by or greeted according to the soul's dictate. If it be a great soul, it will be worshipped in the road.

The love of man and woman: a recognition of souls, and a 490 communion of worship. The love of comrades: a recognition of souls, and a communion of worship. Democracy: a recognition of souls, all down the open road, and a great soul seen in its greatness, as it travels on foot among the rest, down the common way of the living. A glad recognition of souls, and a gladder worship of great and greater souls, because they are the only riches.

Love, and Merging, brought Whitman to the Edge of Death! Death! Death!

But the exultance of his message still remains. Purified of MERGING, purified of MYSELF, the exultant message of American Democracy, of souls in the Open Road, full of glad recognition, full of fierce readiness, full of the joy of worship, when one soul sees a greater soul.

The only riches, the great souls.

HIBISCUS AND SALVIA FLOWERS

Hark! Hark!
The dogs do bark!
It's the socialists come to town,
None in rags and none in tags,
Swaggering up and down.

Sunday morning,
And from the Sicilian townlets skirting Etna
The socialists have gathered upon us, to look at us.

How shall we know them when we see them?
How shall we know them now they've come?

Not by their rags and not by their tags,
Nor by any distinctive gown;
The same unremarkable Sunday suit
And hats cocked up and down.

Yet there they are, youths, loutishly
Strolling in gangs and staring along the Corso
With the gang-stare
And a half-threatening envy

At every *forestière*,
Every lordly tuppenny foreigner from the hotels, fattening on the
    exchange.   20

Hark! Hark!
The dogs do bark!
It's the socialists in the town.

Sans rags, sans tags,
Sans beards, sans bags,
Sans any distinction at all except loutish commonness.

How do we know then, that they are they?
Bolshevists.
Leninists.
Communists.   30
Socialists.
-Ists! -Ists!

Alas, salvia and hibiscus flowers.
Salvia and hibiscus flowers.

Listen again.
Salvia and hibiscus flowers.
Is it not so?
Salvia and hibiscus flowers.

Hark! Hark!
The dogs do bark!   40
Salvia and hibiscus flowers.

Who smeared their doors with blood?
Who on their breasts
Put salvias and hibiscus?

Rosy, rosy scarlet,
And flame-rage, golden-throated
Bloom along the Corso on the living, perambulating bush

Who said they might assume these blossoms?
What god did they consult?

Rose-red, princess hibiscus, rolling her pointed Chinese petals!   50

Azalea and camellia, single peony
And pomegranate bloom and scarlet mallow-flower
And all the eastern, exquisite royal plants
That noble blood has brought us down the ages!
Gently nurtured, frail and splendid
Hibiscus flower –
Alas, the Sunday coats of Sicilian bolshevists!

Pure blood, and noble blood, in the fine and rose-red veins;
Small, interspersed with jewels of white gold
Frail-filigreed among the rest;   60
Rose of the oldest races of princesses, Polynesian
Hibiscus.

Eve, in her happy moments,
Put hibiscus in her hair,
Before she humbled herself, and knocked her knees with repentance.

Sicilian bolshevists,
With hibiscus flowers in the buttonholes of your Sunday suits,
Come now, speaking of rights, what right have you to this flower?

The exquisite and ageless aristocracy
Of a peerless soul,   70
Blessed are the pure in heart and the fathomless in bright pride;
The loveliness that knows *noblesse oblige*;
The native royalty of red hibiscus flowers;
The exquisite assertion of new delicate life
Risen from the roots:
Is this how you'll have it, red-decked socialists,
Hibiscus-breasted?

If it be so, I fly to join you,
And if it be not so, brutes to pull down hibiscus flowers!

Or salvia!   80
Or dragon-mouthed salvia with gold throat of wrath!
Flame-flushed, enraged, splendid salvia,
Cock-crested, crowing your orange scarlet like a tocsin
Along the Corso all this Sunday morning.

Is your wrath red as salvias,
You socialists?
You with your grudging, envious, furtive rage,
In Sunday suits and yellow boots along the Corso.
You look well with your salvia flowers, I must say.
Warrior-like, dawn-cock's-comb flaring flower   90
Shouting forth flame to set the world on fire,
The dust-heap of man's filthy world on fire,
And burn it down, the glutted, stuffy world,
And feed the young new fields of life with ash,
With ash I say,
Bolshevists,
Your ashes even, my friends,
Among much other ash.

If there were salvia-savage bolshevists
To burn the world back to manure-good ash,   100
Wouldn't I stick the salvia in my coat!
But these themselves must burn, these louts!

The dragon-faced,
The anger-reddened, golden-throated salvia
With its long antennæ of rage put out
Upon the frightened air.
Ugh, how I love its fangs of perfect rage
That gnash the air;
The molten gold of its intolerable rage
Hot in the throat.   110

I long to be a bolshevist
And set the stinking rubbish-heap of this foul world
Afire at a myriad scarlet points,
A bolshevist, a salvia-face
To lick the world with flame that licks it clean.

I long to see its chock-full crowdedness
And glutted squirming populousness on fire
Like a field of filthy weeds
Burnt back to ash,
And then to see the new, real souls sprout up.   120

Not this vast rotting cabbage patch we call the world;
But from the ash-scarred fallow
New wild souls.

Nettles, and a rose sprout,
Hibiscus, and mere grass,
Salvia still in a rage
And almond honey-still,
And fig-wort stinking for the carrion wasp;
All the lot of them, and let them fight it out.

But not a trace of foul equality,   130
Nor sound of still more foul human perfection.
You need not clear the world like a cabbage patch for me;
Leave me my nettles,
Let me fight the wicked, obstreperous weeds myself, and put them
     in their place,
Severely in their place.
I don't at all want to annihilate them,
I like a row with them,
But I won't be put on a cabbage-idealistic level of equality with them.

What rot, to see the cabbage and hibiscus-tree
As equals!   140
What rot, to say the louts along the Corso
In Sunday suits and yellow shoes
Are my equals!
I am their superior, saluting the hibiscus flower, not them.
The same I say to the profiteers from the hotels, the money-fat-ones,
Profiteers here being called dog-fish, stinking dog-fish, sharks.
The same I say to the pale and elegant persons,
Pale-face authorities loitering tepidly:
That I salute the red hibiscus flowers
And send mankind to its inferior blazes.   150
Mankind's inferior blazes,
And these along with it, all the inferior lot –
These bolshevists,
These dog-fish,

These precious and ideal ones,
All rubbish ready for fire.

And I salute hibiscus and the salvia flower
Upon the breasts of loutish bolshevists,
Damned loutish bolshevists,
Who perhaps will do the business after all,   160
In the long run, in spite of themselves.

Meanwhile, alas
For me no fellow-men,
No salvia-frenzied comrades, antennæ
Of yellow-red, outreaching, living wrath
Upon the smouldering air,
And throat of brimstone-molten angry gold.
Red, angry men are a race extinct, alas!

Never
To be a bolshevist   170
With a hibiscus flower behind my ear
In sign of life, of lovely, dangerous life
And passionate disquality of men;
In sign of dauntless, silent violets,
And impudent nettles grabbing the under-earth,
And cabbages born to be cut and eat,
And salvia fierce to crow and shout for fight,
And rosy-red hibiscus wincingly
Unfolding all her coiled and lovely self
In a doubtful world.   180

Never, bolshevistically
To be able to stand for all these!
Alas, alas, I have got to leave it all
To the youths in Sunday suits and yellow shoes
Who have pulled down the salvia flowers
And rosy delicate hibiscus flowers
And everything else to their disgusting level,
Never, of course, to put anything up again.

But yet
If they pull all the world down,   190

The process will amount to the same in the end.
Instead of flame and flame-clean ash
Slow watery rotting back to level muck
And final humus,
Whence the re-start.

And still I cannot bear it
That they take hibiscus and the salvia flower.

Taormina

POMEGRANATE

You tell me I am wrong.
Who are you, who is anybody to tell me I am wrong?
I am not wrong.

In Syracuse, rock left bare by the viciousness of Greek
    women,
No doubt you have forgotten the pomegranate-trees in flower,
Oh so red, and such a lot of them.

Whereas at Venice
Abhorrent, green, slippery city
Whose Doges were old, and had ancient eyes,
In the dense foliage of the inner garden   10
Pomegranates like bright green stone,
And barbed, barbed with a crown.
Oh, crown of spiked green metal
Actually growing!

Now in Tuscany,
Pomegranates to warm your hands at;
And crowns, kingly, generous, tilting crowns
Over the left eyebrow.

And, if you dare, the fissure!

Do you mean to tell me you will see no fissure?   20
Do you prefer to look on the plain side?

111

For all that, the setting suns are open.
The end cracks open with the beginning:
Rosy, tender, glittering within the fissure.

Do you mean to tell me there should be no fissure?
No glittering, compact drops of dawn?
Do you mean it is wrong, the gold-filmed skin, integument, shown
    ruptured?

For my part, I prefer my heart to be broken.
It is so lovely, dawn-kaleidoscopic within the crack.

                                        San Gervasio in Tuscany

MEDLARS AND SORB-APPLES

I love you, rotten,
Delicious rottenness.

I love to suck you out from your skins
So brown and soft and coming suave,
So morbid, as the Italians say.

What a rare, powerful, reminiscent flavour
Comes out of your falling through the stages of decay:
Stream within stream.

Something of the same flavour as Syracusan muscat wine
Or vulgar Marsala.   10

Though even the word Marsala will smack of preciosity
Soon in the pussy-foot West.

What is it?
What is it, in the grape turning raisin,
In the medlar, in the sorb-apple,
Wineskins of brown morbidity,
Autumnal excrementa;
What is it that reminds us of white gods?

Gods nude as blanched nut-kernels,
Strangely, half-sinisterly flesh-fragrant   20

112

As if with sweat,
And drenched with mystery.

Sorb-apples, medlars with dead crowns.

I say, wonderful are the hellish experiences
Orphic, delicate
Dionysos of the Underworld.

A kiss, and a vivid spasm of farewell, a moment's orgasm of rupture,
Then along the damp road alone, till the next turning.
And there, a new partner, a new parting, a new unfusing into twain,
A new gasp of further isolation,   30
A new intoxication of loneliness, among decaying, frost-cold leaves.

Going down the strange lanes of hell, more and more intensely alone,
The fibres of the heart parting one after the other
And yet the soul continuing, naked-footed, ever more vividly
    embodied
Like a flame blown whiter and whiter
In a deeper and deeper darkness
Ever more exquisite, distilled in separation.

So, in the strange retorts of medlars and sorb-apples
The distilled essence of hell.
The exquisite odour of leave-taking.   40
        Jamque vale!
Orpheus, and the winding, leaf-clogged, silent lanes of hell.

Each soul departing with its own isolation,
Strangest of all strange companions,
And best.

Medlars, sorb-apples
More than sweet
Flux of autumn
Sucked out of your empty bladders
And sipped down, perhaps, with a sip of Marsala   50
So that the rambling, sky-dropped grape can add its music to yours,

Orphic farewell, and farewell, and farewell
And the *ego sum* of Dionysos
The *sono io* of perfect drunkenness
Intoxication of final loneliness.

San Gervasio

FIGS

The proper way to eat a fig, in society,
Is to split it in four, holding it by the stump,
And open it, so that it is a glittering, rosy, moist, honied, heavy-
  petalled four-petalled flower.

Then you throw away the skin
Which is just like a four-sepalled calyx,
After you have taken off the blossom with your lips.

But the vulgar way
Is just to put your mouth to the crack, and take out the flesh in one
  bite.

Every fruit has its secret.

The fig is a very secretive fruit.   10
As you see it standing growing, you feel at once it is symbolic:
And it seems male.
But when you come to know it better, you agree with the Romans,
  it is female.

The Italians vulgarly say, it stands for the female part; the fig-fruit:
The fissure, the yoni,
The wonderful moist conductivity towards the centre.

Involved,
Inturned,
The flowering all inward and womb-fibrilled;
And but one orifice.   20

The fig, the horse-shoe, the squash-blossom.
Symbols.

There was a flower that flowered inward, womb-ward;
Now there is a fruit like a ripe womb.

It was always a secret.
That's how it should be, the female should always be secret.

There never was any standing aloft and unfolded on a bough
Like other flowers, in a revelation of petals;
Silver-pink peach, venetian green glass of medlars and sorb-apples,
Shallow wine-cups on short, bulging stems   30
Openly pledging heaven:
Here's to the thorn in flower! Here is to Utterance!
The brave, adventurous rosaceæ.

Folded upon itself, and secret unutterable,
And milky-sapped, sap that curdles milk and makes *ricotta*,
Sap that smells strange on your fingers, that even goats won't taste it;
Folded upon itself, enclosed like any Mohammedan woman,
Its nakedness all within-walls, its flowering forever unseen,
One small way of access only, and this close-curtained from the light;
Fig, fruit of the female mystery, covert and inward,   40
Mediterranean fruit, with your covert nakedness,
Where everything happens invisible, flowering and fertilisation, and
    fruiting
In the inwardness of your you, that eye will never see
Till it's finished, and you're over-ripe, and you burst to give up your
    ghost.

Till the drop of ripeness exudes,
And the year is over.

And then the fig has kept her secret long enough.
So it explodes, and you see through the fissure the scarlet.
And the fig is finished, the year is over.

That's how the fig dies, showing her crimson through the purple slit   50
Like a wound, the exposure of her secret, on the open day.
Like a prostitute, the bursten fig, making a show of her secret.

That's how women die too.

The year is fallen over-ripe,
The year of our women.
The year of our women is fallen over-ripe.
The secret is laid bare.
And rottenness soon sets in.
The year of our women is fallen over-ripe.

When Eve once knew *in her mind* that she was naked   60
She quickly sewed fig-leaves, and sewed the same for the man.
She'd been naked all her days before,
But till then, till that apple of knowledge, she hadn't had the fact
    on her mind.

She got the fact on her mind, and quickly sewed fig-leaves.
And women have been sewing ever since.
But now they stitch to adorn the bursten fig, not to cover it
They have their nakedness more than ever on their mind,
And they won't let us forget it.

Now, the secret
Becomes an affirmation through moist, scarlet lips   70
That laugh at the Lord's indignation.

What then, good Lord! cry the women.
We have kept our secret long enough.
We are a ripe fig.
Let us burst into affirmation.

They forget, ripe figs won't keep.
Ripe figs won't keep.

Honey-white figs of the north, black figs with scarlet inside, of the
    south.
Ripe figs won't keep, won't keep in any clime.
What then, when women the world over have all bursten into
    affirmation?   80
And bursten figs won't keep?

                                        San Gervasio

116

THE MOSQUITO

When did you start your tricks,
Monsieur?

What do you stand on such high legs for?
Why this length of shredded shank,
You exaltation?

Is it so that you shall lift your centre of gravity upwards
And weigh no more than air as you alight upon me,
Stand upon me weightless, you phantom?

I heard a woman call you the Winged Victory
In sluggish Venice.   10
You turn your head towards your tail, and smile.

How can you put so much devilry
Into that translucent phantom shred
Of a frail corpus?

Queer, with your thin wings and your streaming legs
How you sail like a heron, or a dull clot of air,
A nothingness.

Yet what an aura surrounds you;
Your evil little aura, prowling, and casting a numbness on my mind.

That is your trick, your bit of filthy magic: 20
Invisibility, and the anæsthetic power
To deaden my attention in your direction.

But I know your game now, streaky sorcerer.

Queer, how you stalk and prowl the air
In circles and evasions, enveloping me,
Ghoul on wings
Winged Victory.

Settle, and stand on long thin shanks
Eyeing me sideways, and cunningly conscious that I am aware,
You speck.   30

I hate the way you lurch off sideways into air
Having read my thoughts against you.

Come then, let us play at unawares,
And see who wins in this sly game of bluff,
Man or mosquito.

You don't know that I exist, and I don't know that you exist.
Now then!

It is your trump,
It is your hateful little trump,
You pointed fiend,   40
Which shakes my sudden blood to hatred of you:
It is your small, high, hateful bugle in my ear.

Why do you do it?
Surely it is bad policy.

They say you can't help it.

If that is so, then I believe a little in Providence protecting the
    innocent.
But it sounds so amazingly like a slogan,
A yell of triumph as you snatch my scalp.

Blood, red blood
Super-magical   50
Forbidden liquor.

I behold you stand
For a second enspasmed in oblivion,
Obscenely ecstasied
Sucking live blood,
My blood.

Such silence, such suspended transport,
Such gorging,
Such obscenity of trespass.

You stagger   60
As well as you may.

118

Only your accursed hairy frailty,
Your own imponderable weightlessness
Saves you, wafts you away on the very draught my anger makes in
    its snatching.

Away with a pæan of derision,
You winged blood-drop.

Can I not overtake you?
Are you one too many for me,
Winged Victory?
Am I not mosquito enough to out-mosquito you?   70

Queer, what a big stain my sucked blood makes
Beside the infinitesimal faint smear of you!
Queer, what a dim dark smudge you have disappeared into!

                                                  Siracusa

FISH

Fish, oh Fish,
So little matters!

Whether the waters rise and cover the earth
Or whether the waters wilt in the hollow places,
All one to you.

Aqueous, subaqueous,
Submerged
And wave-thrilled.

As the waters roll
Roll you.
The waters wash,   10
You wash in oneness
And never emerge.

Never know,
Never grasp.

Your life a sluice of sensation along your sides,
A flush at the flails of your fins, down the whorl of your tail,
And water wetly on fire in the grates of your gills;
Fixed water-eyes.

Even snakes lie together.   20

But oh, fish, that rock in water,
You lie only with the waters;
One touch.
No fingers, no hands and feet, no lips;
No tender muzzles,
No wistful bellies,
No loins of desire,
None.

You and the naked element,
Sway-wave.   30
Curvetting bits of tin in the evening light.

Who is it ejects his sperm to the naked flood?
In the wave-mother?
Who swims enwombed?
Who lies with the waters of his silent passion, womb-element?
– Fish in the waters under the earth.

What price *his* bread upon the waters?

Himself all silvery himself
In the element
No more.   40

Nothing more.

Himself,
And the element.
Food, of course!
Water-eager eyes,
Mouth-gate open
And strong spine urging, driving;
And desirous belly gulping.

Fear also!
He knows fear!   50
Water-eyes craning,
A rush that almost screams,
Almost fish-voice
As the pike comes. . . .
Then gay fear, that turns the tail sprightly, from a shadow.

Food, and fear, and joie de vivre,
Without love.

The other way about:
Joie de vivre, and fear, and food,
All without love.   60

Quelle joie de vivre
Dans l'eau!
Slowly to gape through the waters,
Alone with the element;
To sink, and rise, and go to sleep with the waters;
To speak endless inaudible wavelets into the wave;
To breathe from the flood at the gills,
Fish-blood slowly running next to the flood, extracting fish-fire;
To have the element under one, like a lover;
And to spring away with a curvetting click in the air,   70
Provocative.
Dropping back with a slap on the face of the flood.
And merging oneself!

To be a fish!
So utterly without misgiving
To be a fish
In the waters.

Loveless, and so lively!
Born before God was love,
Or life knew loving.   80
Beautifully beforehand with it all.

Admitted, they swarm in companies,
Fishes.

121

They drive in shoals.
But soundless, and out of contact.
They exchange no word, no spasm, not even anger.
Not one touch.
Many suspended together, forever apart,
Each one alone with the waters, upon one wave with the rest.

A magnetism in the water between them only.   90

I saw a water-serpent swim across the Anapo,
And I said to my heart, *look, look at him!*
With his head up, steering like a bird!
He's a rare one, but he belongs . . .

But sitting in a boat on the Zeller lake
And watching the fishes in the breathing waters
Lift and swim and go their way –

I said to my heart, *who are these?*
And my heart couldn't own them. . . .

A slim young pike, with smart fins   100
And grey-striped suit, a young cub of a pike
Slouching along away below, half out of sight,
Like a lout on an obscure pavement. . . .

Aha, there's somebody in the know!

But watching closer
That motionless deadly motion,
That unnatural barrel body, that long ghoul nose, . . .
I left off hailing him.

I had made a mistake, I didn't know him,
This grey, monotonous soul in the water,   110
This intense individual in shadow,
Fish-alive.

I didn't know his God,
I didn't know his God.

Which is perhaps the last admission that life has to wring out of us.

I saw, dimly,
Once a big pike rush,
And small fish fly like splinters.
And I said to my heart, *there are limits*
To you, my heart;   120
And to the one God.
Fish are beyond me.

Other Gods
Beyond my range . . . gods beyond my God . . .

They are beyond me, are fishes.
I stand at the pale of my being
And look beyond, and see
Fish, in the outerwards,
As one stands on a bank and looks in.

I have waited with a long rod   130
And suddenly pulled a gold-and-greenish, lucent fish from below,
And had him fly like a halo round my head,
Lunging in the air on the line.

Unhooked his gorping, water-horny mouth,
And seen his horror-tilted eye,
His red-gold, water-precious, mirror-flat bright eye;
And felt him beat in my hand, with his mucous, leaping
    life-throb.

And my heart accused itself
Thinking: *I am not the measure of creation.*
This is beyond me, this fish.   140
His God stands outside my God.

And the gold-and-green pure lacquer-mucus comes off in my hand,
And the red-gold mirror-eye stares and dies,
And the water-suave contour dims.

But not before I have had to know
He was born in front of my sunrise,
Before my day.

He outstarts me.
And I, a many-fingered horror of daylight to him,
Have made him die.   150

Fishes,
With their gold, red eyes, and green-pure gleam, and under-gold,
And their pre-world loneliness,
And more-than-lovelessness,
And white meat;
They move in other circles.

Outsiders.
Water-wayfarers.
Things of one element.
Aqueous,   160
Each by itself.

Cats, and the Neapolitans,
Sulphur sun-beasts,
Thirst for fish as for more-than-water;
Water-alive
To quench their over-sulphureous lusts.

But I, I only wonder
And don't know.
I don't know fishes.

In the beginning   170
Jesus was called The Fish. . . .
And in the end.

Zell-am-See

BAT

At evening, sitting on this terrace,
When the sun from the west, beyond Pisa, beyond the mountains
    of Carrara
Departs, and the world is taken by surprise . . .

When the tired flower of Florence is in gloom beneath the glowing
Brown hills surrounding . . .

When under the arches of the Ponte Vecchio
A green light enters against stream, flush from the west,
Against the current of obscure Arno . . .

Look up, and you see things flying
Between the day and the night;
Swallows with spools of dark thread sewing the shadows together.

A circle swoop, and a quick parabola under the bridge arches
Where light pushes through;
A sudden turning upon itself of a thing in the air.
A dip to the water.

And you think:
'The swallows are flying so late!'

Swallows?

Dark air-life looping
Yet missing the pure loop . . .
A twitch, a twitter, an elastic shudder in flight
And serrated wings against the sky,
Like a glove, a black glove thrown up at the light,
And falling back.

Never swallows!
Bats!
The swallows are gone.

At a wavering instant the swallows gave way to bats
By the Ponte Vecchio . . .
Changing guard.

Bats, and an uneasy creeping in one's scalp
As the bats swoop overhead!
Flying madly.

Pipistrello!
Black piper on an infinitesimal pipe.
Little lumps that fly in air and have voices indefinite, wildly
    vindictive;

125

Wings like bits of umbrella.

Bats!

Creatures that hang themselves up like an old rag, to sleep;
And disgustingly upside down.   40
Hanging upside down like rows of disgusting old rags
And grinning in their sleep.
Bats!

Not for me!

SNAKE

A snake came to my water-trough
On a hot, hot day, and I in pyjamas for the heat,
To drink there.

In the deep, strange-scented shade of the great dark carob-tree
I came down the steps with my pitcher
And must wait, must stand and wait, for there he was at the trough
    before me.

He reached down from a fissure in the earth-wall in the gloom
And trailed his yellow-brown slackness soft-bellied down, over the
    edge of the stone trough
And rested his throat upon the stone bottom,
And where the water had dripped from the tap, in a small clearness,   10
He sipped with his straight mouth,
Softly drank through his straight gums, into his slack long body,
Silently.

Someone was before me at my water-trough,
And I, like a second comer, waiting.

He lifted his head from his drinking, as cattle do,
And looked at me vaguely, as drinking cattle do,
And flickered his two-forked tongue from his lips, and mused a
    moment,
And stooped and drank a little more,

Being earth-brown, earth-golden from the burning bowels of the
    earth   20
On the day of Sicilian July, with Etna smoking.

The voice of my education said to me
He must be killed,
For in Sicily the black, black snakes are innocent, the gold are
    venomous.

And voices in me said, If you were a man
You would take a stick and break him now, and finish him off.

But must I confess how I liked him,
How glad I was he had come like a guest in quiet, to drink at my
    water-trough
And depart peaceful, pacified, and thankless,
Into the burning bowels of this earth?   30

Was it cowardice, that I dared not kill him?
Was it perversity, that I longed to talk to him?
Was it humility, to feel so honoured?
I felt so honoured.

And yet those voices:
If you were not afraid, you would kill him!

And truly I was afraid, I was most afraid,
But even so, honoured still more
That he should seek my hospitality
From out the dark door of the secret earth.   40

He drank enough
And lifted his head, dreamily, as one who has drunken,
And flickered his tongue like a forked night on the air, so black,
Seeming to lick his lips,
And looked around like a god, unseeing, into the air,
And slowly turned his head,
And slowly, very slowly, as if thrice adream,
Proceeded to draw his slow length curving round
And climb again the broken bank of my wall-face.

And as he put his head into that dreadful hole, 50
And as he slowly drew up, snake-easing his shoulders, and entered
    farther,
A sort of horror, a sort of protest against his withdrawing into that
    horrid black hole,
Deliberately going into the blackness, and slowly drawing himself
    after,
Overcame me now his back was turned.

I looked round, I put down my pitcher,
I picked up a clumsy log
And threw it at the water-trough with a clatter.

I think it did not hit him,
But suddenly that part of him that was left behind convulsed in
    undignified haste,
Writhed like lightning, and was gone 60
Into the black hole, the earth-lipped fissure in the wall-front,
At which, in the intense still noon, I stared with fascination.

And immediately I regretted it.
I thought how paltry, how vulgar, what a mean act!
I despised myself and the voices of my accursed human education.

And I thought of the albatross,
And I wished he would come back, my snake.

For he seemed to me again like a king,
Like a king in exile, uncrowned in the underworld,
Now due to be crowned again. 70

And so, I missed my chance with one of the lords
Of life.
And I have something to expiate;
A pettiness.

Taormina

TORTOISES

BABY TORTOISE

You know what it is to be born alone,
Baby tortoise!

128

The first day to heave your feet little by little from the shell,
Not yet awake,
And remain lapsed on earth,
Not quite alive.

A tiny, fragile, half-animate bean.

To open your tiny beak-mouth, that looks as if it would never open,
Like some iron door;
To lift the upper hawk-beak from the lower base   10
And reach your skinny little neck
And take your first bite at some dim bit of herbage,
Alone, small insect,
Tiny bright-eye,
Slow one.

To take your first solitary bite
And move on your slow, solitary hunt.
Your bright, dark little eye,
Your eye of a dark disturbed night,
Under its slow lid, tiny baby tortoise,   20
So indomitable.

No one ever heard you complain.

You draw your head forward, slowly, from your little wimple
And set forward, slow-dragging, on your four-pinned toes,
Rowing slowly forward.
Whither away, small bird?

Rather like a baby working its limbs,
Except that you make slow, ageless progress
And a baby makes none.

The touch of sun excites you,   30
And the long ages, and the lingering chill
Make you pause to yawn,
Opening your impervious mouth,
Suddenly beak-shaped, and very wide, like some suddenly gaping
    pincers;
Soft red tongue, and hard thin gums,

Then close the wedge of your little mountain front,
Your face, baby tortoise.

Do you wonder at the world, as slowly you turn your head in its
    wimple
And look with laconic, black eyes?
Or is sleep coming over you again,   40
The non-life?

You are so hard to wake.

Are you able to wonder?
Or is it just your indomitable will and pride of the first life
Looking round
And slowly pitching itself against the inertia
Which had seemed invincible?

The vast inanimate,
And the fine brilliance of your so tiny eye,
Challenger.   50

Nay, tiny shell-bird,
What a huge vast inanimate it is, that you must row against,
What an incalculable inertia.

Challenger,
Little Ulysses, fore-runner,
No bigger than my thumb-nail,
Buon viaggio.

All animate creation on your shoulder,
Set forth, little Titan, under your battle-shield.
The ponderous, preponderate,   60
Inanimate universe;
And you are slowly moving, pioneer, you alone.

How vivid your travelling seems now, in the troubled sunshine,
Stoic, Ulyssean atom;
Suddenly hasty, reckless, on high toes.

Voiceless little bird,
Resting your head half out of your wimple

In the slow dignity of your eternal pause.
Alone, with no sense of being alone,
And hence six times more solitary;   70
Fulfilled of the slow passion of pitching through immemorial ages
Your little round house in the midst of chaos.

Over the garden earth,
Small bird,
Over the edge of all things.

Traveller,
With your tail tucked a little on one side
Like a gentleman in a long-skirted coat.

All life carried on your shoulder,
Invincible fore-runner.   80

TORTOISE-SHELL

The Cross, the Cross
Goes deeper in than we know,
Deeper into life;
Right into the marrow
And through the bone.

Along the back of the baby tortoise
The scales are locked in an arch like a bridge,
Scale-lapping, like a lobster's sections
Or a bee's.

Then crossways down his sides   10
Tiger-stripes and wasp-bands.

Five, and five again, and five again,
And round the edges twenty-five little ones,
The sections of the baby tortoise shell.

Four, and a keystone;
Four, and a keystone;

Four, and a keystone;
Then twenty-four, and a tiny little keystone.

It needed Pythagoras to see life playing with counters on the living
    back
Of the baby tortoise;   20
Life establishing the first eternal mathematical tablet,
Not in stone, like the Judean Lord, or bronze, but in life-clouded,
    life-rosy tortoise shell.

The first little mathematical gentleman
Stepping, wee mite, in his loose trousers
Under all the eternal dome of mathematical law.
Fives, and tens,
Threes and fours and twelves,
All the *volte face* of decimals,
The whirligig of dozens and the pinnacle of seven.

Turn him on his back,   30
The kicking little beetle,
And there again, on his shell-tender, earth-touching belly,
The long cleavage of division, upright of the eternal cross
And on either side count five,
On each side, two above, on each side, two below
The dark bar horizontal.

The Cross!
It goes right through him, the sprottling insect,
Through his cross-wise cloven psyche,
Through his five-fold complex-nature.   40

So turn him over on his toes again;
Four pin-point toes, and a problematical thumb-piece,
Four rowing limbs, and one wedge-balancing head,
Four and one makes five, which is the clue to all mathematics.

The Lord wrote it all down on the little slate
Of the baby tortoise.
Outward and visible indication of the plan within,
The complex, manifold involvedness of an individual creature

Plotted out
On this small bird, this rudiment,   50
This little dome, this pediment
Of all creation,
This slow one.

TORTOISE FAMILY CONNECTIONS

On he goes, the little one,
Bud of the universe,
Pediment of life.

Setting off somewhere, apparently.
Whither away, brisk egg?

His mother deposited him on the soil as if he were no more than
    droppings,
And now he scuffles tinily past her as if she were an old rusty tin.

A mere obstacle,
He veers round the slow great mound of her –
Tortoises always foresee obstacles.   10

It is no use my saying to him in an emotional voice:
'This is your Mother, she laid you when you were an egg.'

He does not even trouble to answer: 'Woman, what have I to do with
    thee?'
He wearily looks the other way,
And she even more wearily looks another way still,
Each with the utmost apathy,
Incognizant,
Unaware,
Nothing.

As for papa,   20
He snaps when I offer him his offspring,
Just as he snaps when I poke a bit of stick at him,
Because he is irascible this morning, an irascible tortoise
Being touched with love, and devoid of fatherliness.

Father and mother,
And three little brothers,
And all rambling aimless, like little perambulating pebbles scattered
   in the garden,
Not knowing each other from bits of earth or old tins.

Except that papa and mama are old acquaintances, of course,
Though family feeling there is none, not even the beginnings.   30

Fatherless, motherless, brotherless, sisterless
Little tortoise.

Row on then, small pebble,
Over the clods of the autumn, wind-chilled sunshine,
Young gaiety.

Does he look for a companion?

No, no, don't think it.
He doesn't know he is alone;
Isolation is his birthright,
This atom.   40

To row forward, and reach himself tall on spiny toes,
To travel, to burrow into a little loose earth, afraid of the night,
To crop a little substance,
To move, and to be quite sure that he is moving:
Basta!
To be a tortoise!
Think of it, in a garden of inert clods
A brisk, brindled little tortoise, all to himself –
Crœsus!

In a garden of pebbles and insects   50
To roam, and feel the slow heart beat
Tortoise-wise, the first bell sounding
From the warm blood, in the dark-creation morning.

Moving, and being himself,
Slow, and unquestioned,
And inordinately there, O stoic!

Wandering in the slow triumph of his own existence,
Ringing the soundless bell of his presence in chaos,
And biting the frail grass arrogantly,   60
Decidedly arrogantly.

LUI ET ELLE

She is large and matronly
And rather dirty,
A little sardonic-looking, as if domesticity had driven her to it.

Though what she does, except lay four eggs at random in the garden
    once a year
And put up with her husband,
I don't know.

She likes to eat.
She hurries up, striding reared on long uncanny legs,
When food is going.
Oh yes, she can make haste when she likes.   10

She snaps the soft bread from my hand in great mouthfuls,
Opening her rather pretty wedge of an iron, pristine face
Into an enormously wide-beaked mouth
Like sudden curved scissors,
And gulping at more than she can swallow, and working her thick,
    soft tongue,
And having the bread hanging over her chin.

O Mistress, Mistress,
Reptile mistress,
Your eye is very dark, very bright,
And it never softens   20
Although you watch.

She knows,
She knows well enough to come for food,
Yet she sees me not;
Her bright eye sees, but not me, not anything,

135

Sightful, sightless, seeing and visionless,
Reptile mistress.

Taking bread in her curved, gaping, toothless mouth,
She has no qualm when she catches my finger in her steel overlapping
   gums,
But she hangs on, and my shout and my shrinking are nothing to her,   30
She does not even know she is nipping me with her curved beak.
Snake-like she draws at my finger, while I drag it in horror away.

Mistress, reptile mistress,
You are almost too large, I am almost frightened.

He is much smaller,
Dapper beside her,
And ridiculously small.

Her laconic eye has an earthy, materialistic look,
His, poor darling, is almost fiery.

His wimple, his blunt-prowed face,   40
His low forehead, his skinny neck, his long, scaled, striving legs,
So striving, striving,
Are all more delicate than she,
And he has a cruel scar on his shell.

Poor darling, biting at her feet,
Running beside her like a dog, biting her earthy, splay feet,
Nipping her ankles,
Which she drags apathetic away, though without retreating into her
   shell.

Agelessly silent,
And with a grim, reptile determination,   50
Cold, voiceless age-after-age behind him, serpents' long obstinacy
Of horizontal persistence.

Little old man
Scuffling beside her, bending down, catching his opportunity,
Parting his steel-trap face, so suddenly, and seizing her scaly ankle,
And hanging grimly on,

Letting go at last as she drags away,
And closing his steel-trap face.

His steel-trap, stoic, ageless, handsome face.
Alas, what a fool he looks in this scuffle.   60

And how he feels it!
The lonely rambler, the stoic, dignified stalker through chaos,
The immune, the animate,
Enveloped in isolation,
Forerunner.
Now look at him!

Alas, the spear is through the side of his isolation.
His adolescence saw him crucified into sex,
Doomed, in the long crucifixion of desire, to seek his consummation
    beyond himself.
Divided into passionate duality,   70
He, so finished and immune, now broken into desirous
    fragmentariness,
Doomed to make an intolerable fool of himself
In his effort toward completion again.

Poor little earthy house-inhabiting Osiris,
The mysterious bull tore him at adolescence into pieces,
And he must struggle after reconstruction, ignominiously.

And so behold him following the tail
Of that mud-hovel of his slowly rambling spouse,
Like some unhappy bull at the tail of a cow,
But with more than bovine, grim, earth-dank persistence,   80
Suddenly seizing the ugly ankle as she stretches out to walk,
Roaming over the sods,
Or, if it happen to show, at her pointed, heavy tail
Beneath the low-dropping back-board of her shell.

Their two shells like domed boats bumping,
Hers huge, his small;
Their splay feet rambling and rowing like paddles,
And stumbling mixed up in one another,

137

In the race of love –
Two tortoises,   90
She huge, he small.

She seems earthily apathetic,
And he has a reptile's awful persistence.

I heard a woman pitying her, pitying the Mère Tortue.
While I, I pity Monsieur.
'He pesters her and torments her,' said the woman.
How much more is *he* pestered and tormented, say I.

What can he do?
He is dumb, he is visionless,
Conceptionless.   100
His black, sad-lidded eye sees but beholds not
As her earthen mound moves on,
But he catches the folds of vulnerable, leathery skin,
Nail-studded, that shake beneath her shell,
And drags at these with his beak,
Drags and drags and bites,
While she pulls herself free, and rows her dull mound along.

TORTOISE GALLANTRY

Making his advances
He does not look at her, nor sniff at her,
No, not even sniff at her, his nose is blank.

Only he senses the vulnerable folds of skin
That work beneath her while she sprawls along
In her ungainly pace,
Her folds of skin that work and row
Beneath the earth-soiled hovel in which she moves.

And so he strains beneath her housey walls
And catches her trouser-legs in his beak   10
Suddenly, or her skinny limb,
And strange and grimly drags at her

138

Like a dog,
Only agelessly silent, with a reptile's awful persistency

Grim, gruesome gallantry, to which he is doomed.
Dragged out of an eternity of silent isolation
And doomed to partiality, partial being,
Ache, and want of being,
Want,
Self-exposure, hard humiliation, need to add himself on to her   20

Born to walk alone,
Fore-runner,
Now suddenly distracted into this mazy side-track,
This awkward, harrowing pursuit,
This grim necessity from within.

Does she know
As she moves eternally slowly away?
Or is he driven against her with a bang, like a bird flying in the dark
    against a window,
All knowledgeless?

The awful concussion,   30
And the still more awful need to persist, to follow, follow, continue,

Driven, after æons of pristine, fore-god-like singleness and oneness,
At the end of some mysterious, red-hot iron,
Driven away from himself into her tracks,
Forced to crash against her.

Stiff, gallant, irascible, crook-legged reptile,
Little gentleman,
Sorry plight,
We ought to look the other way.

Save that, having come with you so far,   40
We will go on to the end.

TORTOISE SHOUT

I thought he was dumb,
I said he was dumb,
Yet I've heard him cry.

First faint scream,
Out of life's unfathomable dawn,
Far off, so far, like a madness, under the horizon's dawning rim,
Far, far off, far scream.

Tortoise *in extremis*.

Why were we crucified into sex?
Why were we not left rounded off, and finished in ourselves,   10
As we began,
As he certainly began, so perfectly alone?

A far, was-it-audible scream,
Or did it sound on the plasm direct?

Worse than the cry of the new-born,
A scream,
A yell,
A shout,
A pæan,
A death-agony,   20
A birth-cry,
A submission,
All tiny, tiny, far away, reptile under the first dawn.

War-cry, triumph, acute-delight, death-scream reptilian,
Why was the veil torn?
The silken shriek of the soul's torn membrane?
The male soul's membrane
Torn with a shriek half music, half horror.

Crucifixion.
Male tortoise, cleaving behind the hovel-wall of that dense female,   30
Mounted and tense, spread-eagle, out-reaching out of the shell
In tortoise-nakedness,
Long neck, and long vulnerable limbs extruded, spread-eagle over her
    house-roof,
And the deep, secret, all-penetrating tail curved beneath her
    walls,

140

Reaching and gripping tense, more reaching anguish in uttermost
    tension
Till suddenly, in the spasm of coition, tupping like a jerking leap,
    and oh!
Opening its clenched face from his outstretched neck
And giving that fragile yell, that scream,
Super-audible,
From his pink, cleft, old-man's mouth,   40
Giving up the ghost,
Or screaming in Pentecost, receiving the ghost.

His scream, and his moment's subsidence,
The moment of eternal silence,
Yet unreleased, and after the moment, the sudden, startling jerk of
    coition, and at once
The inexpressible faint yell –
And so on, till the last plasm of my body was melted back
To the primeval rudiments of life, and the secret.

So he tups, and screams
Time after time that frail, torn scream   50
After each jerk, the longish interval,
The tortoise eternity,
Agelong, reptilian persistence,
Heart-throb, slow heart-throb, persistent for the next spasm.

I remember, when I was a boy,
I heard the scream of a frog, which was caught with his foot in the
    mouth of an up-starting snake;
I remember when I first heard bull-frogs break into sound in the
    spring;
I remember hearing a wild goose out of the throat of night
Cry loudly, beyond the lake of waters;
I remember the first time, out of a bush in the darkness, a nightin-
    gale's piercing cries and gurgles startled the depths of my soul;   60
I remember the scream of a rabbit as I went through a wood at
    midnight;
I remember the heifer in her heat, blorting and blorting through the
    hours, persistent and irrepressible;

I remember my first terror hearing the howl of weird, amorous cats;
I remember the scream of a terrified, injured horse, the
sheet-lightning,
And running away from the sound of a woman in labour, something
like an owl whooing,
And listening inwardly to the first bleat of a lamb,
The first wail of an infant,
And my mother singing to herself,
And the first tenor singing of the passionate throat of a young collier,
who has long since drunk himself to death,
The first elements of foreign speech   70
On wild dark lips.

And more than all these,
And less than all these,
This last,
Strange, faint coition yell
Of the male tortoise at extremity,
Tiny from under the very edge of the farthest far-off horizon of life.

The cross,
The wheel on which our silence first is broken,
Sex, which breaks up our integrity, our single inviolability, our deep
silence   80
Tearing a cry from us.

Sex, which breaks us into voice, sets us calling across the deeps,
calling, calling for the complement,
Singing, and calling, and singing again, being answered, having
found;

Torn, to become whole again, after long seeking for what is lost,
The same cry from the tortoise as from Christ, the Osiris-cry of
abandonment,
That which is whole, torn asunder,
That which is in part, finding its whole again throughout the
universe.

EAGLE IN NEW MEXICO

Towards the sun, towards the south-west
A scorched breast.
A scorched breast, breasting the sun like an answer,
Like a retort.

An eagle at the top of a low cedar-bush
On the sage-ash desert
Reflecting the scorch of the sun from his breast;
Eagle, with the sickle dripping darkly above.

Erect, scorched-pallid out of the hair of the cedar,
Erect, with the god-thrust entering him from below,   10
Eagle gloved in feathers
In scorched white feathers
In burnt dark feathers
In feathers still fire-rusted;
Sickle-overswept, sickle dripping over and above.

Sun-breaster,
Staring two ways at once, to right and left;
Masked-one
Dark-visaged
Sickle-masked   20
With iron between your two eyes;
You feather-gloved
To the feet;
Foot-fierce;
Erect one;
The god-thrust entering you steadily from below.

You never look at the sun with your two eyes.
Only the inner eye of your scorched broad breast
Looks straight at the sun.

You are dark   30
Except scorch-pale-breasted;
And dark cleaves down and weapon-hard downward curving
At your scorched breast,

Like a sword of Damocles,
Beaked eagle.

You've dipped it in blood so many times
That dark face-weapon, to temper it well,
Blood-thirsty bird.

Why do you front the sun so obstinately,
American eagle?   40
As if you owed him an old, old grudge, great sun: or an old, old
    allegiance.

When you pick the red smoky heart from a rabbit or a light-
    blooded bird
Do you lift it to the sun, as the Aztec priests used to lift red hearts
    of men?

Does the sun need steam of blood do you think
In America, still,
Old eagle?

Does the sun in New Mexico sail like a fiery bird of prey in the sky
Hovering?

Does he shriek for blood?
Does he fan great wings above the prairie, like a hovering, blood-
    thirsty bird?   50

And are you his priest, big eagle
Whom the Indians aspire to?
Is there a bond of bloodshed between you?

Is your continent cold from the ice-age still, that the sun is so angry?
Is the blood of your continent somewhat reptilian still,
That the sun should be greedy for it?

I don't yield to you, big, jowl-faced eagle.
Nor you nor your blood-thirsty sun
That sucks up blood
Leaving a nervous people.   60

Fly off, big bird with a big black back,

144

Fly slowly away, with a rust of fire in your tail,
Dark as you are on your dark side, eagle of heaven.

Even the sun in heaven can be curbed and chastened at last
By the life in the hearts of men.
And you, great bird, sun-starer, heavy black beak
Can be put out of office as sacrifice bringer.

Taos

THE ASS

The long-drawn bray of the ass
In the Sicilian twilight –

All mares are dead!
All mares are dead!
Oh-h!
Oh-h-h!
Oh-h-h-h-h – h!!
I can't bear it, I can't bear it,
I can't!
Oh, I can't!
Oh –
There's one left!
There's one left!
One!
There's one . . . left. . . .

10

So ending on a grunt of agonised relief.

This is the authentic Arabic interpretation of the braying of the ass.
And Arabs should know.

And yet, as his brass-resonant howling yell resounds through the
    Sicilian twilight
I am not sure –

20

His big, furry head,
His big, regretful eyes,

145

His diminished, drooping hindquarters,
His small toes.

Such a dear!
Such an ass!
With such a knot inside him!
He regrets something that he remembers.
That's obvious.

The Steppes of Tartary,   30
And the wind in his teeth for a bit,
And *noli me tangere*.

Ah then, when he tore the wind with his teeth,
And trod wolves underfoot,
And over-rode his mares as if he were savagely leaping an obstacle,
    to set his teeth in the sun. . . .

Somehow, alas, he fell in love,
And was sold into slavery.

He fell into the rut of love,
Poor ass, like man, always in a rut,
The pair of them alike in that.   40

All his soul in his gallant member
And his head gone heavy with the knowledge of desire
And humiliation.

The ass was the first of all animals to fall finally into love,
From obstacle-leaping pride,
Mare obstacle,
Into love, mare-goal, and the knowledge of love.

Hence Jesus rode him in the Triumphant Entry.
Hence his beautiful eyes.
Hence his ponderous head, brooding over desire, and down-fall,
    Jesus, and a pack-saddle,   50
Hence he uncovers his big ass-teeth and howls in that agony that is
    half-insatiable desire and half-unquenchable humiliation.
Hence the black cross on his shoulders.

146

The Arabs were only half right, though they hinted the whole;
Everlasting lament in everlasting desire.

See him standing with his head down, near the Porta Cappuccini,
Asinello,
Somaro;
With the half-veiled, beautiful eyes, and the pensive face not asleep,
Motionless, like a bit of rock.

Has he seen the Gorgon's head, and turned to stone?   60
Alas, Love did it.
Now he's a jackass, a pack-ass, a donkey, somaro, burro, with a boss
     piling loads on his back.
Tied by the nose at the Porta Cappuccini.
And tied in a knot, inside, dead-licked between two desires:
To overleap like a male all mares as obstacles
In a leap at the sun;
And to leap in one last heart-bursting leap like a male at the goal of
     a mare,
And there end.
Well, you can't have it both roads.

Hee! Hee! Ehee! Ehow! Ehaw!! Oh! Oh! Oh-h-h!!   70
The wave of agony bursts in the stone that he was,
Bares his long ass's teeth, flattens his long ass's ears, straightens his
     donkey neck,
And howls his pandemonium on the indignant air.

Yes, it's a quandary.
Jesus rode on him, the first burden on the first beast of burden.
Love on a submissive ass.
So the tale began.

But the ass never forgets.

The horse, being nothing but a nag, will forget.
And men, being mostly geldings and knacker-boned hacks, have
     almost all forgot.   80
But the ass is a primal creature, and never forgets.

The Steppes of Tartary,

And Jesus on a meek ass-colt: mares: Mary escaping to Egypt:
   Joseph's cudgel.

Hee! Hee! Ehee! Ehow-ow-!-ow!-aw!-aw!-aw!
All mares are dead!
Or else I am dead!
One of us, or the pair of us,
I don't know-ow!-ow!
Which!
Not sure-ure-ure   90
Quite which!
Which!

                                                              Taormina

HE-GOAT

See his black nose snubbed back, pressed over like a whale's
   blow-holes,
As if his nostrils were going to curve back to the root of his tail.

As he charges slow among the herd
And rows among the females like a ship pertinaciously,
Heavy with a rancid cargo, through the lesser ships –
Old father
Sniffing forever ahead of him, at the rear of the goats, that they lift
   the little door,
And rowing on, unarrived, no matter how often he enter:
Like a big ship pushing her bowsprit over the little ships
Then swerving and steering afresh   10
And never, never arriving at journey's end, at the rear of the female
   ships.

Yellow eyes incomprehensible with thin slits
To round-eyed us.

Yet if you had whorled horns of bronze in a frontal dark wall
At the end of a back-bone ridge, like a straight sierra roquena,
And nerves urging forward to the wall, you'd have eyes like his,

148

Especially if, being given a needle's eye of egress elsewhere
You tried to look back to it, and couldn't.

Sometimes he turns with a start, to fight, to challenge, to suddenly
    butt.
And then you see the God that he is, in a cloud of black hair   20
And storm-lightning-slitted eye.
Splendidly planting his feet, one rocky foot striking the ground with
    a sudden rock-hammer announcement.

I am here!
And suddenly lowering his head, the whorls of bone and of horn
Slowly revolving towards unexploded explosion,
As from the stem of his bristling, lightning-conductor tail
In a rush up the shrieking duct of his vertebral way
Runs a rage drawn in from the other divinely through him
Towards a shock and a crash and a smiting of horns ahead.

That is a grand old lust of his, to gather the great   30
Rage of the sullen-stagnating atmosphere of goats
And bring it hurtling to a head, with crash of horns against the horns
Of the opposite enemy goat,
Thus hammering the mettle of goats into proof, and smiting out
The godhead of goats from the shock.
Things of iron are beaten on the anvil,
And he-goat is anvil to he-goat, and hammer to he-goat
In the business of beating the mettle of goats to a god-head.

But they've taken his enemy from him
And left him only his libidinousness,   40
His nostrils turning back, to sniff at even himself
And his slitted eyes seeking the needle's eye,
His own, unthreaded, forever.

So it is, when they take the enemy from us,
And we can't fight.

He is not fatherly, like the bull, massive Providence of hot blood;
The goat is an egoist, aware of himself, devilish aware of himself,
And full of malice prepense, and overweening, determined to stand
    on the highest peak

149

Like the devil, and look on the world as his own.

And as for love: 50
With a needle of long red flint he stabs in the dark
At the living rock he is up against;
While she with her goaty mouth stands smiling the while as he
    strikes, since sure
He will never *quite* strike home, on the target-quick, for her quick
Is just beyond range of the arrow he shoots
From his leap at the zenith in her, so it falls just short of the mark,
    far enough.
It is over before it is finished.
She, smiling with goaty munch-mouth, Mona Lisa, arranges it so
Orgasm after orgasm after orgasm
And he smells so rank and his nose goes back,   60
And never an enemy brow-metalled to thresh it out with in the open
    field;
Never a mountain peak, to be king of the castle.
Only those eternal females to overleap and surpass, and never succeed.

The involved voluptuousness of the soft-footed cat
Who is like a fur folding a fur,
The cat who laps blood, and knows
The soft welling of blood invincible even beyond bone or metal of
    bone.

The soft, the secret, the unfathomable blood
The cat has lapped
And known it subtler than frisson-shaken nerves,   70
Stronger than multiplicity of bone on bone
And darker than even the arrows of violentest will
Can pierce, for that is where will gives out, like a sinking stone that
    can sink no further.

But he-goat,
Black procreant male of the selfish will and libidinous desire,
God in black cloud with curving horns of bronze,
Find an enemy, Egoist, and clash the cymbals in face-to-face defiance,
And let the lightning out of your smothered dusk.

150

Forget the female herd for a bit,
And fight to be boss of the world.   80
Fight, old Satan with a selfish will, fight for your selfish will;
Fight to be the devil on the tip of the peak
Overlooking the world for his own.

But bah, how can he, poor domesticated beast.

                                                        Taormina

SHE-GOAT

Goats go past the back of the house like dry leaves in the dawn,
And up the hill like a river, if you watch.

At dusk they patter back like a bough being dragged on the ground,
Raising dusk and acridity of goats, and bleating.

Our old goat we tie up at night in the shed at the back of the broken
    Greek tomb in the garden,
And when the herd goes by at dawn she begins to bleat for me to
    come down and untie her.

Merr-err-err! Merr-er-errr! Mer! Mé!
Wait, wait a bit, I'll come when I've lit the fire.
Merrr!
Exactly.   10
Mé! Mer! Merrrrrr!!!
Tace, tu, crapa, bestia!
Merr-ererrr-ererrrr! Merrrr!

She is such an alert listener, with her ears wide, to know am I coming!
Such a canny listener, from a distance, looking upwards, lending first
    one ear, then another.

There she is, perched on her manger, looking over the boards into
    the day
Like a belle at her window.

And immediately she sees me she blinks, stares, doesn't know me,

turns her head and ignores me vulgarly with a wooden blank on
    her face.

What do I care for her, the ugly female, standing up there with her
    long tangled sides like an old rug thrown over a fence.
But she puts her nose down shrewdly enough when the knot is
    untied,   20
And jumps staccato to earth, a sharp, dry jump, still ignoring me,
Pretending to look round the stall.

Come on, you, crapa! I'm not your servant!

She turns her head away with an obtuse, female sort of deafness, bête.
And then invariably she crouches her rear and makes water.
That being her way of answer, if I speak to her. – Self-conscious!
Le bestie non parlano, poverine!

She was bought at Giardini fair, on the sands, for six hundred lire.

An obstinate old witch, almost jerking the rope from my hands to
    eat the acanthus, or bite at the almond buds, and make me wait.
Yet the moment I hate her she trips mild and smug like a woman
    going to mass.   30
The moment I really detest her.

Queer it is, suddenly, in the garden
To catch sight of her standing like some huge, ghoulish grey bird
    in the air, on the bough of the leaning almond-tree,
Straight as a board on the bough, looking down like some hairy
    horrid God the Father in a William Blake imagination.
Come down, crapa, out of that almond tree!

Instead of which she strangely rears on her perch in the air, vast beast,
And strangely paws the air, delicate,
And reaches her black-striped face up like a snake, far up,
Subtly, to the twigs overhead, far up, vast beast,
And snaps them sharp, with a little twist of her anaconda head;   40
All her great hairy-shaggy belly open against the morning.

At seasons she curls back her tail like a green leaf in the fire,
Or like a lifted hand, hailing at her wrong end.

And having exposed the pink place of her nakedness, fixedly,
She trots on blithe toes,
And if you look at her, she looks back with a cold, sardonic stare.
Sardonic, sardonyx, rock of cold fire.
See me? She says, *That's me!*

That's her.

Then she leaps the rocks like a quick rock,   50
Her back-bone sharp as a rock,
Sheer will.

Along which ridge of libidinous magnetism
Defiant, curling the leaf of her tail as if she were curling her lip behind
    her at all life,
Libidinous desire runs back and forth, asserting itself in that little
    lifted bare hand.

Yet she has such adorable spurty kids, like spurts of black ink.
And in a month again is as if she had never had them.

And when the billy goat mounts her
She is brittle as brimstone.
While his slitted eyes squint back to the roots of his ears.   60

Taormina

KANGAROO

In the northern hemisphere
Life seems to leap at the air, or skim under the wind
Like stags on rocky ground, or pawing horses, or springy scut-tailed
    rabbits.

Or else rush horizontal to charge at the sky's horizon,
Like bulls or bisons or wild pigs.

Or slip like water slippery towards its ends,
As foxes, stoats, and wolves, and prairie dogs.

Only mice, and moles, and rats, and badgers, and beavers, and
   perhaps bears
Seem belly-plumbed to the earth's mid-navel.
Or frogs that when they leap come flop, and flop to the centre of
   the earth.   10

But the yellow antipodal Kangaroo, when she sits up,
Who can unseat her, like a liquid drop that is heavy, and just touches
   earth.

The downward drip.
The down-urge.
So much denser than cold-blooded frogs.

Delicate mother Kangaroo
Sitting up there rabbit-wise, but huge, plumb-weighted,
And lifting her beautiful slender face, oh! so much more gently and
   finely lined than a rabbit's, or than a hare's,
Lifting her face to nibble at a round white peppermint drop, which
   she loves, sensitive mother Kangaroo.

Her sensitive, long, pure-bred face.   20
Her full antipodal eyes, so dark,
So big and quiet and remote, having watched so many empty dawns
   in silent Australia.

Her little loose hands, and drooping Victorian shoulders.
And then her great weight below the waist, her vast pale belly
With a thin young yellow little paw hanging out, and straggle of
   a long thin ear, like ribbon,
Like a funny trimming to the middle of her belly, thin little dangle
   of an immature paw, and one thin ear.

Her belly, her big haunches
And in addition, the great muscular python-stretch of her tail.

There, she shan't have any more peppermint drops.
So she wistfully, sensitively sniffs the air, and then turns, goes off
   in slow sad leaps   30
On the long flat skis of her legs,
Steered and propelled by that steel-strong snake of a tail.

Stops again, half turns, inquisitive to look back.

While something stirs quickly in her belly, and a lean little face comes
    out, as from a window,

Peaked and a bit dismayed,

Only to disappear again quickly away from the sight of the world,
    to snuggle down in the warmth,

Leaving the trail of a different paw hanging out.

Still she watches with eternal, cocked wistfulness!

How full her eyes are, like the full, fathomless, shining eyes of an
    Australian black-boy

Who has been lost so many centuries on the margins of existence!   40

She watches with insatiable wistfulness.

Untold centuries of watching for something to come,

For a new signal from life, in that silent lost land of the South.

Where nothing bites but insects and snakes and the sun, small life.

Where no bull roared, no cow ever lowed, no stag cried, no leopard
    screeched, no lion coughed, no dog barked,

But all was silent save for parrots occasionally, in the haunted blue
    bush.

Wistfully watching, with wonderful liquid eyes.

And all her weight, all her blood, dripping sack-wise down towards
    the earth's centre,

And the live little one taking in its paw at the door of her belly.

Leap then, and come down on the line that draws to the earth's deep,
    heavy centre.   50

Sydney

MOUNTAIN LION

Climbing through the January snow, into the Lobo canyon

Dark grow the spruce trees, blue is the balsam, water sounds still
    unfrozen, and the trail is still evident.

Men!

Two men!

Men! The only animal in the world to fear!

They hesitate.
We hesitate.
They have a gun.
We have no gun.

Then we all advance, to meet.   10

Two Mexicans, strangers, emerging out of the dark and snow and
    inwardness of the Lobo valley.
What are they doing here on this vanishing trail?

What is he carrying?
Something yellow.
A deer?

Qué tiene, amigo? –
León –

He smiles, foolishly, as if he were caught doing wrong.
And we smile, foolishly, as if we didn't know.
He is quite gentle and dark-faced.   20

It is a mountain lion,
A long, slim cat, yellow like a lioness.
Dead.

He trapped her this morning, he says, smiling foolishly.

Lift up her face,
Her round, bright face, bright as frost.
Her round, fine-fashioned head, with two dead ears:
And stripes in the brilliant frost of her face, sharp, fine dark rays,
Dark, keen, fine rays in the brilliant frost of her face.
Beautiful dead eyes.   30

Hermoso es!

They go out towards the open;
We go on into the gloom of Lobo.

And above the trees I found her lair,

A hole in the blood-orange brilliant rocks that stick up, a little cave.
And bones, and twigs, and a perilous ascent.

So, she will never leap up that way again, with the yellow flash of
    a mountain lion's long shoot!
And her bright striped frost-face will never watch any more, out of
    the shadow of the cave in the blood-orange rock,
Above the trees of the Lobo dark valley-mouth!

Instead, I look out.   40
And out to the dim of the desert, like a dream, never real;
To the snow of the Sangre de Cristo mountains, the ice of the
    mountains of Picoris,
And near across at the opposite steep of snow, green trees motionless
    standing in snow, like a Christmas toy.

And I think in this empty world there was room for me and a
    mountain lion.
And I think in the world beyond, how easily we might spare a million
    or two of humans
And never miss them.
Yet what a gap in the world, the missing white frost-face of that slim
    yellow mountain lion!

LOBO

A SECOND CONTEMPORARY VERSE ANTHOLOGY

'It is not merely an assembly of verse, but the spiritual record of an
entire people.' – This from the wrapper of *A Second Contemporary
Verse Anthology*. The spiritual record of an entire people sounds rather
impressive. The book as a matter of fact is a collection of pleasant
verse, neat and nice and easy as eating candy.

Naturally, any collection of contemporary verse in any country at
any time is bound to be more or less a box of candy. Days of Horace,
days of Milton, days of Whitman, it would be pretty much the same,
more or less a box of candy. Would it be at the same time the spiritual
record of an entire people? Why not? If we had a good representative   10
anthology of the poetry of Whitman's day, and if it contained two

poems by Whitman, then it would be a fairly true spiritual record of the American people of that day. As if the whole nation had whispered or chanted its inner experience into the horn of a gramophone.

And the bulk of the whisperings and murmurings would be candy: sweet nothings, tender trifles and amusing things. For of such is the bulk of the spiritual experience of any entire people.

The Americans have always been good at 'occasional' verse. Sixty years ago they were very good indeed: making their little joke against themselves and their century. To-day there are fewer jokes. There are also fewer footprints on the sands of time. Life is still earnest, but a little less real. And the soul has left off asserting that dust it isn't nor to dust returneth. The spirit of verse prefers now a 'composition salad' of fruits of sensation, in a cooked mayonnaise of sympathy. Odds and ends of feelings smoothed into unison by some prevailing sentiment:

> My face is wet with the rain
> But my heart is warm to the core. . . .

Or you can call it a box of chocolate candies. Let me offer you a sweet! Candy! Isn't everything candy?

> There be none of Beauty's daughters
>   With a magic like thee –
> And like music on the waters
>   Is thy sweet voice to me.

Is that candy? Then what about this?

> But you are a girl and run
>   Fresh bathed and warm and sweet,
> After the flying ball
>   On little, sandalled feet.

One of those two fragments is a classic. And one is a scrap from the contemporary spiritual record.

> The river boat had loitered down its way,
> The ropes were coiled, and business for the day
> Was done —

158

> Now fades the glimmering landscape on the sight,
> And all the air a solemn stillness holds;
> Save where —

Two more bits. Do you see any intrinsic difference between them? After all, the one *means* as much as the other. And what is there in the mere stringing together of words?

For some mysterious reason, there is everything.

> When lilacs last in the dooryard bloomed —

It is a string of words, but it makes me prick my innermost ear. So do I prick my ear to: 'Fly low, vermilion dragon.' But the next line: 'With the moon horns,' makes me lower that same inward ear once more, in indifference. 40

There is an element of danger in all new utterance. We prick our ears like an animal in a wood at a strange sound.

Alas! though there is a modicum of 'strange sound' in this contemporary spiritual record, we are not the animal to prick our ears at it. Sounds sweetly familiar, linked in a new crochet pattern. 'Christ, what are patterns for?' But why invoke Deity? Ask the *Ladies' Home Journal*. You may know a new utterance by the element of danger in it. 'My heart aches,' says Keats, and you bet it's no joke.

> Why do I think of stairways
> With a rush of hurt surprise?

Heaven knows, my dear, unless you once fell down.

The element of danger. Man is always, all the time and for ever 50 on the brink of the unknown. The minute you realise this, you prick your ears in alarm. And the minute any man steps alone, with his whole naked self, emotional and mental, into the everlasting hinterland of consciousness, you hate him and you wonder over him. Why can't he stay cozily playing word-games around the camp fire?

Now it is time to invoke the Deity, who made man an adventurer into the everlasting unknown of consciousness.

The spiritual record of any people is 99 per cent a record of games around a camp fire: word-games and picture-games. But the one per cent is a step into the grisly dark, which is for ever dangerous and 60 wonderful. Nothing is wonderful unless it is dangerous. Dangerous

159

to the *status quo* of the soul. And therefore to some degree detestable.

When the contemporary spiritual record warbles away about the wonder of the blue sky and the changing seas, etc., etc., etc., it is all candy. The sky is a blue hand-mirror to the modern poet and he goes on smirking before it. The blue sky of our particular heavens is painfully well known to us all. In fact, it is like the glass bowl to the goldfish, a *ne plus ultra* in which he sees himself as he goes round and round.

The actual heavens can suddenly roll up like the heavens of Ezekiel. 70 That's what happened at the Renaissance. The old heavens shrivelled and men found a new empyrean above them. But they didn't get at it by playing word-games around the camp fire. Somebody has to jump like a desperate clown through the vast blue hoop of the upper air. Or hack a slow way through the dome of crystal.

Play! Play! Play! All the little playboys and playgirls of the western world, playing at goodness, playing at badness, playing at sadness, and playing deafeningly at gladness. Playboys and playgirls of the western world, harmlessly fulfilling their higher destinies and registering the spiritual record of an entire people. Even playing at death, 80 and playing with death. Oh, poetry, you child in a bathing-dress, playing at ball!

You say nature is always nature, the sky is always the sky. But sit still and consider for one moment what sort of nature it was the Romans saw on the face of the earth, and what sort of heavens the medievals knew above them, and your sky will begin to crack like glass. The world is what it is, and the chimerical universe of the ancients was always child's play. The camera cannot lie. And the eye of man is nothing but a camera photographing the outer world in colour-process. 90

This sounds very well. But the eye of man photographs the chimera of nature, as well as the so-called scientific vision. The eye of man photographs gorgons and chimeras, as the eye of the spider photographs images unrecognisable to us and the eye of the horse photographs flat ghosts and looming motions. We are at the phase of scientific vision. This phase will pass and this vision will seem as chimerical to our descendants as the medieval vision seems to us.

The upshot of it all is that we are pot-bound in our consciousness.

160

We are like a fish in a glass bowl, swimming round and round and
gaping at our own image reflected on the walls of the infinite: the   100
infinite being the glass bowl of our conception of life and the universe. We are prisoners inside our own conception of life and being.
We have exhausted the possibilities of the universe, as we know it.
All that remains is to telephone to Mars for a new word of advice.

Our consciousness is pot-bound. Our ideas, our emotions, our
experiences are all pot-bound. For us there is nothing new under the
sun. What there is to know, we know it already, and experience adds
little. The girl who is going to fall in love knows all about it
beforehand from books and the movies. She knows what she wants
and she wants what she knows. Like candy. It is still nice to eat candy,   110
though one has eaten it every day for years. It is still nice to eat candy.
But the spiritual record of eating candy is a rather thin noise.

There is nothing new under the sun, once the consciousness
becomes pot-bound. And this is what ails all art to-day. But particularly American art. The American consciousness is peculiarly pot-
bound. It doesn't even have that little hole in the bottom of the pot
through which desperate roots straggle. No, the American consciousness is not only potted in a solid and everlasting pot, it is placed
moreover in an immovable ornamental vase. A double hide to bind
it and a double bond to hide it.   120

European consciousness still has cracks in its vessel and a hole in
the bottom of its absoluteness. It still has strange roots of memory
groping down to the heart of the world.

But American consciousness is absolutely free of such danglers. It
is free from all loop-holes and crevices of escape. It is absolutely safe
inside a solid and ornamental concept of life. There it is Free! Life
is good, and all men are meant to have a good time. Life is good!
that is the flower-pot. The ornamental vase: Having a good time.

So they proceed to have it, even with their woes. The young
maiden knows exactly when she falls in love: she knows exactly how   130
she feels when her lover or husband betrays her or when she betrays
him: she knows precisely what it is to be a forsaken wife, an adoring
mother, an erratic grandmother. All at the age of eighteen.

Vive la vie!

There is nothing new under the sun, but you can have a jolly good old time all the same with the old things. A nut sundae or a new beau, a baby or an automobile, a divorce or a troublesome appendix: my dear, that's Life! You've got to get a good time out of it, anyhow, so here goes!

In which attitude there is a certain piquant stoicism. The stoicism 140 of having a good time. The heroism of enjoying yourself. But, as I say, it makes rather thin hearing in a spiritual record. *Rechauffés* of *rechauffés*. Old soup of old bones of life, heated up again for a new consommé. Nearly always called *printanière*.

> I know a forest, stilly-deep . . .

Mark the poetic novelty of stilly-deep, and then say there is nothing new under the sun.

> My soul-harp never thrills to peaceful tunes;

I should say so.

> For after all, the thing to do
> Is just to put your heart in song —

Or in pickle.

> I sometimes wish that God were back
>   In this dark world and wide;
> For though some virtues he might lack,
>   He had his pleasant side.

'Getting on the pleasant side of God, and how to stay there.' –
Hints by a Student of Life.   150

> Oh, ho! Now I am masterful!
> Now I am filled with power.
> Now I am brutally myself again
> And my own man.

> For I have been among my hills today,
> On the scarred dumb rocks standing;

And it made a man of him . . .
Open confession is good for the soul.
The spiritual record of an entire . . . what?

CORASMIN AND THE PARROTS

One says Mexico: one means, after all, one little town away South in the Republic: and in this little town, one rather crumbly adobe house built round two sides of a garden *patio*: and of this house, one spot on the deep, shady veranda facing inwards to the trees, where there are an onyx table and three rocking-chairs and one little wooden chair, a pot with carnations, and a person with a pen. We talk so grandly, in capital letters, about Morning in Mexico. All it amounts to is one little individual looking at a bit of sky and trees, then looking down at the page of his exercise book.

It is a pity we don't always remember this. When books come out   10
with grand titles, like *The Future of America*, or *The European Situation*, it's a pity we don't immediately visualize a thin or a fat person, in a chair or in bed, dictating to a bob-haired stenographer or making little marks on paper with a fountain pen.

Still, it is morning, and it is Mexico. The sun shines. But then, during the winter, it always shines. It is pleasant to sit out of doors and write, just fresh enough and just warm enough. But then it is Christmas next week, so it ought to be just right.

There is a little smell of carnations, because they are the nearest thing. And there is a resinous smell of ocote wood, and a smell of   20
coffee, and a faint smell of leaves, and of Morning, and even of Mexico. Because when all is said and done, Mexico has a faint, physical scent of her own, as each human being has. And this is a curious, inexplicable scent, in which there are resin and perspiration and sunburned earth and urine among other things.

And cocks are still crowing. The little mill where the natives have their own corn ground is puffing rather languidly. And because some women are talking in the entrance-way, the two tame parrots in the trees have started to whistle.

The parrots, even when I don't listen to them, have an extra-   30
ordinary effect on me. They make my diaphragm convulse with little laughs, almost mechanically. They are a quite commonplace pair of green birds, with bits of bluey red, and round, disillusioned eyes, and heavy, overhanging noses. But they listen intently. And they repro-duce. The pair whistle now like Rosalino, who is sweeping the *patio* with a twig broom; and yet it is so unlike him, to be whistling full

163

vent, when any of us is around, that one looks at him to see. And the moment one sees him, with his black head bent rather drooping and hidden as he sweeps, one laughs.

The parrots whistle exactly like Rosalino, only a little more so. 40 And this little-more-so is extremely sardonically funny. With their sad old long-jowled faces and their flat disillusioned eyes, they reproduce Rosalino and a little-more-so without moving a muscle. And Rosalino, sweeping the *patio* with his twig broom, scraping and tittering leaves into little heaps, covers himself more and more with the cloud of his own obscurity. He doesn't rebel. He is powerless. Up goes the wild, sliding Indian whistle into the morning, very powerful, with an immense energy seeming to drive behind it. And always, always a little more than life-like.

Then they break off into a cackling chatter, and one knows they 50 are shifting their clumsy legs, perhaps hanging on with their beaks and clutching with their cold, slow claws, to climb to a higher bough, like rather raggedy green buds climbing to the sun. And suddenly the penetrating, demonish mocking voices:

'Perro! Oh, Perro! Perr-rro! Oh, Perr-rro! Perro!'

They are imitating somebody calling the dog. *Perro* means dog. But that any creature should be able to pour such a suave, prussic-acid sarcasm over the voice of a human being calling a dog, is incredible. One's diaphragm chuckles involuntarily. And one thinks: *Is it possible?* Is it possible that we are so absolutely, so innocently, so *ab* 60 *ovo* ridiculous?

And not only is it possible, it is patent. We cover our heads in confusion.

Now they are yapping like a dog: exactly like Corasmin. Corasmin is a little fat, curly white dog who was lying in the sun a minute ago, and has now come into the veranda shade, walking with slow resignation, to lie against the wall near-by my chair. 'Yap-yap-yap! Wouf! Wouf! Yapyapyapyap!' go the parrots, exactly like Corasmin when some stranger comes into the *zaguán*, Corasmin and a little-more-so.

With a grin on my face I look down at Corasmin. And with a 70 silent, abashed resignation in his yellow eyes, Corasmin looks up at me, with a touch of reproach. His little white nose is sharp, and under his eyes there are dark marks, as under the eyes of one who has known

164

much trouble. All day he does nothing but walk resignedly out of the sun, when the sun gets too hot, and out of the shade, when the shade gets too cool. And bite ineffectually in the region of his fleas.

Poor old Corasmin: he is only about six, but resigned, unspeakably resigned. Only not humble. He does not kiss the rod. He rises in spirit above it, letting his body lie.

'Perro! Oh, Perr-rro! Perr-rro! Perr-rr-rro!!' shriek the parrots,   80 with that strange penetrating, antediluvian malevolence that seems to make even the trees prick their ears. It is a sound that penetrates one straight at the diaphragm, belonging to the ages before brains were invented. And Corasmin pushes his sharp little nose into his bushy tail, closes his eyes because I am grinning, feigns to sleep and then, in an orgasm of self-consciousness, starts up to bite in the region of his fleas.

'Perr-rro! Perr-rro!' And then a restrained, withheld sort of yapping. The fiendish rolling of the Spanish 'r', malevolence rippling out of all the vanished spiteful aeons. And following it, the small,   90 little-curly-dog sort of yapping. They can make their voices so devilishly small and futile, like a little curly dog. And follow it up with that ringing malevolence that swoops up the ladders of the sunbeams right to the stars, rolling the Spanish 'r'.

Corasmin slowly walks away from the veranda, his head drooped, and flings himself down in the sun. No! He gets up again, in an agony of self-control, and scratches the earth loose a little, to soften his lie. Then flings himself down again.

Invictus! The still-unconquered Corasmin! The sad little white curly pendulum oscillating ever slower between the shadow and the   100 sun.

> In the fell clutch of circumstance
> > I have not winced nor cried aloud,
> Under the bludgeonings of chance
> > My head is bloody, but unbowed.

But that is human bombast, and a little too ridiculous even for Corasmin. Poor old Corasmin's clear yellow eyes! He is going to be master of his own soul, under all the vitriol those parrots pour over him. But he's not going to throw out his chest in a real lust of self-

165

pity. That belongs to the next cycle of evolution.

I wait for the day when the parrots will start throwing English at us, in the pit of our stomachs. They cock their heads and listen to our gabble. But so far they haven't got it. It puzzles them. Castilian, and Corasmin, and Rosalino come more natural.   110

Myself, I don't believe in evolution, like a long string hooked on to a First Cause, and being slowly twisted in unbroken continuity through the ages. I prefer to believe in what the Aztecs called Suns: that is, Worlds successively created and destroyed. The sun itself convulses, and the worlds go out like so many candles when somebody coughs in the middle of them. Then subtly, mysteriously, the sun convulses again, and a new set of worlds begins to flicker alight.

This pleases my fancy better than the long and weary twisting of the rope of Time and Evolution, hitched on to the revolving hook   120
of a First Cause. I like to think of the whole show going bust, *bang!* – and nothing but bits of chaos flying about. Then out of the dark, new little twinklings reviving from nowhere, nohow.

I like to think of the world going pop! when the lizards had grown too unwieldy, and it was time they were taken down a peg or two. Then the little humming birds beginning to spark in the darkness, and a whole succession of birds shaking themselves clean of the dark matrix, flamingoes rising upon one leg like dawn commencing, parrots shrieking about at midday, *almost* able to talk, then peacocks unfolding at evening like the night with stars. And apart from these   130
little pure birds, a lot of unwieldy skinny-necked monsters bigger than crocodiles, barging through the mosses; till it was time to put a stop to them. When someone mysteriously touched the button, and the sun went bang, with smithereens of birds bursting in all directions. On a few parrots' eggs and peacocks' eggs and eggs of flamingoes smuggling in some safe nook, to hatch on the next Day, when the animals arose.

Up reared the elephant, and shook the mud off his back. The birds watched him in sheer stupefaction. What? *What in heaven's name is this wingless, beakless old perambulator?*   140

No good, oh birds! Curly, little white Corasmin ran yapping out of the undergrowth, the new undergrowth, till parrots, going white at the gills, flew off into the ancientest recesses. Then the terrific neighing of the wild horse was heard in the twilight for the first time, and the bellowing of lions through the night.

And the birds were sad. What is this? they said. A whole vast gamut of new noises. A universe of new voices.

Then the birds under the leaves hung their heads and were dumb. No good our making a sound, they said. We are superseded.

The great big, booming, half-naked birds were blown to   150
smithereens. Only the real little feathery individuals hatched out again and remained. This was a consolation. The larks and warblers cheered up, and began to say their little say, out of the old 'Sun', to the new sun. But the peacock, and the turkey, and the raven, and the parrot above all, they could not get over it. Because, in the old days of the Sun of Birds, they had been the big guns. The parrot had been the old boss of the flock. He was so clever.

Now he was, so to speak, up a tree. Nor dare he come down, because of the toddling little curly white Corasmin, and such-like, down below. He felt absolutely bitter. That wingless, beakless,   160
featherless, curly, misshapen bird's nest of a Corasmin had usurped the face of the earth, waddling about, whereas his Grace, the heavy-nosed old Duke of a parrot, was forced to sit out of reach up a tree, dispossessed.

So, like the riff-raff up in the gallery at the theatre, aloft in the Paradiso of the vanished Sun, he began to whistle and jeer. 'Yap-yap!' said his new little lordship of a Corasmin. 'Ye Gods!' cried the parrot. 'Hear him forsooth! *Yap-yap!* he says! Could anything be more imbecile? Yap-yap! Oh, Sun of the Birds, hark at that! *Yap-yap-yap!* Perro! *Perro! Perr-rro!* Oh, *Perr-rr-rro!*'   170

The parrot had found his cue. Stiff-nosed, heavy-nosed old duke of the birds, he wasn't going to give in and sing a new song, like those fool brown thrushes and nightingales. Let them twitter and warble. The parrot was a gentleman of the old school. He was going to jeer now! Like an ineffectual old aristocrat.

'*Oh, Perr-rro! Perr-rro-o-o-!*'

The Aztecs say there have been four Suns and ours is the fifth. The first Sun, a tiger, or a jaguar, a night-spotted monster of rage, rose out of nowhere and swallowed it, with all its huge, mercifully

forgotten insects along with it. The second Sun blew up in a great   180
wind: that was when the big lizards must have collapsed. The third
Sun burst in water, and drowned all the animals that were considered
unnecessary, together with the first attempts at animal men.

Out of the floods rose our own Sun, and little naked man. 'Hello!'
said the old elephant. 'What's that noise?' And he pricked his ears,
listening to a new voice on the face of the earth. The sound of man,
and *words* for the first time. Terrible, unheard-of sound. The elephant
dropped his tail and ran into the deep jungle, and there stood looking
down his nose.

But little white curly Corasmin was fascinated. '*Come on! Perro!*   190
Perro!' called the naked two-legged one. And Corasmin, fascinated,
said to himself: 'Can't stand out against that name. Shall have to go!'
so off he trotted, at the heels of the naked one. Then came the horse,
then the elephant, spell-bound at being given a name. The other
animals ran for their lives and stood quaking.

In the dust, however, the snake, the oldest dethroned king of all,
bit his tail once more and said to himself: '*Here's another! No end to
these new lords of creation! But I'll bruise his heel! Just as I swallow the eggs
of the parrot, and lick up the little Corasmin-pups.*'

And in the branches, the parrot said to himself: '*Hello! What's this*   200
*new sort of half-bird? Why, he's got Corasmin trotting at his heels! Must
be a new sort of boss! Let's listen to him, and see if I can't take him off.*'

Perr-rro! Perr-rr-rro-oo! Oh, Perro!

The parrot had hit it.

And the monkey, cleverest of creatures, cried with rage when he
heard men speaking. '*Oh, why couldn't I do it!*' he chattered. But no
good, he belonged to the old Sun. So he sat and gibbered across the
invisible gulf in time, which is the 'other dimension' that clever
people gas about: calling it 'fourth dimension', as if you could
measure it with a foot-rule, the same as the obedient other three   210
dimensions.

If you come to think of it, when you look at the monkey, you are
looking straight into the other dimension. He's got length and
breadth and height all right, and he's in the same universe of Space
and Time as you are. But there's another dimension. He's different.
There's no rope of evolution linking him to you, like a navel string.

168

No! Between you and him there's a cataclysm and another dimension. It's no good. You can't link him up. Never will. It's the other dimension.

He mocks at you and gibes at you and imitates you. Sometimes 220 he is even more *like* you than you are yourself. It's funny, and you laugh just a bit on the wrong side of your face. It's the other dimension.

He stands in one Sun, you in another. He whisks his tail in one Day, you scratch your head in another. He jeers at you, and is afraid of you. You laugh at him and are frightened of him.

What's the length and the breadth, what's the height and the depths between you and me? says the monkey.

You get out a tape-measure, and he flies into an obscene mockery of you. 230

It's the other dimension, put the tape-measure away, it won't serve.

'Perro! Oh, Perr-rro!' shrieks the parrot.

Corasmin looks up at me, as much as to say:

'It's the other dimension. There's no help for it. Let us agree about it.'

And I look down into his yellow eyes, and say:

'You're quite right, Corasmin, it's the other dimension. You and I, we admit it. But the parrot won't, and the monkey won't, and the crocodile won't, neither the earwig. They all wind themselves 240 up and wriggle inside the cage of the other dimension, hating it. And those that have voices jeer, and those that have mouths bite, and the insects that haven't even mouths, they turn up their tails and nip with them, or sting. Just behaving according to their own dimension: which, for me, is the other dimension.'

And Corasmin wags his tail mildly, and looks at me with real wisdom in his eyes. He and I, we understand each other in the wisdom of the other dimension.

But the flat, saucer-eyed parrot won't have it. Just won't have it.

'Oh, Perro! Perr-rro! Perr-rro-o-o-o! Yap-yap-yap!' 250

And Rosalino, the Indian *mozo*, looks up at me with his eyes veiled by their own blackness. We won't have it either: he is hiding and repudiating. Between us also is the gulf of the other dimension, and he wants to bridge it with the foot-rule of the three-dimensional space. He knows it can't be done. So do I. Each of us knows the other knows.

But he can imitate me, even more than life-like. As the parrot can him. And I have to laugh at his *me*, a bit on the wrong side of my face, as he has to grin on the wrong side of his face when I catch his eye as the parrot is whistling *him*. With a grin, with a laugh we pay 260 tribute to the other dimension. But Corasmin is wiser. In his clear, yellow eyes is the self-possession of full admission.

The Aztecs said this world, our Sun, would blow up from inside, in earthquakes. Then what will come, in the other dimension, when we are superseded?

EXTRACT FROM THE NIGHTINGALE

. . . The nightingale, let us repeat, is the most unsad thing in the world; even more unsad than the peacock full of gleam. He has nothing to be sad about. He feels perfect with life. It isn't conceit. He just feels life-perfect, and he trills it out – shouts, jugs, gurgles, trills, gives long, mock-plaintiff calls, makes declarations, assertions, and triumphs; but he never reflects. It is pure music, in so far as you could never put words to it. But there are words for the feelings aroused in us by the song. No, even that is not true. There are no words to tell what one really feels, hearing the nightingale. It is something so much purer than words, which are all tainted. Yet we 10 can say, it is some sort of feeling of triumph in one's own life-perfection.

> 'Tis not through envy of thy happy lot,
>> But being too happy in thy happiness, –
>>> That thou, light-wingèd Dryad of the trees,
>>>> In some melodious plot
> Of beechen green, and shadows numberless,
>> Singest of summer in full-throated ease.

Poor Keats, he has to be 'too happy' in the nightingale's happiness, not being very happy in himself at all. So he wants to drink the blushful Hippocrene, and fade away with the nightingale into the forest dim.

Fade far away, dissolve, and quite forget
   What thou among the leaves hast never known,
The weariness, the fever, and the fret. . . .

It is such sad, beautiful poetry of the human male. Yet the next
line strikes me as a bit ridiculous.

Here, where men sit and hear each other groan;
   Where palsy shakes a few, sad, last gray hairs. . . .

This is Keats, not at all the nightingale. But the sad human male
still tries to break away, and get over into the nightingale world.   20
Wine will not take him across. Yet he will go.

Away! away! for I will fly to thee,
   Not charioted by Bacchus and his pards,
But on the viewless wings of Poesy. . . .

He doesn't succeed, however. The viewless wings of Poesy carry
him only into the bushes, not into the nightingale world. He is still
outside.

Darkling I listen; and for many a time
   I have been half in love with easeful Death. . . .

The nightingale never made any man in love with easeful death,
except by contrast. The contrast between the bright flame of positive
pure self-aliveness, in the bird, and the uneasy flickering of yearning
selflessness, for ever yearning for something outside himself, which
is Keats:

To cease upon the midnight with no pain,
   While thou art pouring forth thy soul abroad
      In such an ecstasy!
Still wouldst thou sing, and I have ears in vain, –
   To thy high requiem become a sod.

How astonished the nightingale would be if he could be made to   30
realise what sort of answer the poet was answering to his song. He
would fall off the bough with amazement.

Because a nightingale, when you answer him back, only shouts and

sings louder. Suppose a few other nightingales pipe up in neigh-
bouring bushes – as they always do. Then the blue-white sparks of
sound go dazzling up to heaven. And suppose you, mere mortal,
happen to be sitting on the shady bank having an altercation with
the mistress of your heart, hammer and tongs, then the chief nightingale swells and goes at it like Caruso in the Third Act –
simply a brilliant, bursting frenzy of music, singing you down, till   40
you simply can't hear yourself speak to quarrel.

There was, in fact, something very like a nightingale in Caruso –
that bird-like, bursting, miraculous energy of song, and fullness of
himself, and self-luxuriance.

> Thou wast not born for death, immortal Bird!
> No hungry generations tread thee down.

Not yet in Tuscany, anyhow. They are twenty to the dozen.
Whereas the cuckoo seems remote and low-voiced, calling his low,
half secretive call as he flies past. Perhaps it really is different in
England.

> The voice I hear this passing night was heard
> In ancient days by emperor and clown:
> Perhaps the self-same song that found a path
> Through the sad heart of Ruth, when, sick for home,
> She stood in tears amid the alien corn.

And why in tears? Always tears. Did Diocletian, I wonder, among
the emperors, burst into tears when he heard the nightingale, and   50
Æsop among the clowns? And Ruth, really? Myself, I strongly
suspect that young lady of setting the nightingale singing, like the
nice damsel in Boccaccio's story, who went to sleep with the lively
bird in her hand, ' – *tua figliuola è stata sì vaga dell'usignuolo, ch'ella l'ha
preso e tienlosi in mano!'*

And what does the hen nightingale think of it all, as she mildly
sits upon the eggs and hears milord giving himself forth? Probably
she likes it, for she goes on breeding him as jaunty as ever. Probably
she prefers his high cockalorum to the poet's humble moan:

> Now more than ever seems it rich to die,
> To cease upon the midnight with no pain. . . .

172

That wouldn't be much use to the hen nightingale. And one sym- 60
pathises with Keats's Fanny, and understands why she wasn't having
any. Much good such a midnight would have been to *her*!

Perhaps, when all's said and done, the female of the species gets
more out of life when the male isn't wanting to cease upon the
midnight, with or without pain. There are better uses for midnights.
And a bird that sings because he's full of his own bright life, and leaves
her to keep the eggs cosy, is perhaps preferable to one who moans,
even with love of her.

Of course, the nightingale is utterly unconscious of the little dim
hen, while he sings. And he never mentions her name. But she knows 70
well enough that the song is half her: just as she knows the eggs are
half him. And just as she doesn't want him coming in and putting
a heavy foot down on her little bunch of eggs, he doesn't want her
poking into his song, and fussing over it, and mussing it up. Every
man to his trade, and every woman to hers:

Adieu! adieu! thy plaintive anthem fades. . . .

It never was a plaintive anthem – it was Caruso at his jauntiest. But
don't try to argue with a poet.

EXTRACT FROM CHAOS IN POETRY

Poetry, they say, is a matter of words. And this is just as much true
as that pictures are a matter of paint, and frescoes a matter of water
and colour-wash. It is such a long way from being the whole truth
that it is slightly silly if uttered sententiously.

Poetry is a matter of words. Poetry is a stringing together of words
into a ripple and jingle and a run of colours. Poetry is an interplay
of images. Poetry is the iridescent suggestion of an idea. Poetry is all
these things, and still it is something else. Given all these ingredients,
you have something very like poetry, something for which we might
borrow the old romantic name of poesy. And poesy, like bric-à-brac, 10
will for ever be in fashion. But poetry is still another thing.

The essential quality of poetry is that it makes a new effort of
attention, and 'discovers' a new world within the known world.
Man, and the animals, and the flowers, all live within a strange and

for ever surging chaos. The chaos which we have got used to we call a cosmos. The unspeakable inner chaos of which we are composed we call consciousness, and mind, and even civilisation. But it is, ultimately, chaos, lit up by visions, or not lit up by visions. Just as the rainbow may or may not light up the storm. And, like the rainbow, the vision perisheth. 20

But man cannot live in chaos. The animals can. To the animal all is chaos, only there are a few recurring motions and aspects within the surge. And the animal is content. But man is not. Man must wrap himself in a vision, make a house of apparent form and stability, fixity. In his terror of chaos he begins by putting up an umbrella between himself and the everlasting whirl. Then he paints the underside of his umbrella like a firmament. Then he parades around, lives and dies under his umbrella. Bequeathed to his descendants, the umbrella becomes a dome, a vault, and men at last begin to feel that something is wrong. 30

Man fixes some wonderful erection of his own between himself and the wild chaos, and gradually goes bleached and stifled under his parasol. Then comes a poet, enemy of convention, and makes a slit in the umbrella; and lo! the glimpse of chaos is a vision, a window to the sun. But after a while, getting used to the vision, and not liking the genuine draught from chaos, commonplace man daubs a simulacrum of the window that opens on to chaos, and patches the umbrella with the painted patch of the simulacrum. That is, he has got used to the vision; it is part of his house-decoration. So that the umbrella at last looks like a glowing open firmament, of many 40 aspects. But alas! it is all simulacrum, in innumerable patches. Homer and Keats, annotated and with glossary.

This is the history of poetry in our era. Someone sees Titans in the wild air of chaos, and the Titan becomes a wall between succeeding generations and the chaos they should have inherited. The wild sky moved and sang. Even that became a great umbrella between mankind and the sky of fresh air; then it became a painted vault, a fresco on a vaulted roof, under which men bleach and go dissatisfied. Till another poet makes a slit on to the open and windy chaos.

But at last our roof deceives us no more. It is painted plaster, and 50 all the skill of all the human ages won't take us in. Dante or Leonardo,

Beethoven or Whitman: lo! it is painted on the plaster of our vault.
Like St. Francis preaching to the birds in Assisi. Wonderfully like air
and birdy space and chaos of many things – partly because the fresco
is faded. But even so, we are glad to get out of that church, and into
the natural chaos.

This is the momentous crisis for mankind, when we have to get
back to chaos. So long as the umbrella serves, and poets make slits
in it, and the mass of people can be gradually educated up to the vision
in the slit: which means they patch it over with a patch that looks   60
just like the vision in the slit: so long as this process can continue,
and mankind can be educated up, and thus built in, so long will a
civilisation continue more or less happily, completing its own painted
prison. It is called completing the consciousness.

The joy men had when Wordsworth, for example, made a slit, and
saw a primrose! Till then, men had only seen a primrose dimly, in
the shadow of the umbrella. They saw it through Wordsworth in
the full gleam of chaos. Since then, gradually, we have come to see
primavera nothing but primrose. Which means, we have patched
over the slit.   70

And the greater joy when Shakespeare made a big rent and saw
emotional, wistful man outside in the chaos, beyond the conventional
idea and painted umbrella of moral images and iron-bound paladins,
which had been put up in the Middle Ages. But now, alas, the roof
of our vault is simply painted dense with Hamlets and Macbeths, the
side walls too, and the order is fixed and complete. Man can't be any
different from his image. Chaos is all shut out.

The umbrella has got so big, the patches and plaster are so tight
and hard, it can be slit no more. If it were slit, the rent would no
more be a vision, it would only be an outrage. We should dab it over   80
at once, to match the rest.

So the umbrella is absolute. And so the yearning for chaos becomes
a nostalgia. And this will go on till some terrific wind blows the
umbrella to ribbons, and much of mankind to oblivion. The rest will
shiver in the midst of chaos. For chaos is always there, and always
will be, no matter how we put up umbrellas of visions.

What about the poets, then, at this juncture? They reveal the
inward desire of mankind. What do they reveal? They show the

desire for chaos, and the fear of chaos. The desire for chaos is the
breath of their poetry. The fear of chaos is in their parade of forms   90
and technique. Poetry is made of words, they say. So they blow
bubbles of sound and image, which soon burst with the breath of
longing for chaos, which fills them. But the poetasters can make
pretty shiny bubbles for the Christmas-tree, which never burst,
because there is no breath of poetry in them, but they remain till we
drop them.

INTRODUCTION TO THE PRIVATELY PRINTED EDITION
OF *PANSIES*, PUBLISHED AUGUST 1929

This little bunch of fragments is offered as a bunch of *pensées, anglicé*
pansies; a handful of thoughts. Or, if you will have the other
derivation of pansy, from *panser*, to dress or soothe a wound, these
are my tender administrations to the mental and emotional wounds
we suffer from. Or you can have heartsease if you like, since the
modern heart could certainly do with it.

Each little piece is a thought; not a bare idea or an opinion or a
didactic statement, but a true thought, which comes as much from
the heart and the genitals as from the head. A thought, with its own
blood of emotion and instinct running in it like the fire in a fire-opal,   10
if I may be so bold. Perhaps if you hold up my pansies properly to
the light, they may show a running vein of fire. At least, they do
not pretend to be half-baked lyrics or melodies in American measure.
They are thoughts which run through the modern mind and body,
each having its own separate existence, yet each of them combining
with all the others to make up a complete state of mind.

It suits the modern temper better to have its state of mind made
up of apparently irrelevant thoughts that scurry in different directions, yet belong to the same nest; each thought trotting down the
page like an independent creature, each with its own small head and   20
tail, trotting its own little way, then curling up to sleep. We prefer
it, at least the young seem to prefer it to those solid blocks of mental
pabulum packed like bales in the pages of a proper heavy book. Even
we prefer it to those slightly didactic opinions and slices of wisdom
which are laid horizontally across the pages of Pascal's *Pensées* or

La Bruyère's *Caractères*, separated only by *pattes de mouches*, like faint sprigs of parsley. Let every *pensée* trot on its own little paws, not be laid like a cutlet trimmed with a *patte de mouche*.

Live and let live, and each pansy will tip you its separate wink. The fairest thing in nature, a flower, still has its roots in earth and manure; and in the perfume there hovers still the faint strange scent of earth, the under-earth in all its heavy humidity and darkness. Certainly it is so in pansy-scent, and in violet-scent; mingled with the blue of the morning the black of the corrosive humus. Else the scent would be just sickly sweet.

So it is: we all have our roots in earth. And it is our roots that now need a little attention, need the hard soil eased away from them, and softened so that a little fresh air can come to them, and they can breathe. For by pretending to have no roots, we have trodden the earth so hard over them that they are starving and stifling below the soil. We have roots, and our roots are in the sensual, instinctive and intuitive body, and it is here we need fresh air of open consciousness.

I am abused most of all for using the so-called 'obscene' words. Nobody quite knows what the word 'obscene' itself means, or what it is intended to mean: but gradually all the *old* words that belong to the body below the navel, have come to be judged obscene. Obscene means today that the policeman thinks he has a right to arrest you, nothing else.

Myself, I am mystified at this horror over a mere word, a plain simple word that stands for a plain simple thing. 'In the beginning was the Word, and the Word was God and the Word was with God.' If that is true, then we are very far from the beginning. When did the Word 'fall'? When did the Word become unclean 'below the navel'? Because today, if you suggest that the word arse was in the beginning and was God and was with God, you will just be put in prison at once. Though a doctor might say the same of the word *ischial tuberosity*, and all the old ladies would piously murmur 'Quite!' Now that sort of thing is idiotic and humiliating. Whoever the God was that made us, He made us complete. He didn't stop at the navel and leave the rest to the devil. It is too childish. And the same with the Word which is God. If the Word is God – which in the sense of the human it is – then you can't suddenly say that all the words

which belong below the navel are obscene. The word arse is as much
god as the word face. It must be so, otherwise you cut off your god
at the waist.

What is obvious is that the words in these cases have been dirtied
by the mind, by unclean mental associations. The words themselves
are clean, so are the things to which they apply. But the mind drags
in a filthy association, calls up some repulsive emotion. Well then,
cleanse the mind, that is the real job. It is the mind which is the 70
Augean stables, not language. The word arse is clean enough. Even
the part of the body it refers to is just as much me as my hand and
my brain are me. It is not for *me* to quarrel with my own natural
make-up. If I am, I am all that I am. But the impudent and dirty mind
won't have it. It hates certain parts of the body, and makes the words
representing these parts scapegoats. It pelts them out of the consciousness with filth, and there they hover, never dying, never dead,
slipping into the consciousness again unawares, and pelted out again
with filth, haunting the margins of the consciousness like jackals or
hyenas. And they refer to parts of our own living bodies, and to our 80
most essential acts. So that man turns himself into a thing of shame
and horror. And his consciousness shudders with horrors that he has
made for himself.

That sort of thing has got to stop. We can't have the consciousness
haunted any longer by repulsive spectres which are no more than poor
simple scapegoat words representing parts of man himself; words that
the cowardly and unclean mind has driven out into the limbo of the
unconscious, whence they return upon us looming and magnified out
of all proportion, frightening us beyond all reason. We must put an
end to that. It is the self divided against itself most dangerously. The 90
simple and natural 'obscene' words must be cleaned up of all their
depraved fear-associations, and re-admitted into the consciousness to
take their natural place. Now they are magnified out of all proportion, so is the mental fear they represent. We must accept the
word arse as we accept the word face, since arses we have and always
shall have. We can't start cutting off the buttocks of unfortunate
mankind, like the ladies in the Voltaire story, just to fit the mental
expulsion of the word.

This scapegoat business does the mind itself so much damage.

There is a poem of Swift's which should make us pause. It is written   100
to Celia, his Celia – and every verse ends with the mad, maddened
refrain: 'But – Celia, Celia, Celia shits!' Now that, stated baldly, is
so ridiculous it is almost funny. But when one remembers the
gnashing insanity to which the great mind of Swift was reduced by
that and similar thoughts, the joke dies away. Such thoughts
poisoned him, like some terrible constipation. They poisoned his
mind. And why, in heaven's name? The *fact* cannot have troubled
him, since it applied to himself and to all of us. It was not the fact
that Celia shits which so deranged him, it was the *thought*. His mind
couldn't bear the thought. Great wit as he was, he could not see how   110
ridiculous his revulsions were. His arrogant mind overbore him. He
couldn't even see how much worse it would be if Celia didn't shit.
His physical sympathies were too weak, his guts were too cold to
sympathize with poor Celia in her natural functions. His insolent and
sicklily squeamish mind just turned her into a thing of horror, because
she was merely natural and went to the w.c. It is monstrous! One
feels like going back across all the years to poor Celia, to say to her:
It's all right, don't you take any notice of that mental lunatic.

And Swift's form of madness is very common today. Men with
cold guts and over-squeamish minds are always thinking those things   120
and squirming. Wretched man is the victim of his own little
revulsions, which he magnifies into great horrors and terrifying
taboos. We are all savages, we all have taboos. The Australian black
may have the kangaroo for his taboo. And then he will probably die
of shock and terror if a kangaroo happens to touch him. Which is
what I would call a purely unnecessary death. But modern men have
even more dangerous taboos. To us, certain words, certain ideas are
taboo, and if they come upon us and we can't drive them away, we
die or go mad with a degraded sort of terror. Which is what happened
to Swift. He was such a great wit. And the modern mind altogether   130
is falling into this form of degraded taboo-insanity. I call it a waste
of sane human consciousness. But it is very dangerous, dangerous to
the individual and utterly dangerous to society as a whole. Nothing
is so fearful in a mass-civilization like ours as a mass-insanity.

The remedy is, of course, the same in both cases: lift off the taboo.
The kangaroo is a harmless animal, the word shit is a harmless word.

Make either into a taboo, and it becomes most dangerous. The result
of taboo is insanity. And insanity, especially mob-insanity, mass-
insanity, is the fearful danger that threatens our civilization. There
are certain persons with a sort of rabies, who live only to infect the   140
mass. If the young do not watch out, they will find themselves,
before so many years are past, engulfed in a howling manifestation
of mob-insanity, truly terrifying to think of. It will be better to be
dead than to live to see it. Sanity, wholeness, is everything. In the
name of piety and purity, what a mass of disgusting insanity is spoken
and written. We shall have to fight the mob, in order to keep sane,
and to keep society sane.

LIZARD

A lizard ran out on a rock and looked up, listening
no doubt to the sounding of the spheres.
And what a dandy fellow! the right toss of a chin for you
and swirl of a tail!

If men were as much men as lizards are lizards
they'd be worth looking at.

SELF-PROTECTION

When science starts to be interpretive
it is more unscientific even than mysticism.

To make self-preservation and self-protection the first law of
    existence
is about as scientific as making suicide the first law of existence,
and amounts to very much the same thing.

A nightingale singing at the top of his voice
is neither hiding himself nor preserving himself nor propagating his
    species;
he is giving himself away in every sense of the word;
and obviously, it is the culminating point of his existence.

A tiger is striped and golden for his own glory.   10
He would certainly be much more invisible if he were grey-green.

And I don't suppose the ichthyosaurus sparkled like the
    humming-bird,
no doubt he was khaki-coloured with muddy protective coloration,
so why didn't he survive?

As a matter of fact, the only creatures that seem to survive
are those that give themselves away in flash and sparkle
and gay flicker of joyful life;
those that go glittering abroad
with a bit of splendour.

Even mice play quite beautifully at shadows,   20
and some of them are brilliantly piebald.

I expect the dodo looked like a clod,
a drab and dingy bird.

WAGES

The wages of work is cash.
The wages of cash is want more cash.
The wages of want more cash is vicious competition.
The wages of vicious competition is – the world we live in.

The work-cash-want circle is the viciousest circle
that ever turned men into fiends.

Earning a wage is a prison occupation
and a wage-earner is a sort of gaol-bird.

Earning a salary is a prison overseer's job
a gaoler instead of a gaol-bird.   10

Living on our income is strolling grandly outside the prison
in terror lest you have to go in. And since the work-prison
    covers
almost every scrap of the living earth, you stroll up and down
on a narrow beat, about the same as a prisoner taking exercise.

This is called universal freedom.

A SANE REVOLUTION

If you make a revolution, make it for fun,
don't make it in ghastly seriousness,
don't do it in deadly earnest,
do it for fun.

Don't do it because you hate people,
do it just to spit in their eye.

Don't do it for the money,
do it and be damned to the money.

Don't do it for equality,
do it because we've got too much equality   10
and it would be fun to upset the apple-cart
and see which way the apples would go a-rolling.

Don't do it for the working classes.
Do it so that we can all of us be little aristocracies on our own
and kick our heels like jolly escaped asses.

Don't do it, anyhow, for international Labour.
Labour is the one thing a man has had too much of.
Let's abolish labour, let's have done with labouring!
Work can be fun, and men can enjoy it; then it's not labour.
Let's have it so! Let's make a revolution for fun!   20

NOVEMBER BY THE SEA

Now in November nearer comes the sun
down the abandoned heaven.

As the dark closes round him, he draws nearer
as if for our company.

At the base of the lower brain
the sun in me declines to his winter solstice
and darts a few gold rays
back to the old year's sun across the sea.

A few gold rays thickening down to red
as the sun of my soul is setting   10
setting fierce and undaunted, wintry
but setting, setting behind the sounding sea between my ribs.

The wide sea wins, and the dark
winter, and the great day-sun, and the sun in my soul
sinks, sinks to setting and the winter solstice
downward, they race in decline
my sun, and the great gold sun.

FIRE

Fire is dearer to us than love or food,
hot, hurrying, yet it burns if you touch it.

What we ought to do
is not to add our love together, or our goodwill, or any of that,
for we're sure to bring in a lot of lies,
but our fire, our elemental fire
so that it rushes up in a huge blaze like a phallus into hollow space
and fecundates the zenith and the nadir
and sends off millions of sparks of new atoms
and singes us, and burns the house down.   10

BEAUTIFUL OLD AGE

It ought to be lovely to be old
to be full of the peace that comes of experience
and wrinkled ripe fulfilment.

The wrinkled smile of completeness that follows a life
lived undaunted and unsoured with accepted lies.
If people lived without accepting lies
they would ripen like apples, and be scented like pippins
in their old age.

Soothing, old people should be, like apples
when one is tired of love.   10

Fragrant like yellowing leaves, and dim with the soft
stillness and satisfaction of autumn.

And a girl should say:
It must be wonderful to live and grow old.
Look at my mother, how rich and still she is!

And a young man should think: By Jove
my father has faced all weathers, but it's been a life!

GOOD HUSBANDS MAKE UNHAPPY WIVES

Good husbands make unhappy wives
so do bad husbands, just as often;
but the unhappiness of a wife with a good husband
is much more devastating
than the unhappiness of a wife with a bad husband.

TO WOMEN, AS FAR AS I'M CONCERNED

The feelings I don't have, I don't have.
The feelings I don't have, I won't say I have.
The feelings you say you have, you don't have.
The feelings you would like us both to have, we neither of us have.

The feelings people ought to have, they never have.
If people say they've got feelings, you may be pretty sure they haven't
    got them.

So if you want either of us to feel anything at all
you'd better abandon all idea of feelings altogether.

WHEN I WENT TO THE CIRCUS

When I went to the circus that had pitched on the waste lot
it was full of uneasy people
frightened of the bare earth and the temporary canvas
and the smell of horses and other beasts
instead of merely the smell of man.

Monkeys rode rather grey and wizened
on curly plump piebald ponies
and the children uttered a little cry –
and dogs jumped through hoops and turned somersaults
and then the geese scuttled in in a little flock   10
and round the ring they went to the sound of the whip
then doubled, and back, with a funny up-flutter of wings –
and the children suddenly shouted out.

Then came the hush again, like a hush of fear.

The tight-rope lady, pink and blonde and nude-looking, with a few
    gold spangles
footed cautiously out on the rope, turned prettily, spun round
bowed, and lifted her foot in her hand, smiled, swung her parasol
to another balance, tripped round, poised, and slowly sank
her handsome thighs down, down, till she slept her splendid body
    on the rope.
When she rose, tilting her parasol, and smiled at the cautious people   20
they cheered, but nervously.

The trapeze man, slim and beautiful and like a fish in the air
swung great curves through the upper space, and came down like a
    star.
– And the people applauded, with hollow, frightened applause.

The elephants, huge and grey, loomed their curved bulk through the
    dusk
and sat up, taking strange postures, showing the pink soles of their
    feet
and curling their precious live trunks like ammonites
and moving always with soft slow precision
as when a great ship moves to anchor.
The people watched and wondered, and seemed to resent the mystery
    that lies in beasts.   30

Horses, gay horses, swirling round and plaiting
in a long line, their heads laid over each other's necks;
they were happy, they enjoyed it;

185

all the creatures seemed to enjoy the game
in the circus, with their circus people.

But the audience, compelled to wonder
compelled to admire the bright rhythms of moving bodies
compelled to see the delicate skill of flickering human bodies
flesh flamey and a little heroic, even in a tumbling clown,
they were not really happy.   40
There was no gushing response, as there is at the film.

When modern people see the carnal body dauntless and flickering gay
playing among the elements neatly, beyond competition
and displaying no personality,
modern people are depressed.

Modern people feel themselves at a disadvantage.
They know they have no bodies that could play among the elements.
They have only their personalities, that are best seen flat, on the film,
flat personalities in two dimensions, imponderable and touchless.

And they grudge the circus people the swooping gay weight of limbs   50
that flower in mere movement,
and they grudge them the immediate, physical understanding they
    have with their circus beasts,
and they grudge them their circus life altogether.

Yet the strange, almost frightened shout of delight that comes now
    and then from the children
shows that the children vaguely know how cheated they are of their
    birthright
in the bright wild circus flesh.

TWO PERFORMING ELEPHANTS

He stands with his forefeet on the drum
and the other, the old one, the pallid hoary female
must creep her great bulk beneath the bridge of him.

On her knees, in utmost caution
all agog, and curling up her trunk

186

she edges through without upsetting him.
Triumph! the ancient pig-tailed monster!

When her trick is to climb over him
with what shadow-like slow carefulness
she skims him, sensitive   10
as shadows from the ages gone and perished
in touching him, and planting her round feet.

While the wispy, modern children, half-afraid
watch silent. The looming of the hoary, far-gone ages
is too much for them.

NOTTINGHAM'S NEW UNIVERSITY

In Nottingham, that dismal town
where I went to school and college,
they've built a new university
for a new dispensation of knowledge.

Built it most grand and cakeily
out of the noble loot
derived from shrewd cash-chemistry
by good Sir Jesse Boot.

Little I thought, when I was a lad
and turned my modest penny
over on Boot's Cash-Chemist's counter,   10
that Jesse, by turning many

millions of similar honest pence
over, would make a pile
that would rise at last and blossom out
in grand and cakey style

into a university
where smart men would dispense
doses of smart cash-chemistry
in language of common-sense!   20

That future Nottingham lads would be
cash-chemically B.Sc.
that Nottingham lights would rise and say:
– By Boots I am M.A.

From this I learn, though I knew it before
that culture has her roots
in the deep dung of cash, and lore
is a last offshoot of Boots.

WHATEVER MAN MAKES

Whatever man makes and makes it live
lives because of the life put into it.
A yard of India muslin is alive with Hindu life.
And a Navajo woman, weaving her rug in the pattern of her dream
must run the pattern out in a little break at the end
so that her soul can come out, back to her.

But in the odd pattern, like snake-marks on the sand
it leaves its trail.

RED-HERRING

My father was a working man
   and a collier was he,
at six in the morning they turned him down
   and they turned him up for tea.

My mother was a superior soul
   a superior soul was she,
cut out to play a superior role
   in the god-damn bourgeoisie.

We children were the in-betweens
   little non-descripts were we,
indoors we called each other *you*,
   outside, it was *tha* and *thee*.

But time has fled, our parents are dead,
   we've risen in the world all three;

10

but still we are in-betweens, we tread
  between the devil and the deep sad sea.

I am a member of the bourgeoisie
  and a servant-maid brings me my tea –
But I'm always longing for someone to say:
  'ark 'ere, lad! atween thee an' me   20

they're a' a b--- d– lot o' ---s,
  an' I reckon it's nowt but right
we should start an' kick their --ses for 'em
  an' tell 'em to -----.

NO! MR LAWRENCE!

No, Mr Lawrence, it's not like that!
I don't mind telling you
I know a thing or two about love,
perhaps more than you do.

And what I know is that you make it
too nice, too beautiful.
It's not like that, you know; you fake it.
It's really rather dull.

THE LITTLE WOWSER

There is a little wowser
  John Thomas by name,
and for every bloomin', mortal thing
  that little blighter's to blame.

It was 'im as made the first mistake
  of putting us in the world,
forcin' us out of the unawake,
  an' makin' us come uncurled.

And then when you're gettin' nicely on
  an' life seems to begin,   10

that little bleeder comes bustin' in
    with: Hello boy! what about sin?

An' then he leads you by the nose
    after a lot o' women
as strips you stark as a monkey nut
    an' leaves you never a trimmin'.

An' then somebody has ter marry you
    to put him through 'is paces;
then when John Thomas don't worry you,
    it's your wife, wi' her airs an' graces.   20

I think of all the little brutes
    as ever was invented
that little cod's the holy worst.
    I've chucked him, I've repented.

CONUNDRUMS

Tell me a word
that you've often heard,
yet it makes you squint
if you see it in print!

Tell me a thing
that you've often seen,
yet if put in a book
it makes you turn green!

Tell me a thing
that you often do,   10
which, described in a story
shocks you through and through!

Tell me what's wrong
with words or with you
that you don't mind the thing
yet the name is taboo.

WILLY WET-LEG

I can't stand Willy wet-leg,
can't stand him at any price.
He's resigned, and when you hit him
he lets you hit him twice.

CANVASSING FOR THE ELECTION

– Excuse me, but are you a superior person?
– I beg your pardon?
– Oh, I'm sure you'll understand. We're making a census of all the
really patriotic people – the right sort of people, you know – of
course you understand what I mean – so *would* you mind giving
me your word? – and signing here, please – that you *are* a superior
person – that's all we need to know –
– Really, I don't know what you take me for!
– Yes, I know! It's too bad! Of course it's perfectly superfluous to
ask, but the League insists. Thank you so much! No, sign here,   10
please, and there I countersign. That's right! Yes, that's all! – *I
declare I am a superior person* –. Yes, exactly! and here I countersign
your declaration. It's so simple, and really, it's *all* we need to know
about anybody. And do you know, I've never been denied a
signature! We English *are* a solid people, after all. This proves it.
Quite! Thank you so much! We're getting on simply splendidly –
and it *is* a comfort, isn't it? –

LEAVES OF GRASS, FLOWERS OF GRASS

Leaves of grass, what about leaves of grass?
Grass blossoms, grass has flowers, flowers of grass
dusty pollen of grass, tall grass in its midsummer maleness,
hay-seed and tiny grain of grass, graminiferae
not far from the lily, the considerable lily;

even the blue-grass blossoms;
even the bison knew it;

even the stupidest farmer gathers his hay in bloom, in blossom
just before it seeds.

Only the best matters; even the cow knows it;   10
grass in blossom, blossoming grass, risen to its height and its
    natural pride
in its own splendour and its own feathery maleness
the grass, the grass.

Leaves of grass, what are leaves of grass, when at its best grass
    blossoms.

WE DIE TOGETHER

Oh, when I think of the industrial millions, when I see some of them,
a weight comes over me heavier that leaden linings of coffins
and I almost cease to exist, weighed down to extinction
and sunk into a depression that almost blots me out.

Then I say to myself: Am I also dead? is that the truth?
Then I know
that with so many dead men in mills
I too am almost dead.
I know the unliving factory-hand, living-dead millions
is unliving me, living-dead me,   10
I, with them, am living-dead, mechanical at the machine.

And enshrouded in the vast corpse of the industrial millions
embedded in them, I look out on the sunshine of the South.

And though the pomegranate has red flowers outside the window
and oleander is hot with perfume under the afternoon sun
and I am 'il Signore' and they love me here,
yet I am a mill-hand in Leeds
and the death of the Black Country is upon me
and I am wrapped in the lead of a coffin-lining, the living death of
    my fellow men.

THE GODS! THE GODS!

People were bathing and posturing themselves on the beach
and all was dreary, great robot limbs, robot breasts
robot voices, robot even the gay umbrellas.

But a woman, shy and alone, was washing herself under a tap
and the glimmer of the presence of the gods was like lilies,
and like water-lilies.

NAME THE GODS!

I refuse to name the gods, because they have no name.
I refuse to describe the gods, because they have no form nor shape
   nor substance.

Ah, but the simple ask for images!
Then for a time at least, they must do without.

But all the time I see the gods:
the man who is mowing the tall white corn,
suddenly, as it curves, as it yields, the white wheat
and sinks down with a swift rustle, and a strange, falling flatness,
ah! the gods, the swaying body of god!
ah the fallen stillness of god, autumnus, and it is only July   10
the pale-gold flesh of Priapus dropping asleep.

THERE ARE NO GODS

There are no gods, and you can please yourself
have a game of tennis, go out in the car, do some shopping, sit
   and talk, talk, talk
with a cigarette browning your fingers.

There are no gods, and you can please yourself –
go and please yourself –

But leave me alone, leave me alone, to myself!
and then in the room, whose is the presence
that makes the air so still and lovely to me?

Who is it that softly touches the sides of my breast
and touches me over the heart   10
so that my heart beats soothed, soothed, soothed and at peace?

Who is it smooths the bed-sheets like the cool
smooth ocean where the fishes rest on edge
in their own dream?

Who is it that clasps and kneads my naked feet, till they
    unfold,
till all is well, till all is utterly well? the lotus-lilies of the feet!

I tell you, it is no woman, it is no man, for I am alone.
And I fall asleep with the gods, the gods
that are not, or that are
according to the soul's desire,   20
like a pool into which we plunge, or do not plunge.

RETORT TO WHITMAN

And whoever walks a mile full of false sympathy
walks to the funeral of the whole human race.

RETORT TO JESUS

And whoever forces himself to love anybody
begets a murderer in his own body.

SENSE OF TRUTH

You must fuse mind and wit with all the senses
before you can feel truth.
And if you can't feel truth you can't have any other
satisfactory sensual experience.

EDITORIAL OFFICE

Applicant for post as literary critic: Here are my credentials, Sir! –
Editor: Er – quite. But – er – biologically! Have you been fixed? –

194

– *arrangé* – you understand what I mean?

Applicant: I'm afraid I don't.

Editor (sternly): Have you been made safe for the great British Public? Has everything objectionable been removed from you?

Applicant: In what way, quite?

Editor: By surgical operation. Did your parents have you sterilised?

Applicant: I don't think so, Sir. I'm afraid not.

Editor: Good morning! Don't trouble to call again. We have the welfare of the British Public at heart.

THE ENGLISH ARE SO NICE!

The English are so nice
so awfully nice
they're the nicest people in the world.
And what's more, they're very nice about being nice
about your being nice as well!
If you're not nice, they soon make you feel it.

Americans and French and Germans and so on
they're all very well
but they're not *really* nice, you know.
They're not nice in *our* sense of the word, are they now?   10

That's why one doesn't have to take them seriously.
We must be nice to them, of course,
of course, naturally –
But it doesn't really matter what you say to them,
they don't really understand –
you can just say anything to them:
be nice, you know, just be nice –
but you must never take them seriously, they wouldn't understand
just be nice, you know! oh, fairly nice,
not too nice of course, they take advantage –   20
but nice enough, just nice enough
to let them feel they're not quite as nice as they might be.

INNOCENT ENGLAND

Oh what a pity, Oh! don't you agree
that figs aren't found in the land of the free!

Fig-trees don't grow in my native land;
there's never a fig-leaf near at hand

when you want one; so I did without;
and that is what the row's about.

Virginal, pure policemen came
and hid their faces for very shame,

while they carried the shameless things away
to gaol, to be hid from the light of day.   10

And Mr Mead, that old, old lily
said: 'Gross! coarse! hideous!' – and I like a silly

thought he meant the faces of the police-court officials,
and how right he was, and I signed my initials

to confirm what he said; but alas, he meant
my pictures, and on the proceedings went.

The upshot was, my pictures must burn
that English artists might finally learn

when they painted a nude, to put a *cache sexe* on,
a cache sexe, a cache sexe, or else begone!   20

A fig leaf; or, if you cannot find it
a wreath of mist, with nothing behind it.

A wreath of mist is the usual thing
in the north, to hide where the turtles sing.

Though they never sing, they never sing,
don't you dare to suggest such a thing

or Mr Mead will be after you.
– But what a pity I never knew

A wreath of English mist would do
as a cache sexe! I'd have put a whole fog.   30

But once and forever barks the old dog,
so my pictures are in prison, instead of in the Zoo.

THOUGHT

Thought, I love thought.
But not the juggling and twisting of already existent ideas
I despise that self-important game.
Thought is the welling up of unknown life into consciousness,
Thought is the testing of statements on the touchstone of the
    conscience,
Thought is gazing on to the face of life, and reading what can
    be read,
Thought is pondering over experience, and coming to a conclusion.
Thought is not a trick, or an exercise, or a set of dodges,
Thought is a man in his wholeness wholly attending.

BAVARIAN GENTIANS

Not every man has gentians in his house
in soft September, at slow, sad Michaelmas.

Bavarian gentians, tall and dark, but dark
darkening the daytime torch-like with the smoking blueness of
    Pluto's gloom,
ribbed hellish flowers erect, with their blaze of darkness spread blue,
blown flat into points, by the heavy white draught of the day.

Torch-flowers of the blue-smoking darkness, Pluto's dark-blue blaze
black lamps from the halls of Dis, smoking dark blue
giving off darkness, blue darkness, upon Demeter's yellow-pale day
Whom have you come for, here in the white-cast day?   10

Reach me a gentian, give me a torch!
let me guide myself with the blue, forked torch of a flower
down the darker and darker stairs, where blue is darkened on blueness

197

down the way Persephone goes, just now, in first-frosted September
to the sightless realm where darkness is married to dark
and Persephone herself is but a voice, as a bride
a gloom invisible enfolded in the deeper dark
of the arms of Pluto as he ravishes her once again
and pierces her once more with his passion of the utter dark
among the splendour of black-blue torches, shedding fathomless
    darkness on the nuptials.   20

Give me a flower on a tall stem, and three dark flames,
for I will go to the wedding, and be wedding-guest
at the marriage of the living dark.

LUCIFER

Angels are bright still, though the brightest fell.
But tell me, tell me, how do you know
he lost any of his brightness in the falling?
In the dark-blue depths, under layers and layers of darkness,
I see him move like the ruby, a gleam from within
of his own magnificence,
coming like the ruby in the invisible dark, glowing
with his own annunciation, towards us.

IN THE CITIES

In the cities
there is even no more any weather
the weather in town is always benzine, or else petrol fumes
lubricating oil, exhaust gas.

As over some dense marsh, the fumes
thicken, miasma, the fumes of the automobile
densely thicken in the cities.

In ancient Rome, down the thronged streets
no wheels might run, no insolent chariots.
Only the footsteps, footsteps   10

of people
and the gentle trotting of the litter-bearers.

In Minos, in Mycenae
in all the cities with lion gates
the dead threaded the air, lingering
lingering in the earth's shadow
and leaning towards the old hearth.

In London, New York, Paris
in the bursten cities
the dead tread heavily through the muddy air   20
through the mire of fumes
heavily, stepping weary on our hearts.

RED GERANIUM AND GODLY MIGNONETTE

Imagine that any mind ever *thought* a red geranium!
As if the redness of a red geranium could be anything but a sensual
    experience
and as if sensual experience could take place before there were any
    senses.
We know that even God could not imagine the redness of a red
    geranium
nor the smell of mignonette
when geraniums were not, and mignonette neither.
And even when they were, even God would have to have a nose to
    smell at the mignonette.
You can't imagine the Holy Ghost sniffing at cherry-pie heliotrope.
Or the Most High, during the coal age, cudgelling his mighty brains
even if he had any brains: straining his mighty mind   10
to think, among the moss and mud of lizards and mastodons
to think out, in the abstract, when all was twilit green and muddy:
'Now there shall be tum-tiddly-um, and tum-tiddly-um,
hey-presto! scarlet geranium!'
We know it couldn't be done.

But imagine, among the mud and the mastodons

God sighing and yearning with tremendous creative yearning, in that
   dark green mess
oh, for some other beauty, some other beauty
that blossomed at last, red geranium, and mignonette.

THE SHIP OF DEATH

Have you built your ship of death, oh have you?
Oh build your ship of death, for you will need it.

Now in the twilight, sit by the invisible sea
Of peace, and build your little ship
Of death, that will carry the soul
On its last journey, on and on, so still
So beautiful, over the last of seas.

When the day comes, that will come.
Oh think of it in the twilight peacefully!
The last day, and the setting forth   10
On the longest journey, over the hidden sea
To the last wonder of oblivion.

Oblivion, the last wonder!
When we have trusted ourselves entirely
To the unknown, and are taken up
Out of our little ships of death
Into pure oblivion.

Oh build your ship of death, be building it now
With dim, calm thoughts and quiet hands
Putting its timbers together in the dusk,   20

Rigging its mast with the silent, invisible sail
That will spread in death to the breeze
Of the kindness of the cosmos, that will waft
The little ship with its soul to the wonder-goal.

Ah, if you want to live in peace on the face of the earth
Then build your ship of death, in readiness
For the longest journey, over the last of seas.

TABERNACLE

Come, let us build a temple to oblivion
with seven veils, and an innermost
Holy of Holies of sheer oblivion.

And there oblivion dwells, and the silent soul
may sink into god at last, having passed the veils.

But anyone who shall ascribe attributes to God or oblivion
let him be cast out, for blasphemy.
For God is a deeper forgetting far than sleep
and all description is a blasphemy.

SHADOWS

And if tonight my soul may find her peace
in sleep, and sink in good oblivion,
and in the morning wake like a new-opened flower
then I have been dipped again in God, and new-created.

And if, as weeks go round, in the dark of the moon
my spirit darkens and goes out, and soft, strange gloom
pervades my movements and my thoughts and words
then I shall know that I am walking still
with God, we are close together now the moon's in shadow.

And if, as autumn deepens and darkens   10
I feel the pain of falling leaves, and stems that break in storms
and trouble and dissolution and distress
and then the softness of deep shadows folding, folding
around my soul and spirit, around my lips
so sweet, like a swoon, or more like the drowse of a low, sad song
singing darker than the nightingale, on, on to the solstice
and the silence of short days, the silence of the year, the shadow,
then I shall know that my life is moving still
with the dark earth, and drenched
with the deep oblivion of earth's lapse and renewal.   20

And if, in the changing phases of man's life
I fall in sickness and in misery

my wrists seem broken and my heart seems dead
and strength is gone, and my life
is only the leavings of a life:

and still, among it all, snatches of lovely oblivion, and snatches of
    renewal
odd, wintry flowers upon the withered stem, yet new strange flowers
such as my life has not brought forth before, new blossoms of me –

then I must know that still
I am in the hands of the unknown God,   30
he is breaking me down to his own oblivion
to send me forth on a new morning, a new man.

Appendix

THE WILD COMMON

The quick sparks on the gorse-bushes are leaping
Little jets of sunlight texture imitating flame;
Above them, exultant, the peewits are sweeping:
They have triumphed again o'er the ages, their screamings proclaim.

Rabbits, handfuls of brown earth, lie
Low-rounded on the mournful turf they have bitten down to the
    quick.
Are they asleep? – are they living? – Now see, when I
Lift my arms, the hill bursts and heaves under their spurting kick!

The common flaunts bravely; but below, from the rushes
Crowds of glittering king-cups surge to challenge the blossoming
    bushes;
There the lazy streamlet pushes
His bent course mildly; here wakes again, leaps, laughs, and gushes

Into a deep pond, an old sheep-dip,
Dark, overgrown with willows, cool, with the brook ebbing
    through so slow;
Naked on the steep, soft lip
Of the turf I stand watching my own white shadow quivering to and
    fro.

What if the gorse-flowers shrivelled, and I were gone?
What if the waters ceased, where were the marigolds then, and the
    gudgeon?

10

203

What is this thing that I look down upon?
White on the water wimples my shadow, strains like a dog on a
    string, to run on.   20

How it looks back, like a white dog to its master!
I on the bank all substance, my shadow all shadow looking up to me,
    looking back!
And the water runs, and runs faster, runs faster,
And the white dog dances and quivers, I am holding his cord quite
    slack.

But how splendid it is to be substance, here!
My shadow is neither here nor there; but I, I am royally here!
I am here! I am here! screams the peewit; the may-blobs burst out
    in a laugh as they hear!
Here! flick the rabbits. Here! pants the gorse. Here! say the insects
    far and near.

Over my skin in the sunshine, the warm, clinging air
Flushed with the songs of seven larks singing at once, goes kissing
    me glad.   30
You are here! You are here! We have found you! Everywhere
We sought you substantial, you touchstone of caresses, you naked
    lad!

Oh but the water loves me and folds me,
Plays with me, sways me, lifts me and sinks me, murmurs:
    Oh marvellous stuff!
No longer shadow! – and it holds me
Close, and it rolls me, enfolds me, touches me, as if never it could
    touch me enough.

Sun, but in substance, yellow water-blobs!
Wings and feathers on the crying, mysterious ages, peewits
    wheeling!
All that is right, all that is good, all that is God takes substance! a
    rabbit lobs
In confirmation, I hear sevenfold lark-songs pealing.   40

BAVARIAN GENTIANS

Not every man has gentians in his house
in soft September, at slow, sad Michaelmas.

Bavarian gentians, big and dark, only dark
darkening the day-time, torch-like, with the smoking blueness of
    Pluto's gloom,
ribbed and torch-like, with their blaze of darkness spread blue
down flattening into points, flattened under the sweep of white day
torch-flower of the blue-smoking darkness, Pluto's dark-blue daze,
black lamps from the halls of Dis, burning dark blue,
giving off darkness, blue darkness, as Demeter's pale lamps give off
    light,
lead me then, lead the way.   10

Reach me a gentian, give me a torch!
let me guide myself with the blue, forked torch of this flower
down the darker and darker stairs, where blue is darkened on blueness
even where Persephone goes, just now, from the frosted September
to the sightless realm where darkness is awake upon the dark
and Persephone herself is but a voice
or a darkness invisible enfolded in the deeper dark
of the arms Plutonic, and pierced with the passion of dense gloom,
among the splendour of torches of darkness, shedding darkness on
    the lost bride and her groom.

THE SHIP OF DEATH

1

Now it is autumn and the falling fruit
and the long journey towards oblivion.

The apples falling like great drops of dew
to bruise themselves an exit from themselves.

And it is time to go, to bid farewell
to one's own self, and find an exit
from the fallen self.

2

Have you built your ship of death, O have you?
O build your ship of death, for you will need it.

The grim frost is at hand, when the apples will fall   10
thick, almost thundrous, on the hardened earth.

And death is on the air like a smell of ashes!
Ah! can't you smell it?

And in the bruised body, the frightened soul
finds itself shrinking, wincing from the cold
that blows upon it through the orifices.

3

And can a man his own quietus make
with a bare bodkin?

With daggers, bodkins, bullets, man can make
a bruise or break of exit for his life;   20
but is that a quietus, O tell me, is it quietus?

Surely not so! for how could murder, even self-murder
ever a quietus make?

4

O let us talk of quiet that we know,
that we can know, the deep and lovely quiet
of a strong heart at peace!

How can we this, our own quietus, make?

5

Build then the ship of death, for you must take
the longest journey, to oblivion.

And die the death, the long and painful death   30
that lies between the old self and the new.

206

Already our bodies are fallen, bruised, badly bruised,
already our souls are oozing through the exit
of the cruel bruise.

Already the dark and endless ocean of the end
is washing in through the breaches of our wounds,
already the flood is upon us.

Oh build your ship of death, your little ark
and furnish it with food, with little cakes, and wine
for the dark flight down oblivion.   40

6

Piecemeal the body dies, and the timid soul
has her footing washed away, as the dark flood rises.

We are dying, we are dying, we are all of us dying
and nothing will stay the death-flood rising within us
and soon it will rise on the world, on the outside world.

We are dying, we are dying, piecemeal our bodies are dying
and our strength leaves us,
and our soul cowers naked in the dark rain over the flood,
cowering in the last branches of the tree of our life.

7

We are dying, we are dying, so all we can do   50
is now to be willing to die, and to build the ship
of death to carry the soul on the longest journey.

A little ship, with oars and food
and little dishes, and all accoutrements
fitting and ready for the departing soul.

Now launch the small ship, now as the body dies
and life departs, launch out, the fragile soul
in the fragile ship of courage, the ark of faith
with its store of food and little cooking pans
and change of clothes,   60

upon the flood's black waste
upon the waters of the end
upon the sea of death, where still we sail
darkly, for we cannot steer, and have no port.

There is no port, there is nowhere to go
only the deepening blackness darkening still
blacker upon the soundless, ungurgling flood
darkness at one with darkness, up and down
and sideways utterly dark, so there is no direction any more.
And the little ship is there; yet she is gone.   70
She is not seen, for there is nothing to see her by.
She is gone! gone! and yet
somewhere she is there.
Nowhere!

8

And everything is gone, the body is gone
completely under, gone, entirely gone.
The upper darkness is heavy as the lower,
between them the little ship
is gone
she is gone.   80

It is the end, it is oblivion.

9

And yet out of eternity, a thread
separates itself on the blackness,
a horizontal thread
that fumes a little with pallor upon the dark.

Is it illusion? or does the pallor fume
A little higher?
Ah wait, wait, for there's the dawn,
the cruel dawn of coming back to life
out of oblivion.   90

Wait, wait, the little ship
drifting, beneath the deathly ashy grey
of a flood-dawn.

Wait, wait! even so, a flush of yellow
and strangely, O chilled wan soul, a flush of rose.

A flush of rose, and the whole thing starts again.

10

The flood subsides, and the body, like a worn sea-shell
emerges strange and lovely.
And the little ship wings home, faltering and lapsing
on the pink flood,
and the frail soul steps out, into her house again
filling the heart with peace.

Swings the heart renewed with peace
even of oblivion.

Oh build your ship of death, oh build it!
for you will need it.
For the voyage of oblivion awaits you.

Critical commentary

It does not take long to survey the critical history of Lawrence's poetry, for the simple reason that there is little of it. Not only that. Of the few critics who *have* written about the poetry, only one or two have had anything interesting to say. Lawrence has always been regarded as a great novelist and much good work has been devoted to his fiction. But it sometimes seems as though those who have the intensest regard for him as a novelist are incapable of believing that he could also produce good, even great, poetry. F.R. Leavis is an honourable exception. Yet even Leavis wrote comparatively little about Lawrence's poetry, while the title of his study, *D.H. Lawrence: Novelist*, not only puts the emphasis exclusively on the fiction, but implies that that is where it ought to be. I do not suppose that Leavis intended this emphasis, but it is certainly a fact – and it may be a consequence of his work – that books on Lawrence's novels continue to heap up, whereas the poetry goes virtually unremarked.

Perhaps this is no bad thing. At the very least, it enables each generation of readers to discover Lawrence's poetry for themselves. It also means that his poetry is for the most part spared both the niggling, joyless aridities that typically pass for academic criticism and the slavering approach of those adulators who, taking Lawrence the 'life affirmer' for granted, treat his work as holy writ. As Tom Paulin has said, 'For such critics – they are numerous and influential – Lawrence's work is remarkable for an inchoate intensity, and not for a formal beauty.'[1] To put it bluntly, Lawrence has too often been admired (and less often been reviled) for his 'message'. A quick riffle through the many pages of the collected poems is enough to establish just how often they amount to little more than a message; and the message poems become more thickly sown as the years go by. In both *Pansies* and

211

Nettles it is difficult to spot the flowers among the seemingly endless tangle of weeds.

This is a problem and it is compounded by another one. Lawrence wrote far too much poetry. He seems to have written poems as a way of letting off steam. From his early years he composed what amounts to a diary in verse, especially as regards his relationships with women. His mother, Jessie Chambers, Frieda, and – to a lesser extent – Louie Burrows and Helen Corke: they are all the subjects of sequences of poems in which he tries to sort out his feelings, or to discover what they are, or to understand them. Philip Hobsbaum claims that of the 1,037 titles in the collected edition of the poems 'perhaps not more than forty-three can be recommended to the reader without considerable qualification. Lawrence's use of verse as a kind of emotional diary was not likely to result in many fully articulated structures.'[2] This is severe, and the phrase 'articulated structures' poses a further problem, given that so many of Lawrence's poems seem to be – and perhaps are – notation. Is Hobsbaum demanding the wrong kind of thing from Lawrence's poetry? But then the phrase 'formal beauty' raises yet another problem. Tom Paulin no doubt intended that it should. Among certain of Lawrence's critics it will also raise eyebrows, depending on where they stand. Lawrence either blessedly lacks or is cursed by his disregard for 'formal beauty'. There are Lawrentians who see their man as a vast reproof to the idea that art is a matter of composition. There are anti-Lawrentians who see in Lawrence's poetry the woeful outcome of believing that you can do without it. How do we mediate between these views? If form is preconceived, then surely Lawrence is not to be thought of as trapped by formal terms. He is an original, his utterance that of the authentic artist discovering new means for saying what, without those means, cannot be said. He famously derided Arnold Bennett for being an old imitator. He seems to have wanted to 'make it new'. In what sense, then, can his art be spoken of in terms of its formal beauty? Some of Lawrence's most passionate admirers would scorn the application of these words to his poetry.

Unfortunately for them, critics hostile to Lawrence are quick to agree that his poetry is without formal beauty, that it lacks 'articulated structure'. Whatever the differences between such critics as R. P. Blackmur and C. H. Sisson, they are at one in arguing that poetry should be a form of containment. Indeed, they argue that in a poem the individual voice presses against formal structures – of rhyme, metre, stanza – *not* in order to break free, but in order to resolve tensions between the voice and the form through which it speaks. For these critics, and others like them, form operates as a social term. Behind it is the kind of experience that may legitimately be thought of as collective, cumulative, historically derived. Poetic forms have histories, they do not arrive on earth as though born of nothing but 'inspiration'. When Blackmur and Sisson criticize Lawrence for his formlessness, therefore, they are accusing him of lawlessness, or – it isn't quite the same thing – of wanton lawbreaking. The lawless poet knows no better: he is the hopeless innocent, the Caliban of verse. The lawbreaker *does* know what he is doing: his is a conscious decision and he is therefore guilty in a way the hopeless innocent is not. On occasions both Blackmur and Sisson write as though Lawrence is Caliban. On other occasions they treat him as Antonio. But the layer of adamant that runs beneath all they have to say is their belief that Lawrence is a transgressor against the rule of poetic law. As of course he is.

We come here to an absolute divide in ways of thinking about poetry, a gap that cannot be bridged. For where Blackmur and Sisson may be said to uphold a view of art which is conservative, Lawrence's is truly radical. One could put this differently by saying that their convictions are, at bottom, catholic, his are protestant. And this is how W. H. Auden defines Lawrence, in that excellent essay to which I have referred in the Introduction to the present selection.[3] Given that by the time he came to write this essay Auden had himself retreated from his own earlier radicalism, his account is a great act of imaginative sympathy and it remains the best single introduction to Lawrence the poet. Honourable mention must also be made of the essay by A. Alvarez. Less wide-ranging than Auden, Alvarez nevertheless offers a most persuasive justification for Lawrence's way of writing.

It is, however, necessary here to add that the Alvarez who wrote so enthusiastically about Lawrence was also the early champion of Ted Hughes. And Alvarez prefaced his hugely influential Penguin anthology, *The New Poetry*, 1962, by an essay, 'The New Poetry, or Beyond the Gentility Principle', in which he remarked that 'Since about 1930 the machinery of modern English poetry seems to have been controlled by a series of negative feedbacks designed to produce precisely the effect Hardy wanted.' Alvarez has in mind Thomas Hardy's famous remark to the young

Robert Graves that 'All we can do is write on the old themes in the old styles, but try to do a little better than those who went before us.'[4] The year 1930 was that of Lawrence's death, and although Alvarez does not refer to this fact, I suspect that it was the decisive irritant in the shaping of his view of modern English poetry. For Alvarez, such poetry is altogether *too* English. Gentility is its curse, its fatal limitation. I am not concerned here with the rightness of Alvarez's view, nor with the outcome of his hope – as it seems to have been – that Hughes (and possibly Thom Gunn and Sylvia Plath) represented a breakout from the gentility principle. What matters is that Lawrence provides the means, the more powerful for being unconscious, through which Alvarez can confirm his own belief that now, at last, English poetry is ready to trample down the walls set up by English gentility.

It is easy to see why Lawrence would be the unacknowledged leader in this movement. For Lawrence is the great transgressor. 'To transgress: To go beyond the limits prescribed by (a law, command, etc.); to break, violate, infringe, trespass against . . . To offend, sin . . . To offend against (a person); to disobey. To go or pass beyond (any limit or bounds).' The Oxford Dictionary defines the word in ways that seem almost to define Lawrence. The working-class boy from the English midlands broke out of the confines of his class, his upbringing, his education. He married a divorcée, who was by birth a German aristocrat. Leaving England, he and his wife wandered the world, never settling anywhere for long. He became the author of novels which transgressed not only against formal conventions but against moral ones and this led, inevitably (as it must have seemed), to their being banned from sale and publication in the country of his birth. He refused to identify with England and its allies during the Great War. In rejecting his roots and the claims of English gentility, he might have adapted the words of his hero, Walt Whitman, and called himself 'one of the roughs, a kosmos'.

II

He might have done so, but he didn't. Whitman's words suggest a man at ease with himself. Lawrence, on the other hand, was rarely at ease with himself. A major reason for this is that discovering 'the self' was precisely what caused him such trouble. We can get some inkling of the gap between

214

Whitman and Lawrence if we complete the line from which Whitman's words come. It opens section 24 of *Leaves of Grass*. 'Walt Whitman, an American, one of the roughs, a kosmos.' Lawrence could not consent to calling himself 'English', except in a purely legal sense; and although his passport told him he was British he could not have cared to know himself as that, either. What sensitive person would? The transgressor crosses boundaries. He moves beyond limits, including those of class and nationality. But what exactly does he move towards? One way of answering this question is to say that Lawrence moved – or hoped to move – out of history and into metaphysics. This argument has been used about *The Rainbow*, for example. The novel begins in a recognizably placed, social-historical setting: a part of the English midlands in the middle years of the nineteenth century. It ends in the early twentieth century, but by then the social setting has become far less important than the search for intrinsic selfhood in and of the central character of the novel's last section. So at least a powerful critical argument runs, and although there are questions to be raised about it, it does draw attention to the withdrawal of Lawrence's interest from any attempts to define the self in relation to the social world.[5] Or rather, 'self' is held to be discoverable only in its denial of that world's impingement. 'I am' is an assertion that insists on a pre-social sense of identity.

Yet this is to deny a crucial source of power in much of the poetry of the early period. It is not only that in the poems up until 1912 Lawrence is often delightedly in touch with the community in which he grew, but that even when such delight has given way to something more complex and, it has to be said, more anguished, there is no attempt to *deny* this complexity. On the contrary, much of the best work of the early period springs from an attempt to explore the complex sense of belonging, even while feeling separate. This is implicit in the very fine dialect poems. They record, with extraordinary vivacity, speech habits and occurrences of the mining community of which Lawrence, the working-class boy, was part. Very interestingly, of course, his ambitious mother wanted him to shed this local way of speaking. It was not 'educated' speech.

The dialect poems are ballads. They are written, that is, in the form and measure which by tradition and association can be called without condescension the poetry of the people. The staple form of ballad is a four-line stanza often rhyming abcb. (The number of feet per line is more varied.)

It is a form taken over by many of the hymn writers of the eighteenth and nineteenth centuries, whose verses Lawrence would have sung in the Congregationalist chapel his family attended. It is, in other words, a form with a history and a thick layering of cultural associations. For a writer struggling free of these associations it is, then, a form he can use only in the full knowledge that its gifts are ambiguous. To identify himself with the ballad at all closely is to become trapped. Not surprisingly, therefore, Lawrence's dialect ballads are few in number. To have written more would have been to run the risk of seeming merely quaint and thus condescending, or it would have involved his pretending to an identification with a community with which he felt real dissatisfactions, and which ballad poetry could not allow him to express. This is important enough to require some teasing out.

It is often asserted that as Lawrence grew up he came increasingly to identify with his mother and to reject his father's violent, brutish behaviour. Yet any attentive reading of *Sons and Lovers* makes it impossible to uphold this view. At the very least, we have surely to recognize how often Walter Morel seems to be dismissed from the story and from the novelist's sympathetic concern, only to re-emerge in a way that denies us the chance to write him off. Lawrence, it seems clear, was much more deeply divided about, and uncertain of, what he really felt about his father than incautious biographers and critics have assumed. And what of those social and cultural expectations his mother encouraged in him? They surely compose precisely that corrosive image of gentility, that attainment of stifling respectability, against which he would come to rage and which would be one of the major factors in his continuing transgressions against English life. The tensions operating within a family and across its generations are liable to be at the heart of much English experience. They are brought about by a sense of *separation*, a desire for apartness, felt the more acutely simply because such a desire has been fostered by precisely those people, parents, who want to assert or maintain continuity, coherence, mutuality. In other words, the desire for separation is experienced as a guilty desire. This is the deepest, most upsetting experience of what class means for Englishmen and, I suspect, Englishwomen, for whom separation is also a familial experience. Dickens's *Great Expectations* is the definitive exploration of this experience, but when Lawrence said apropos of *Sons and Lovers* that he had written a story which was about the tragedy of thousands of young Englishmen, it is too hastily assumed that he must mean to refer to the relationship between Paul Morel and his mother. The father is there, too; and is there as a peculiarly tragic figure. Of course, it is true that by the end of the novel Paul has distanced himself from his father. But then he has also distanced himself from his mother. As Graham Hough in *The Dark Sun* was the first to point out, Paul as good as kills her by administering an overdose of the medicine which is sustaining her in her mortal illness.

This must not be misunderstood. There is no glib resolution about the ending of the novel. It recognizes the cost of the snapping of those bonds, familial and social, which had tied Paul to a community. Nevertheless, the determination to break out, to break away, is unmistakable. And this is also evident in much of the poetry of the early period. It is often most fully articulated in those poems where Lawrence explores sexuality in a manner that very markedly breaks taboos. I have already drawn attention to the reasons why, in this respect, Whitman was of such importance to Lawrence and others of his generation. It is, however, worth noting that a poem such as 'Snap-Dragon' has an originality to which we should not be blinded merely because it is cumbered by a certain amount of dead language and by Lawrence's uneasy handling of rhyme, at which he was never much good. It is easy to point to the flaws: the use of 'did' as a kind of coy intensifier ('did float', 'did discover'), the unpractised half-repetition of what anyway is a clumsy expression ('My windows of discovery' echoed in 'windows of my mind'). Any good poet could have helped Lawrence get rid of those faults. What I suspect no other poet of the time could have done was to have challenged the poem's astonishing, deep originality.

Originality, like authenticity, can be over-praised. The words have, in fact, become journalistic clichés, for which the rather more damning terms naivety or ignorance could often, and more accurately, be substituted. But in Lawrence's case they have an absolute justification. In his essay on Lawrence's poetry, Auden brilliantly remarked that

Reading Lawrence's early poems, one is continually struck by the originality of the sensibility and the conventionality of the expressive means. For most immature poets, their chief problem is to learn to forget what they have been taught poets are supposed to feel; too often, as Lawrence says, the young man is afraid of his demon, and puts his hand over the demon's mouth and speaks for him. On the other hand, an immature

217

poet, if he has real talent, usually begins to exhibit quite early a distinctive style of his own; however obvious the influence of some older writer may be, there is something original in his manner or, at least, great technical competence. In Lawrence's case, this was not so; he learned quite soon to let his demon speak, but it took him a long time to find the appropriate style for him to speak in.[6]

My only quarrel with this is that it may seem to imply that later in life Lawrence learned to find the means by which the material experience of 'Snap-Dragon' would be more successfully uttered. There are two reasons for querying this. In the first place, 'Snap-Dragon' is very much a young man's poem. It is about those powerful awkward stirrings and difficult sensations of sexual love, in which the developing relationship between the man and woman involves a sensed struggle for domination. Second, and for all that the scene can be thought of as somehow primal – the garden, the sunlight, the man and woman and the snap-dragon, between them inevitably recall Adam and Eve and the snake in Eden – for all this, the social world is there, as, at the very least, an inescapable atmosphere. It is to be noted less in the reference to 'the old grey walls' than in the social constraints that can be felt threading through the protagonists' talk. As a novelist, Lawrence was always alert to these constraints. There is a very funny moment in *Women in Love* when Birkin and Ursula are momentarily recalled from the depths of a quarrel to daily politeness in order to return the greetings of a passing cyclist. But in the poetry this becomes less and less true. Here, however, much of the poem's power can be located in the tensions between the social ambience in which the characters exist, and the deep, isolated self, that would-be essential identity, with which Lawrence tries to grapple at the end of the poem. 'And death, I know, is better than not-to-be.' Tempting though it may be to read this phrase as suggesting that the speaker wants merely to enter a world of sexual experience, we need to recognize that beyond it is a desire to escape from the hindrances to 'being', and that these hindrances must then be identified with community.

Here, we come to a matter of the utmost importance. We can begin to indicate its nature by saying what is surely obvious, that 'Snap-Dragon' could not have been written in dialect. Much later in his career, when Lawrence gave Lady Chatterley's lover a dialect in which to speak his scatological and sexual thoughts, he intended it as a rebuke to the evasions of 'polite' Englishness. But Mellors's programmatic utterances are very unlike, and very much cruder than, the explorations of 'Snap-Dragon'. The reason for this must be that in the poem's struggle to discover and define a kind of selfhood, what is at stake is selfhood as that which exists apart from, even in opposition to, community. It is the nature of this apartness that it should be registered through a language which is emphatically *not* the language of the community. For Lawrence such language points to a socialized self, a self as identified in and through a 'given' language. The language of 'Snap-Dragon' is very different.

> She laughed, she reached her hand out to the flower,
> Closing its crimson throat. My own throat in her power
> Strangled, my heart swelled up so full
> As if it would burst its wine-skin in my throat,
> Choke me in my own crimson. I watched her pull
> The gorge of the gaping flower, till the blood did float
>
> Over my eyes, and I was blind –
> Her large brown hand stretched over
> The windows of my mind . . .

It is easy to laugh at the excesses of this, partly perhaps as a way of forestalling embarrassment. And certainly the nakedness of the writing *is* embarrassing. (The show of 'art', in its very artlessness, serves only to heighten the vulnerability of this confused sexual outpouring.) Hobsbaum speaks of such poems as having 'the raw appeal of autobiography', but adds that few 'could be detached from their plasm of experience and so be termed poems'.[7] This is true, but it underestimates the difficulty that *any* poet would encounter in handling the material of 'Snap-Dragon'. There is something very ungenerous in Hobsbaum's dismissal of the early poems, a failure to acknowledge that Lawrence was after all struggling through to registering the power of experiences that could not have been registered in any other way. Had he been content to remain within the conventions available to him we should have been spared the worst excesses of 'Snap-Dragon'. But we should have also been denied the triumphs of his achieved poems.

This is why 'End of Another Home-Holiday' is a crucial poem of the early period. To what I have said of this poem in the Introduction, I will add here that the pain of wished-for separation, intense as it is, authenticates the courage of the person tearing himself away. In passing we may note that F.R. Leavis rightly indicated how 'Piano' resists the sentimentality of mere nostalgia that it may, at an unwary reading, look to be settling for. Both it and 'End of Another Home-Holiday' are about the complex relationship that exists between Lawrence and his mother. 'Love is the great Asker', he says in the latter; and it then becomes evident that asking is a particularly insidious kind of intrusion into privacy – selfhood – that he must struggle to resist.

> The wild young heifer, glancing distraught,
> With a strange new knocking of life at her side
>   Runs seeking a loneliness.
> The little grain draws down the earth to hide.
> Nay, even the slumberous egg, as it labours under the shell,
>   Patiently to divide, and self-divide,
> Asks to be hidden, and wishes nothing to tell.
>
> But when I draw the scanty cloak of silence over my eyes,
> Piteous Love comes peering under the hood.

Piteous Love is the mother. She is also the cause of guilt and the perceived spinner of emotional entanglements that cannot be severed without acute pain. It is to Lawrence's credit that he manages to register the pain and yet by and large to avoid self-pity. It is this which gives an especial distinction to the sequence of poems about his mother which come as a sort of climax to the early period of his verse.

III

By the time he wrote these poems, Lawrence had put a good deal of distance between himself and his beginnings. Love poems make up much of the work in verse of the following years. They are unlike most other love poems in the language because they are utterly indifferent to a world of sociality. They turn exclusively inwards, towards the narrator and the woman to and about whom they are written. But 'narrator' suggests a gap that hardly ever exists between the creator and the 'I' of the poems. All too clearly this makes for a difficulty which Lawrence rarely manages to resolve. On the one hand, the poems are about Frieda and himself. On the other, he hopes to offer the relationship as paradigmatic. Hence that hysterical title *Look! We Have Come Through!*: it is both autobiographical and instructive. To be sure, the best poems in the sequence escape from the insistence of that title. They are not simply 'messages', in the sense in which Auden uses the term when he remarks that 'Once I have learned his message, I cease to be interested in a messenger and, should I later come to think his message is false or misleading, I shall remember him with resentment and distaste.'[8]

Auden's remark does, however, raise an awkward question. Leave aside the obvious successes, which include such poems as 'Gloire de Dijon' and 'River Roses', and the reader is faced with a number which, in their almost casual notation, seem to exist for the sake of their message or as rather arrogantly offered fragments of autobiography. They are too inconsiderable, that is, to justify themselves as poems. They say, in so many words, 'this happened, therefore it is important'. The result is a gross over-evaluation of the importance of such happenings. That this should be so comes about because of Lawrence's urgent desire to assert selfhood as somehow an essential entity, cut quite free of the social. In this he is therefore very unlike his great predecessor, Robert Browning.

At first glance, one could make out a case for Browning's life as in some ways anticipating Lawrence's. True, he did not come from the working class, but he broke away from his conventional upbringing, joined up with a group of radical intellectuals and writers, and in his marriage to Elizabeth Barrett and their leaving England for Italy he very plainly transgressed against custom and expectation. Moreover, Browning was a great love poet and he concludes 'Love Among the Ruins' with the implacable statement 'Love is best'. The next poem, however, throws this into doubt. It is called 'A Lovers' Quarrel' and although it ends with what seems to be a resolution of the quarrel, 'I shall pull her through the door, / I shall have her / for evermore!', the confident aggression of that commands neither our assent nor our belief that the quarrel can be at an end. Browning delights in upsetting or reversing or at the very least troubling certainties. It is not surprising that the confident conclusion of one poem should be subverted by its successor. And in repeatedly subverting the 'truths' of his love poems, Browning very brilliantly shows the dangers of assuming that a relationship, no matter how familiar and intense, can be thought of as settled. On the contrary, its very intensity makes for the flow and recoil which Lawrence would come to speak of as present in all relationships and which, as both he and Browning before him realized, could allow for murderous passions quite as much as other, more conventionally positive ones.

But the more important point I want to make here is this: that *Men and Women* appeared in 1855, and for all that Browning might assert 'Love is best', he does so at the conclusion of a poem which is about militarism and the ruins of empire. It seems likely that he wrote the poem before the outbreak of the Crimean war; but this serves only to make it all the more significant that he should choose to place it at the beginning of a volume published at its height.

It may seem from this that I therefore expect Lawrence to show some awareness of the Great War in his love poems, which were, after all, published in 1916 (*Amores*) and 1917 (*Look! We Have Come Through!*). Not necessarily. Most, if not all, of the poems were written while he and Frieda were runaway lovers on the continent of Europe, in 1912–13. One might, it is true, expect the poems at publication to reflect something of the vastly changed circumstances that had occurred between when they were written and the years of their appearing in book form, but it could be argued that by implication at least Lawrence is urging 'Love is best'. Certainly he was appalled by the destructiveness and hatred let loose by the war; and he had especial reason to loathe the jingoism and xenophobia directed against his German-born wife. Here, it is worth recalling the pleasure and relief with which E. M. Forster came upon T. S. Eliot's work, in Cairo, in 1917. The poems, he says, 'were innocent of public-spiritness: they sang of private disgust and diffidence, and of people who seemed genuine because they were unattractive or weak. . . . He who would turn aside to complain of ladies and drawing-rooms preserved a tiny drop of our self-respect, he carried on the human heritage.'[9]

It is not, then, Lawrence's refusal to so much as hint at the existence of war that troubles me about the sequence of love poems. What *is* worrying is their failure to register *any* pressures beyond the merely personal. Or, to put the matter rather differently, Lawrence's rejection of the social circumstances in which he had grown up and whose limits he had outgrown is meant to be total. He and Frieda are lovers in a world elsewhere.

It has to be said that such a world cannot exist for more than a succession of moments. And the poetry of moment is essentially the poetry of mood. Perhaps most love poetry is that. But Lawrence wanted *his* love poetry to be a good deal more. He was the self-proclaimed priest of love and the poems were intended to act as his scripture. But because they turn their backs on the social world they are inevitably too narrow in focus to provide the more general vision of love he seems to have hoped they would open up. This is why he is unlike and inferior to Browning. Moreover, at their worst, as all but the most infatuated of his critics acknowledge, the love poems are trivially self-absorbed. They ask the reader to approve them not so much as poems but because they try to record, as faithfully as possible, what 'really' happened. The problem with this is that although confession may be good for the soul, it is bad for art. Even Keith Sagar, one of the most emphatically supportive of Lawrence's commentators, is forced to admit that some of the love poems are 'personal in the restricting sense'.[10] This is a good deal more sensible than Holly Laird's endorsement of what she calls Amy Lowell's 'happy judgement', that '*Look! We Have Come Through!* is an amazing book. It is to my mind a greater novel even than *Sons and Lovers*.'[11] You have only to think of the love poetry of Donne or Robert Browning, or the more recent love poetry of Louis MacNeice, to know why such a claim is simply ridiculous.

There is point to this comparison. Donne, Browning, and MacNeice all recognize the difficulties in trying to ignore or deny the significance of the world from which lovers may wish to remove themselves but to which they have to return. Their best work, and it is among the greatest of all love poetry in the language to be written from a man's point of view, does not scant the power and vitality of relationship, nor of the discovery of a sense of self through such relationship. Donne, it is true, only rarely can then break through to a sense of the other, but in Browning that sense is invariably the matter of the poetry. This is also Lawrence's strength. Unlike Browning, however, Lawrence concentrates the focus of his poetry so exclusively on the lovers, or on the loved one as perceived by the poet, that there is no room for anything or anyone else. The result is that the sequence as a whole feels obsessive, and that this should be so tells us a great deal about Lawrence's desire to probe for and to make authentic the discovery of an essential self, one which exists only in dynamic relationship with the loved other. This is to move from history to metaphysics. It is a move which, as I have said, is arguably worked through in the last part of *The Rainbow* and most of *Women in Love*, where it has received much critical attention. But such attention has not been directed to the poems, even though it is in the poems that a problem that is inseparably connected with this move shows itself, and with especial clarity.

Here, I should note that by 'essential self' I mean that self conceived of as existing apart from any formative influences, whether linguistic, familial, economic, etc. I have already suggested that in his early writing Lawrence recognizes the difficulty of imagining such a self. Yet we have seen that increasingly he comes to assert that it is both desirable and attainable. In this he was by no means alone among his contemporaries. E. M. Forster, for example, liked to set the 'outer world' of 'telegrams and anger' – that is, the social world – against what he called the world of 'personal relationships', and in *A Room with a View* (1907) and, less schematically, in *Howard's End* (1910) he forced the alternatives into a kind of diagrammatic opposition. Lawrence is a far greater writer than Forster. Nevertheless, his imagination yearns towards the achievement of selfhood through a concentration on relationship to the exclusion of all else, which is, perhaps, the ultimate transgression.

There can be no doubt that this produced its successes. And it is why, in the best of the love poems, Lawrence so rejoices in the woman's physical presence. There is nothing voyeuristic about this. On the contrary, the candid relishing of detail in 'Gloire de Dijon' is as unmawkish as it is non-prurient. But, to repeat, this is the poetry of the moment: it celebrates, as it savours, the instant. It is out of time and, therefore, by implication, out of place. It has no social reference. What it *does* have is something of the loving care that Bonnard brought to the many paintings he made of his wife at her toilette. It is, one might say, impressionistic. It is also imagistic.

> She drips herself with water, and her shoulders
> Glisten as silver, they crumple up
> Like wet and falling roses, and I listen
> For the sluicing of their rain-dishevelled petals.

It is difficult to imagine the poet who would not have been glad to have written those lines. They are the quintessence of all that is best about imagism: compact, vivid, unrhetorical. Yet they go beyond the prescriptiveness of imagist theory. Three of the four lines hover near to iambic pentameter, or at least to a five-stress pattern. To say this is, however, to take nothing away from their expressive fluency, nor from that thread of sound that runs through the short 'i' ('drips', 'glisten', 'silver', 'listen', 'dish . . .'), and so links the lines as though the poem has about it the discreet yet detectable repletion of rhyme. This is formal beauty, right enough. If you took away the words 'as' and 'like' you would have images in all their concreteness, according to the theories of imagism at least. It is also obvious that if you took them away you would hurt the poem's sound. Because it was concerned with rendering 'the thing in itself', imagism, as a theory, had nothing to do with sound. Imagists did, however, scorn regular metres, because, so they argued, a line of predetermined length, especially if it was in a stanza of predetermined length and even a poem of predetermined length (a sonnet, say), would inevitably lead to space-filling. Imagists were intent on striking out the inessential. The padding must go.

Lawrence inevitably knew about the imagist movement. He appeared in the pages of their anthologies. But it is clear from 'Gloire de Dijon' that he would never have been content with the idea that the poet operates as a kind of clinician, observing and accurately reporting without involvement what he/she sees. To be fair, the best imagists also rejected this 'objectivist' formula. F.S. Flint's lovely poem 'The Swan' may seem to be objective description, but its concluding lines reveal how far it is from dispassionate observation.

> Over the green cold leaves
> and the rippled silver
> and the tarnished copper
> of its neck and beak,
> toward the deep black water
> beneath the arches
> the swan floats slowly.
>
> Into the dark of the arch the swan floats
> and into the black depth of my sorrow
> it bears a white rose of flame.[12]

Here, the plangent sounds (that repeated, long 'o' has about it an almost Tennysonian melancholy) reveal how far Flint's involvement is more than merely visual. Indeed, the swan, keenly visualized though it is, is also a carrier of significance which is both emotional and psychological. Will the flame light up, or be extinguished by, the darkness? (Roses, after all, fade and fall.) We do not know what the sorrow is, nor why it has come about. (Though swans and roses are traditional enough properties of love poems.) But the major point to make is this, that the poem's slow movement, together with its characteristic sound effects, can leave us in no doubt that it registers the emotion of sorrow every bit as much as it tries to register the visual image of the swan. The image is the occasion for focusing the emotion. Or vice versa. It does not matter. What does is that the emotion and vision – image – cannot be disentangled.

'Gloire de Dijon' is also a poem in which it is impossible to separate out emotion from observation. *What* is seen is *how* it is seen. If Lawrence had learned from the imagists the possibilities of centring his attention, and his poetry with it, on what amounts to the dynamics of vision (using that word in its wider sense), then there is reason to be grateful to them. We must likewise be grateful to them if they were the cause of his breaking with the habits of rhyme and stanza, and even regular metre, none of which formal properties he handled with much skill outside the ballad poems. From now on, the 'articulated structure' of a Lawrence poem will owe little if anything to the traditions which he had inherited and which had galled his early work. It is, however, entirely possible that he arrived at the writing of the best poems in *Look! We Have Come Through!* by his own route. Either way, it is not very important. (Questions of influence are never easy to resolve.) What does count is that once he had freed himself from the trappings of Georgianism which still clung to his earlier verse Lawrence was able to write the great poems that make up the bulk of *Birds, Beasts and Flowers*. For whatever the limitations of the love poems, it is clear that in writing them he found a style which not only allowed the depth and intensity of his vision to prosper, but in which style *was* his vision. The one cannot be imagined without the other. What may at first seem to be a form of casual notation is formal in a far more significant sense. 'Thought is a man in his wholeness wholly attending.' So runs the last line of one of Lawrence's *Pansies*. It is an exact account of how the best of his poems work.

IV

I want to conclude this commentary, then, by saying something about the uniquely valuable poems he wrote in the period between his leaving England after the end of the Great War and before the late, difficult years when, partly through lost energy, partly through a messianic urge to preach, and partly through prolonged periods that seem close to despair, his poetry degenerates into rant or worse. These poems are in what at a casual glance seems to be a minor vein. But nobody who reads them at all attentively can think them accounted for by such a term.

There are two dangers that threaten what may be called the poetry of nature. The first is that, determined to say all that can be said about an animal, a plant, a fish, the poet may eventually become self-regarding in his or her virtuosity. The subject is merely the opportunity for a display of descriptive skills. That this can be enjoyable, if it is well done, is not to be doubted. Badly done – over-elaborate or over-fussy – it is a repository of tiresome stylistic mannerisms. Here, for example, are some lines by the American poet Amy Clampitt about the clearing of a sea-fog: 'a lifting / of wisps and scarves, of smoke-rings / from about the islands, disclosing / what had been wavering / fishnet plisse as a smoothness / of peau-de-soie or just-ironed / percale . . .'.[13] This seems ready-made for pseuds' corner. In a recent essay contrasting Basil Bunting with both Ted Hughes and Charles Tomlinson, Donald Davie argues that Bunting's power lies in his compactness, his refusal to say more than is absolutely necessary. Davie then quotes Hughes's 'Rhododendrons', which among much else 'Dripped a chill virulence / Into my nape – / Rubberised prison-wear of suppression!' Davie is surely right to say of this that it 'has the air of showing how much can be found in, or made up of, or "worked up out of" the one word "rhododendrons" '. He makes an equally convincing case against Tomlinson's poem 'Mackinnon's Boat', in which there is a prolonged description of 'what lobsters do after they have been caught and are in the boat'.[14]

The interesting thing is, of course, that neither Hughes's nor Tomlinson's poem could have been written without the influence of the Lawrence of *Birds, Beasts and Flowers*. For although I do not suppose Lawrence wrote the poems that make up the volume in order to invent a genre, that is what he did. And poets have been living off it ever since. With very few exceptions, however, they have failed to equal his work. And this is not merely because they lack his descriptive skills. More importantly, they lack the absolute attentiveness which such skills exist to serve. And it is the attentiveness which for the most part saves Lawrence from the other danger into which poems of nature can and often do fall – the danger of anthropomorphism. Because they are free of that danger, the majority of the poems that make up *Birds, Beasts and Flowers* are blessedly free of the besetting sin of the poetry of nature – sentimentality. Only one modern poet can be sensibly compared with Lawrence in this respect, the great American poet

Marianne Moore. Her wonderful poem, 'The Pangolin', far too long to quote in its entirety, begins:

> Another armoured animal – scale
>   lapping scale with spruce-cone regularity until they
> form the uninterrupted central
>   tail-row! This near artichoke with head and legs and
>   grit-equipped gizzard,
> the night miniature artist engineer is,
>   yes, Leonardo's – da Vinci's replica –
>   impressive animal and toiler of whom we seldom hear.[15]

But as this must surely reveal, her versification is very different from Lawrence's. 'The Pangolin' delicately picks its way from line to line, and each stanza is structured in a way quite unlike any of the poems of *Birds, Beasts and Flowers*. Lawrence's poems are not composed by stanza, any more than they have a regular metrical pattern that can compare with her extraordinary syllabic inventions. Moreover, Moore's tone is both more glancing, loath to settle, and thus more quizzically varied than his. It is, in fact, more social. 'Another armoured animal' – this suggests that conversation is starting up, or at the very least that the poet's musings are intended for another's ear. With Lawrence, on the other hand, we do not feel this to be the case. Not at first, anyway. His absorption with his subject – almost, one might say, his absorption *into* it – leaves no room for him to consider a possible auditor. And yet on closer inspection this turns out not to be quite true. The poems *are* social. Not in the sense that they chatter, but in the sense that they are not at all private. They convey a flow of thoughts, observations, instinct with feeling, which takes for granted an interested listener: 'There, she shan't have any more peppermint drops.' When Lawrence says that (in 'Kangaroo') he is not talking to the animal. He doesn't say 'you shan't'. But nor is he talking to himself – quite. For although the tone, balanced between the comic and the ruefully emphatic, implies words in the head, the exclamation 'There' indicates speech. In short, the poem is properly sociable, in a way that some of the love poems are not. And if it is said that love poems don't have to be sociable we are entitled to retort that in that case Lawrence has no business commanding us to 'Look!' Whereas in the poems of *Birds, Beasts and Flowers* we look and see. We see the kangaroo, presented to us with an unrivalled exactness: 'the long flat skis of her legs, / Steered and propelled by that steel-strong snake of a tail.' We also recognize the unique value of a poet so utterly alert to what he sees (and more than sees) that we can enter into that wholeness of response which any attentive reader must surely acknowledge to be the unimprovable worth of Lawrence's writing at its best. To adapt a fine remark of Geoffrey Grigson's, these poems offer exact prescriptions for being human, the more so in that they aren't obsessively concerned with the human. In this respect the great ending of 'Tortoise Shout' is exemplary. For here, in a rhapsodic, almost psalmic utterance, Lawrence links cry after cry in a manner that brings the universe of living things into the most primal dynamic of separateness and union:

> That which is whole, torn asunder,
> That which is in part, finding its whole again throughout
> the universe.

There are, however, a few occasions on which alertness dulls over. At these points the wholly attentive man is replaced by a very much less attractive writer. Hence, 'Eagle in New Mexico', with its heavy, almost incantatory rhythms, its brooding fascination with blood-sacrifice, with ritual murder. This devilish strand weaves its way through many of the *Pansies* and *Nettles*. Yet even here, Lawrence offers a number of jaunty *aperçus*. They are the shavings from the workshop of a great writer. And it would be impossible to pass by without mentioning the worth of one or two of the late poems in which Lawrence broods over death, in particular 'The Ship of Death' and 'Bavarian Gentians'. The latter of these is certainly a remarkable poem, although I cannot agree with Philip Hobsbaum, who thinks it Lawrence's greatest poetic achievement. The language, Hobsbaum says, 'creates concept after concept of darkness, each one more intense than the last, until in the end we have entered an underworld far darker than the gloom of the slow, sad Michaelmas of the beginning. . . . The verbs carry out a concept of dying; the nouns project darkness. And death is welcomed as marriage in the final apotheosis:

> among the splendour of torches of darkness, shedding
> darkness on the lost bride and her groom.[16]

The difficulty here is not that I disagree with Hobsbaum's account of the poem, but that I cannot share his evaluation of it. He says that it is to be read alongside Donne's 'A Hymn to God my God, in my sickness', Herbert's 'Affliction', and Vaughan's 'They are all gone into the world of light'. I am not sure about the last of these, but both the Donne and Herbert poems have more in them than does 'Bavarian Gentians'. By which I mean that they contain qualities that are central to the poets who wrote them, whereas by the time he came to write 'Bavarian Gentians' Lawrence had left behind much of the vivid, multi-faceted wholeness of *Birds, Beasts and Flowers*. In saying this I in no sense intend to denigrate the poem. I wish simply to emphasize the irreplaceable worth of poems like 'Snake', 'Kangaroo', and the entire Tortoise sequence. There, it seems to me, Lawrence is at his richest.

NOTES TO THE CRITICAL COMMENTARY

1 See Tom Paulin, *Ireland and the English Crisis*, London, Bloodaxe Books, 1985, p. 117.

2 Philip Hobsbaum, *A Reader's Guide to D. H. Lawrence*, London, Thames & Hudson, 1988, p. 147.

3 In *The Dyer's Hand*, New York, Vintage Books, 1968.

4 Quoted by Alvarez, *The New Poetry*, Harmondsworth, Penguin, 1962, p. 17.

5 It is an argument developed by Mark Kinkead-Weekes, in his essay on the novel in *D. H. Lawrence and the Modern World*, London, Macmillan, 1980.

6 Auden, op. cit., p. 285.

7 Hobsbaum, op. cit., p. 8.

8 ibid., p. 278.

9 E. M. Forster, *Abinger Harvest*, London, Edward Arnold, 1936, pp. 87–8.

10 *D. H. Lawrence: Poems*, selected and introduced by Keith Sagar, revised edition, Harmondsworth, Penguin, 1986, p. 15.

11 Holly Laird, *Self and Sequence: The Poetry of D. H. Lawrence*, Charlottesville, Va, University of Virginia Press, 1988, p. 48.

12 Flint's poem may be found in *Imagist Poetry*, edited by Peter Jones, Harmondsworth, Penguin, 1972, p. 80.

13 Amy Clampitt's poem 'Gradual Clearing' is in her collection, *The Kingfisher*, London, Faber, 1984, p. 18.

14 Donald Davie, *Under Briggflats, A History of Poetry in Great Britain,*

1960–1988, Manchester, Carcanet, 1989, p. 128.

15 The poem is to be found in Marianne Moore, *Complete Poems*, London, Faber, 1984, pp. 117–20.

16 Hobsbaum, op. cit., p. 147.

Reading list

The standard edition of the poems is *The Complete Poems of D. H. Lawrence*, edited by Vivian de Sola Pinto and Warren Roberts, Harmondsworth, Penguin, 1977. (The edition was first published in two volumes by Heinemann, 1964.)

The key individual volumes of poems which appeared in Lawrence's lifetime are:

Love Poems and Others, London, Duckworth, 1913
Amores, London, Duckworth, 1916
Look! We Have Come Through!, London, Chatto & Windus, 1917
New Poems, London, Secker, 1918; New York, 1920
Birds, Beasts and Flowers, London, Secker, 1923
Collected Poems, London, Secker, 1928; this is important for Lawrence's own introductory notes as well as for revisions to early poems
Pansies, London, Secker, 1929.

The Phoenix edition of the *Complete Poems*, in three volumes, was published in 1957. There is also a Penguin selection, by Keith Sagar, Harmondsworth, 1972, revised, 1986.

So far two volumes of the letters have appeared in *The Cambridge Edition of the Letters of D. H. Lawrence*, under the general editorship of James T. Boulton. There is also a two-volume edition by Harry T. Moore, London, Heinemann, 1962, although this leaves out letters included in Aldous Huxley's edition of 1932 from which a Penguin selection was made in 1950.

There is a good selection of Lawrence's literary criticism made by

Anthony Beal, London, Mercury Press, 1961, and the Penguin *Selected Essays* (1st edn 1950) is also to be recommended.

For biography see Harry T. Moore, *The Intelligent Heart*, Harmondsworth, Penguin, 1960. There are also Paul Delany's *D.H. Lawrence's Nightmare: The Writer and his Circle in the Years of the Great War*, Hassocks, Harvester Press, 1979, which is invaluable on Lawrence during the years of the Great War, and Martin Green's *Mountain of Truth: The Counter Culture Begins, Ascona 1900–1920*, New Jersey, University Press of New England, 1986, which has a fascinating account of the cultural ethos to which Frieda belonged and to which she introduced Lawrence. Also to be noted is Emile Delavenay's *D.H. Lawrence and Edward Carpenter: A Study in Edwardian Transition*, London, Heinemann, 1971, which usefully establishes the context in which 'Whitmania' developed in England during the last years of the nineteenth century and the early years of this century.

There is not very much criticism of Lawrence's poetry, and of what there is by no means all is to be recommended. A recent full-length study by Holly A. Laird, *Self and Sequence: The Poetry of D.H. Lawrence*, Charlottesville, Va, University of Virginia Press, 1988, valuably establishes the chronology of the poems and therefore helps us to understand the ordering of the major sequences. There are two excellent general essays: by A. Alvarez in his *The Shaping Spirit: Studies in Modern English and American Poets*, first published in London by Chatto & Windus, 1958, reprinted in London by Grey Arrow, 1963; and by W.H. Auden, in his *The Dyer's Hand*, New York, Viking, 1968, first published in England by Faber & Faber in 1963. There is also an enthusiastic pamphlet on the poems, especially *Pansies*, by Charles Davey, *D.H. Lawrence: A Living Poet*, London, Brentham Press, 1985. Graham Hough has a useful chapter on the poems in *The Dark Sun: A Study of D.H. Lawrence*, Harmondsworth, Penguin, 1961, first published in London by Duckworth, 1956, as does Keith Sagar in his *D.H. Lawrence: Life Into Art*, Harmondsworth, Penguin, 1985. There are also two chapters of interest in Philip Hobsbawm's *Reader's Guide to D.H. Lawrence*, London, Thames & Hudson, 1988. Two important essays on individual poems are: Tom Paulin, ' "Hibiscus and Salvia Flowers": the Puritan Imagination', in *D.H. Lawrence in the Modern World*, edited by Peter Preston and Peter Hoare, London, Macmillan, 1988, and F.R. Leavis, on 'Piano', in 'Thought and emotional quality in poetry', *Scrutiny*, vol. 13, no. 1, Spring, 1945. Part of this essay is reprinted by H. Coombes, in his *D.H. Lawrence: Penguin Critical*

Anthology, Harmondsworth, Penguin, 1973, which also contains reviews of Lawrence's poetry by, among others, Edward Thomas and Ezra Pound. Essays on the poetry also occur from time to time in *The D.H. Lawrence Review*. I also recommend the essay by R.P. Blackmur, 'D.H. Lawrence and expressive form', in his *Language as Gesture*, London, Allen & Unwin, 1954. Blackmur's essay seems to me entirely wrongheaded but invaluable in making one realize why that particular formalist approach to Lawrence can never cope with his best poetry.

Notes

HYMNS IN A MAN'S LIFE

This brief essay first appeared in *The Evening News*, London, 13 October 1928. It is invaluable to an understanding of Lawrence, both in its Blakeian insistence on 'the sheer delight of a child's apperception . . . based on *wonder*', and because of the preference Lawrence shows for 'healthy hymns' over 'sentimental messes'. The man who voices this preference is recognizably the same man who said that tragedy should be a great kick at misery. However, it needs to be said that Lawrence's poems do not have the regular, emphatic metres of the hymns he here writes about so lovingly. Unlike Thomas Hardy, who made much use of the metres – and even diction – of hymns, Lawrence felt himself too separated from the community in which as a boy he had sung the hymns to be able to make use of them.

THE WILD COMMON

A later version of this poem is printed in the Appendix. This later version is Lawrence's attempt to 'let the demon say his say'. Yet in many ways the first version feels preferable. For all that Lawrence begins with a basically four-stress line, this is soon lost and as a result the poem gains in rhythmic suppleness; and although there are awkward syntactic inversions – often in the interest of securing rhyme – the poem is more adventurous than most verse of the period. Its 'paganism', its celebration of the body, may seem very much a then contemporary cliché, but to compare it with the swimming scene in *A Room with a View*, or the pallid eroticism of Rupert Brooke's circle, is to recognize that while Lawrence's poem may in some senses derive from the same sources, it has an energy and a quick intensity that set it apart. (For the Brooke circle see Paul Delany, *The Neo-Pagans: Friendship and Love in the Rupert Brooke Circle*, London, Hamish Hamilton, 1988.) The influence of Whitman, via Edward Carpenter, is also important in this context. It was Carpenter who had predicted the coming of a newly liberated post-Christian man: 'Once more in sacred groves will he reunite the passion and the delight of human love with his deepest feelings of the sanctity and beauty of Nature; or in the open, standing uncovered to the Sun, will adore the emblem of the everlasting splendour which shines within.' (*Civilisation: Its Cause and Cure*, 1889, reprinted 1906). Whether Lawrence had read the book I do not know, but he would have heard of the Sheffield-based Carpenter from his socialist friend, Willie Hopkin. I doubt even so that it can fairly be claimed that Lawrence was deeply influenced by Carpenter, although Emile Delavenay thinks otherwise. It is more that Carpenter gives utterance to ideas that were 'in the air'; and it is typical of Lawrence to seize on what he wants and turn that to his own account. The poem's title is then important. 'The *Wild* Common' is a place of untamed and unenclosed activity: of a life not fenced in by law and – by implication – moderation, constraint, denial. It is moreover a place where anyone can go: a spot of old, unregenerate England.

DISCORD IN CHILDHOOD

A poem which draws on much of the same autobiographical material as *Sons and Lovers*. As with the novel, Lawrence is less ready to apportion blame than is often asserted. The 'slender lash / Whistling delirious rage' may be drowned by the other 'in a silence of blood', but this does not make that other, male voice, the more guilty. Besides the 'silence of blood' perhaps means that love-making replaces the quarrel, leaving the 'noise of the ash' to drown the sounds of such love-making. If so, the poem is about anguish which is not confined to the narrator's recall of parental antagonism.

CHERRY ROBBERS, CRUELTY AND LOVE, SNAP-DRAGON

Very much a young man's poems, but unusual because of the candour with which sexual longings are expressed. 'Cruelty and Love' inaugurates a way of thinking about relationships between women and men that intermittently obsesses Lawrence, and which finds late and unpleasant expression in *The Plumed Serpent* and 'The Woman Who Rode Away'. In both these works women gladly, so we are told, surrender themselves to masterful, even murderous, men.

A COLLIER'S WIFE, VIOLETS, THE BEST OF SCHOOL

Early reviewers rightly praised the two dialect poems when they appeared in Lawrence's first volume of poems. Lawrence also used the subject-matter of both in short stories and plays. He was deeply impressed by the vivacity of vocabulary and rhythms of Nottingham dialect. 'Dialect' poetry in English coincides with the rise of 'orthodox' or 'standard' English, in the middle years of the eighteenth century. Like Hardy's Tess, the young Lawrence spoke two languages: standard English at school, dialect at home. His mother's aspirations pushed him away from the language he spoke as a child and from the culture that went with it. Becoming a schoolteacher was, for the class from which Lawrence came, an attainment of very great respectability. 'The Best of School' reads in part like a recruitment speech for the teaching profession, especially where Lawrence talks of the stem of his life 'That bears aloft towards rarer skies / My top of life, that buds on high / Amid the high wind's enterprise'. On the other hand, the sense of the boys' separate lives is a matter Lawrence will explore in the section in *The Rainbow* that deals with Ursula's experiences as a schoolteacher. And this belongs to his great work as an imaginative writer.

END OF ANOTHER HOME-HOLIDAY

There is a good account of this in A. Alvarez's essay. See also the Introduction.

THE BRIDE, SORROW, PIANO

A natural sequence. There is an excellent account of the last poem in the essay by F. R. Leavis referred to in the *Reading list*. It is important that Lawrence, for all his anguished feelings, does not yield to 'sentimental mess'. To 'weep like a child for the past' is to acknowledge that you aren't a child;

and the terrible sadness of watching the grey hairs 'float up the dark chimney' is to acknowledge the inevitability of death, and thus to transcend morbidity. It is also worth noting the delicately repeated rhymes that sew together the stanzas of 'Sorrow'. Their very unobtrusiveness both connects the present musing to a particular moment in the past and refuses to overemphasize it. The kind of recall is post-Wordsworthian. The poem's imaginative movement is entirely Lawrence's. What is inevitable also permits a certain freeing from the past. This is handled with the utmost scrupulousness, but it means that in no sense can the poem be thought of as emotionally regressive, because it is too aware of the dangers of such regression. However, for a more critical view, see Philip Hobsbaum's remarks in *A Reader's Guide to D.H. Lawrence*, pp. 15–16.

PARLIAMENT HILL IN THE EVENING

A post-Whistlerian piece of verse impressionism of a kind to be found among such poets as Arthur Symons (1865–1945) and the Rhymers Club, that group of London poets whose fame during the 1890s and the early years of this century has now more or less faded into nothing. Lawrence, it is clear, could manage this kind of poem as well as any of them. So much for C.H. Sisson's claim that he lacked an ear or metrical skill. For examples of the kind of poem Lawrence is imitating see *British Poetry and Prose 1870–1905*, edited by I. Fletcher (London, Oxford University Press, 1987).

THE NORTH COUNTRY

Here, the influence of Whitman is clear, both in the diction and in the attitudinizing. 'The moaning of sleep-bound beings in travail that toil and are will-less there / In the spell-bound north . . .' See the Introduction for further comment.

GIORNO DEI MORTI

Of this poem, written in 1912, Philip Hobsbaum says: 'The economy of meaning is at one with the precision of language. This experience is not only seen but recreated and projected. It was a poet who found those precise particulars – the round dark heads of the men, the black-scarved faces of the women, the *forgotten*, folded hands of the father, the pale *shut* face of the mother. The poem is lucid without being commonplace and it is vivid without becoming hectic' (*A Reader's Guide to D.H. Lawrence*, p. 21). Hobsbaum is also surely right to draw attention to the less than heavy stressing of rhyme, so that what we have is 'a para-rhyme varying in assonance according to the degree of emphasis required'. Moreover, the poem finely catches Lawrence's ability to enter into the entire meaning of a scene, so that what is recorded is by no means limited to the purely visual, but takes up the emotional involvement of a community in the fact and yet mystery of death. In its absorption of the mystery, its implicit rejection of mere matter-of-fact rationalism, the poem therefore anticipates such late works as 'Bavarian Gentians' and 'The Ship of Death'.

EDWARD THOMAS: REVIEW OF *LOVE POEMS AND OTHERS*

This review appeared in the *Bookman*, April 1913. Thomas (1878–1917) was a wonderfully gifted critic, as Edna Longley's generous selection of his prose reveals (*A Language Not to Be Betrayed*, Manchester, Carcanet, 1981). At the time he wrote this review Thomas was beginning to produce the poems he had denied that he was capable of writing and which make him one of the finest of all English poets of the twentieth century. It is tempting to think that the appearance of *Love Poems and Others* may have helped spring his own poems from the dark where they had for so long gestated.

REVIEW OF *GEORGIAN POETRY, 1911–1912*

Lawrence's review appeared in the journal *Rhythm*, in March 1913. For his brief involvement with the anthology and its joint editor, Edward Marsh, see the Introduction.

EXTRACTS FROM TWO LETTERS TO EDWARD MARSH

Written in October and November 1913. In the first of these Lawrence distances himself from his fellow-contributors to the Georgian anthology. W.H. Davies (1871–1940) had become famous following the publication of his *Autobiography of a Super-Tramp* (1908). His first volume of poems,

The Soul's Destroyer and Other Poems, had been published in 1905, and in spite of the fame his autobiography won him he wanted always to be thought of as a poet. Ralph Hodgson (1871–1962) was another contributor to the anthology. He is probably best remembered now for T.S. Eliot's lines, 'How delightful to meet Mr. Hodgson', although the publication of *The Last Blackbird and Other Poems* (1907) secured him a contemporary reputation. For more on Davies and Hodgson, and the Georgians as a whole, see Delany's *The Neo-Georgians*, C.K. Stead's *The New Poetic* (London, Hutchinson, 1964), and Joy Grant's *Harold Munro and the Poetry Bookshop* (London, Routledge & Kegan Paul, 1967). The second letter is crucial because of Lawrence's statement that for him metre is to be thought of as 'a bird with broad wings flying and lapsing through the air'. The poem chosen to demonstrate his theory of scansion is Ernest Dowson's 'Non sum qualis eram bonae sub regno Cynarae', one of the most famous of all poems of the 1890s. Lawrence's poem, 'Roses on the Breakfast Table', was one of the sequence that became *Look! We Have Come Through!* It is worth noting how aggressive-defensive he becomes about his use of rhyme. The ballad referred to is a poor one, 'The Ballad of a Wayward Woman', which Marsh was right to criticize.

56 *the Sapphic form* Derived from the Greek lyric poet, Sappho, it is a four-line stanza with a short final line. Swinburne used it in a poem called, in fact, 'Sapphics'.

> All the night sleep came not upon my eyelids,
> Shed not dew, nor shook nor unclosed a feather,
> Yet with lips shut close and with eyes of iron
>   Stood and beheld me.

EXTRACT FROM A LETTER TO HENRY SAVAGE

Savage was a literary journalist and would-be poet with whom Lawrence had much correspondence at this period of his life. The account of Whitman is of crucial importance to an understanding of Lawrence's abiding preoccupation with the great American poet. The liking for Gilbert Murray's pre-Raphaelite-style translations is rather more surprising, but at least reminds us that Lawrence had grown up in the heyday of the reputation of Swinburne and Morris as poets.

Harriet Monroe (1860–1936) in 1912 founded and edited *Poetry: A Magazine of Verse*. Ezra Pound acted as her English editor/adviser and pressed on her many poets, including his cluster of imagists, among them Lawrence.

3 *Amy* Amy Lowell, who took over from Pound the editing of imagist anthologies ('Amygism' was Pound's term for the work she promoted); Lawrence is here referring to her prose poem, 'Bombardment'.

7 *Aldington* Richard Aldington, later to become Lawrence's biographer, and at this time part of literary London and married to Hilda Doolittle, had published 'War Yawp' in *Poetry*.

9 *'Hero'* McCarthy's 'Hero' is about rape and slaughter as was much of the literature and art of the early war years.

27 *'Campfollower'* a poem by the American poet, Maxwell Bodenheim

30 *my poem* Lawrence's own poem seems to have been 'Eloi, Eloi, Lama Sabachthani', which was published in the *Egoist* in 1915, and never collected.

For all this information see *The Cambridge Edition of the Letters of D.H. Lawrence*, Volume II, pp. 232–3. Note that already Lawrence is anti-war, and this at the moment when war hysteria had gripped the vast majority of Europe.

POEM AND LETTER TO LADY CYNTHIA ASQUITH

This poem was enclosed with a letter to Lady Asquith and, according to a helpful note of the Cambridge editors of the *Letters*, was, so she confided to her diary, part of Lawrence's attempt to convince her 'that we ought to "down tools". He appears to think that I could stop the war, if only I really wanted to! He writes wildly about the disintegrating process of war etc. . . .' (quoted in the Cambridge edition of the *Letters*, Volume II, p. 424). Not all of us would want to share Lady Asquith's conviction that Lawrence's remarks are wild, but they certainly indicate the intensity of his hatred for the war. For more on this, see the Introduction.

THE SEA

A strange poem which may owe something to Whitman (and to the use of Whitman which Vaughan Williams had made in *A Sea Symphony*, first performed in 1910). Lawrence takes the sea as a kind of male principle, also as associated with non-communicability, chaste and alone. It is a poem of posture, its rhythms ample but unauthentic: very literary. And very unlike the poems that follow.

GREEN, RIVER ROSES, GLOIRE DE DIJON, A DOE AT EVENING, CRAVING FOR SPRING

From the sequence *Look! We Have Come Through!*; Lawrence adds the place to which the scene of each poem applies because he regards the sequence as a kind of progress, if an erratic one. He and Frieda had stayed at Icking, on the River Isar, between June and August 1912. This is their 'honeymoon period'. Irschenhausen is about a mile north of Icking. Zennor is in Cornwall, where the Lawrences lived for a miserable time during the war years, and when the early joy of married life had departed for something more complex and, often, troubling. The fullest and most generous account of the poems that make up the sequence is to be found in Holly Laird's *Self and Sequence: The Poetry of D. H. Lawrence* (Charlottesville, Va, University of Virginia Press, 1988). Lawrence's plea in 'Craving for Spring' for spring to 'stir the rotten globe of the world' should be compared to the letter from Zennor quoted in the Introduction (pp. 14–15) and to Paul Delany's *D. H. Lawrence's Nightmare*. The poem is written out of a mood which fluctuates between despair and ardent desire for the renovation of 'world anew'. Laird refers to Shelley's 'Ode to the West Wind' which Lawrence certainly knew, but the echo is inconsiderable.

AFTER THE OPERA

This anticipates the method of *Pansies*, but is better written than most of them and has about it the novelist's ready response to a social scene which comes to involve him more deeply and problematically than initially seemed possible. The observant, slightly condescending outsider who stands and smiles, suddenly finds himself drawn into keener awareness of – not tragedy, certainly, but pain, exhaustion, human accountability. 'But when I meet the weary eyes / The reddened aching eyes of the bar-man with thin arms, / I am glad to go back where I came from.' The poem was probably written at the end of the war, in London; and it does suggest that 'where

I came from' isn't to be read merely literally. Lawrence catches himself out, as it were, and suddenly realizes that he has less in common with the social world of 'girls with their large eyes wide with tragedy' than the 'bar-man with thin arms'. This is not to make him a socialist, but we cannot avoid recognizing that the issue here touched on will be confronted again, most revealingly, perhaps, in 'Hibiscus and Salvia Flowers'. And we may then wish to consider whether Lawrence's ferocious outburst to David Garnett, quoted in the Introduction, might not have as much to do with the class of the people at whom he directed it as with England itself. Or alternatively, it might be that he could see no hope for an England which even after the events of the war years was, he sensed, about to return to the stewardship of those people for whom 'tragedy' was almost certainly as unreal as the *grand guignol* of opera.

JOHN GOULD FLETCHER: FROM A REVIEW OF *LOOK! WE HAVE COME THROUGH!*

This review appeared in Harriet Monroe's *Poetry* in August 1918. Gould Fletcher (1886–1950) was an American poet and critic closely associated with *Poetry*. The review usefully identifies the importance of Whitman to Lawrence, and in view of how little of Edward Thomas's poetry had by then been published, Gould Fletcher's dismissal of him is to be forgiven.

INTRODUCTION TO *NEW POEMS*

New Poems was first published in England by Secker in 1918 and crept almost unnoticed into the world. It was a tiny paperbound volume which sold for two shillings and sixpence and Lawrence's advance was £6/5 shillings. When it was published he was in deep depression. But by the time of the American edition, 1920, Lawrence's life had undergone a great change for the better as the joyous introduction he wrote for the new edition suggests. Here, he sets out most compellingly his commitment to free verse, significantly distinguishing it from *vers libre*, which he dismisses as 'fragments', without 'the instant; the quick; the very jetting source of all will-be and has-been'. It is of course easy to see in this orgasmic language the self-styled priest of love 'off on the preach again'. But it is important to notice that Lawrence had served a long apprenticeship as poet, and that when he wrote these words he had not only produced more poetry than many poets manage in a lifetime, but that – as the letter on scansion to Edward Marsh makes clear – he had thought deeply about poetic rhythm. If we take this introduction together with the essay on Whitman, it enables us to see how the seeds for the great poems of the following years had been nurtured and could now spring up with such seemingly effortless energy and delight.

HUMAN RELATIONS AND THE UNCONSCIOUS, FROM *PSYCHOANALYSIS AND THE UNCONSCIOUS*

Written in 1920 and published in 1921. This is the last chapter of a book which according to Philip Rieff was 'laughed away by the reviewers, without exception' (Introduction to the 1959 Viking Press edition). However, the young W. H. Auden admired it very much indeed. There are several allusions to the book in his early work and he was obviously much taken by Lawrence's desire to free sex from the rational will and to return it to concrete unconsciousness. 'Human Relations and the Unconscious' provides a way of breaking free of what Lawrence calls the hideous tyranny 'of an automatically ideal humanity'. This is why he asserts that 'Man doth not live by bread alone. It is time we made haste to settle the bread question, which after all is only the A B C of social economies, and proceeded to devote our attention to this much more profound and vital question: how to establish and maintain the circuit of vital polarity from which the psyche actually develops.' We need to recall that this was being written in the context of the aftermath of the Russian revolution, of the post-war humili-ation of Germany and the struggle of the socialists there to establish a new, radical democracy (a struggle which the army and police of course put an end to); and the radical energies of the anarchists and socialists in Italy, whom Lawrence confronts in 'Hibiscus and Salvia Flowers'. All over Europe, in fact, the possibilities of socialism seemed to be moving towards realization, either immediately or in the foreseeable future.

WHITMAN

Although this was not published in book form until 1924, in *Studies in Classic American Literature*, it was written in 1918.

375 *Henley's rant* a reference to the English poet and literary journalist W. E. Henley (1849–1903), from whose 'Out of the night that covers me' Lawrence quotes the last two lines.

HIBISCUS AND SALVIA FLOWERS

The context in which to place this poem is now, I hope, established. As Tom Paulin says, it was written ' "to the moment", and represents a volatile complex engagement with Italian socialism'. Paulin's essay deserves close attention, although I think he perhaps narrows the poem's range of implicit references when he says that it depends 'on an interplay between [Lawrence's] sense of the condition of Britain and the developing political situation in Italy'. Still, that situation was undoubtedly volatile: either socialists or fascists might have won. But what Lawrence yearns for is the destruction of 'this vast rotting cabbage patch we call the world', and the birth of 'New wild souls'. These are the souls – the psyches – whose development from 'the circuit of vital polarity' he desires at the end of *Psychoanalysis and the Unconscious*.

POMEGRANATE

Note that both here and in 'The Mosquito' Venice is treated at best dismissively. Earlier generations of English writers had seen Venice as the most enchanting and liberated of all Italian cities, but by the time Lawrence came to it it was, or so he said in his letters, chiefly remarkable for its stink. It was also, therefore, a place of death – the stink of the canals indicative of the malarial fevers which struck down inhabitants and visitors alike. Thomas Mann's great story, *Death in Venice*, was published in German in 1911, and by 1913 Lawrence was becoming familiar with Mann's work (see Volume II of the Cambridge edition of the *Letters*, p. 147).

The poems from *Birds, Beasts and Flowers* which appear in this selection are not printed in the order in which they were written, but in the order in which Lawrence arranged them. They are thus out of order chronologically and with regard to where they were written; but they are in order of: 'Fruits', 'Creatures', 'Reptiles', 'Birds', 'Animals'. Lawrence put 'Pomegranate' at the beginning of the volume presumably because he wanted the opening lines to act as a calculated affront to the reader. From this challenging opening he moves on to consider the pomegranate within various places where it grows. It means most to him in Tuscany because there is an old, aristocratic way of life associated with Florence which is in some way – how is not made clear – connected to fullness and sexuality, where these things are themselves intimately connected to a manner of social living that isn't 'on the plain side'. Yeats had already made this connection in certain poems in *Responsibilities* (1914). The 'you' who tries to tell Lawrence he is wrong is, presumably, representative of modern prudential values. Tuscan Italy is therefore not merely an embodiment of freedom, it signals traditional values, of order and rootedness.

MEDLARS AND SORB-APPLES

Medlars are small fruit, resembling crab apples, which become edible only when they start to decay. The same is apparently true of sorb-apples. Through associations of colour and fermentation Lawrence connects the fruit to Marsala, a dark, sweet wine made in Sicily. Sicily was where Persephone was carried off to hell by Pluto. Lawrence then links this primal myth of death and rebirth of the seasons to Orpheus descending to the underworld in pursuit of Eurydice. A further link is made to Dionysos, the Greek god of wine, whose festival revelries are associated with fertility myths and the regeneration of the earth by sacrifice (wine poured on it, symbolic of blood). The poem is, then, a part playful, part searching evocation and probing for these deep connections of sexuality with the rhythms of birth and death.

FIGS

As with the preceding poems, Lawrence daringly imagines the fruit in terms of female sexuality, and this is expressive of his deepening concern to search out that cosmic wholeness which he writes about most emphatically in *Apocalypse*.

33 *rosaceæ* a family of flowering plants, including many types of fruit tree.

35 *ricotta* a soft, white, unsalted cheese made from sheep's milk.

9 *Winged Victory*   The joke is, of course, that the goddess so worshipped
by the Greeks and the Romans, sister of Strength and Valour and one
of the attendants of Jupiter, winged and crowned with laurel, should
here have degenerated to an insect. But in 'sluggish Venice' the winged
victory would presumably be at least potentially a killer, since
mosquitoes were the carriers of malaria.

SNAKE

A great poem. In his biography of Lawrence, *The Intelligent Heart*, Harry
T. Moore helpfully quotes something Lawrence had written a few years
previously, in an essay, 'The Reality of Peace'.

> If there is a serpent of secret and shameful desire in my soul, let me not
> beat it out of my consciousness with sticks. . . . For a serpent is a thing
> created. It has its own *raison d'être*. In its own being it has beauty and
> reality. Even my horror is a tribute to its reality. And I must admit the
> genuineness of my horror, accept it, and not exclude it from my under-
> standing. . . . But since it is spring with me, the snake must wreathe
> his way secretly along the paths that belong to him, and when I see him
> asleep in the sunshine I shall admire him in his place.
>
> (*The Intelligent Heart*, Harmondsworth, 1960, p. 332)

By the time he wrote the poem, Lawrence had to some extent moved
beyond the horror: that, now, is at first confined to 'The voice of my
education'. In Taormina, in Sicily, the snake is a god. But as a god of the
underworld he is associated with death and so horror returns. But then
again, Lawrence considers that his action of throwing a stick is like the
mariner's killing of the albatross: an offence against 'one of the lords / Of
life'. Again, acceptance of what *is*, as part of cosmic wholeness, is crucial.
That is why Lawrence must expiate 'a pettiness'. The pettiness is his denial
of a part of creation.

TORTOISES

Six poems which compose a sequence. Graham Hough calls it 'probably the
most sustained attempt in literature to penetrate the mysterious life of a

remote part of the brute creation. From the naked, solitary independence of the baby tortoise to the weird cry of the male tortoise in the extremity of coition a small organic unit of non-human existence is brought as far as it can be within human imaginative comprehension' (*The Dark Sun*, p. 237). This is well put, as is Philip Hobsbaum's remark that the sequence 'is a brilliant amalgam of natural description, comic characterisation and apprehension of the life force which drives the world' (*A Reader's Guide to D.H. Lawrence*, p. 134).

EAGLE IN NEW MEXICO

A deeply disturbing poem. Yeats had already begun to feature the eagle as a symbol of aristocratic hauteur, embodying arrogance, splendour, and a ruthless contempt for littleness. It can stare into the sun. It is the king of the birds. The fascists adopted the eagle as an emblem. For Lawrence, it is associated with a pitiless magnificence, to which he says he will not yield. Yet he is clearly fascinated by the idea of 'a bond of bloodshed' and his invocation of Aztec priests who 'used to lift red hearts of men' anticipates a note that will be heard again, more insistently and much more frighteningly, in *The Plumed Serpent* and 'The Woman Who Rode Away'. While the last lines may initially seem to break the spell the bird has cast, closer inspection shows that if it is 'put out of office as sacrifice bringer', that is because men will take over as sacrificers. And there is nothing to show that Lawrence does not welcome this. The massive, implacable movement about the lines clearly fascinated later poets such as Ted Hughes, who virtually parodies this Lawrence in his famous 'Hawk Roosting'. Hughes's poem is perhaps intended as something of a criticism of Lawrence's poem: the hawk's solipsistic egotism is, finally, absurd. Lawrence, however, grants the eagle a power that is not meant to be absurd and would not have been felt to be so in the 1920s, where the worst, in Yeats's words, 'are full of passionate intensity'. The politics of Lawrence's poem, and it *is* a political poem, is an unhealthy brew of Nietzschean superman strenuousness and that fascism which Lawrence had come into contact with in Italy and to which he had responded with some fervour.

THE ASS, HE-GOAT, SHE-GOAT

By contrast the poem 'The Ass', which was of course written earlier, is an altogether more unproblematic and enjoyable affair, as are the paired poems, 'He-Goat' and 'She-Goat'. It was the former that Auden picked out for especial praise (see his essay in *The Dyer's Hand*).

KANGAROO

The Lawrences sailed to Australia in 1922, having left Sicily in February of that year. Although their stay in Australia lasted only some three months it resulted in the novel *Kangaroo* and this great poem. If I could choose only one poem of Lawrence's to represent him at his best, this would be it. It is beyond criticism, its powers of observation matched by the depths of its apprehension of the sheer strangeness of 'that silent lost land of the South'. Something of that silence, that lost land, is to be found in the paintings of Arthur Boyd and Sidney Nolan, and in the novels of Patrick White. It is also touched on in a poem, 'South Country', by Kenneth Slessor.

> And over the flat earth of empty farms
> The monstrous continent of air floats back
> Coloured with rotting sunlight and the black,
> Bruised flesh of thunderstorms:
>
> Air arched, enormous, pounding the bony ridge,
> Ditches and hutches, with a drench of light,
> So huge, from such infinities of height,
> You walk on the sky's beach
>
> While even the dwindled hills are small and bare,
> As if, rebellious, buried, pitiful,
> Something below pushed up a knob of skull,
> Feeling its way to air.

That is very fine. But then Slessor and the others I have mentioned are all Australasian. Lawrence's grasp of the sheer strangeness of the subcontinent came from a three-month visit.

A poem that again moves towards a disturbing conclusion. 'And I think in the world beyond, how easily we might spare a million or two of humans / And never miss them.' Even if one says that Lawrence came to this mood out of anger at the shooting of the mountain lion, there is a sinister edge to his thoughts, a readiness to entertain the androphobia which had perhaps driven him from Europe and which seemed to flourish in the air of New Mexico.

REVIEW OF *A SECOND CONTEMPORARY VERSE ANTHOLOGY*

This review first appeared in the New York *Evening Post Literary Review*, 29 September 1923. It shows how marvellous a critic Lawrence was. His choice of 'classics' is of course unsurprising: Byron ('There Be None of Beauty's Daughters'), Gray (*Elegy Written in a Country Churchyard* – 'Now fades the glimmering landscape'), and, inevitably, Whitman ('When lilacs last . . .'). I would guess that Lawrence's acquaintance with the poets was limited to the more obvious names of the past. He knew what he liked and, more important, needed; and I doubt that he was much bothered with the rest.

CORASMIN AND THE PARROTS

From *Mornings in Mexico*, published in 1927. The essay was written in 1924. Although the Lawrences lived in Taos, New Mexico, from late 1922 until 1924, they spent much time travelling. The first visit to Mexico took place in March 1923, and there were thereafter regular visits, including one of nearly a year, 1924–5, after which they left for Italy, never to return. 'Corasmin and the Parrots' is a good example of Lawrence at his most informal, delighted (and delightful). He was a great travel writer, as *Twilight in Italy* and perhaps supremely *Sea and Sardinia* (1923) make clear. If it at first seems extraordinary that the man who wrote 'Eagle in New Mexico' should be the same man who could write this enchanting essay, it may help to note that the androphobe of Zennor was also loved by his Zennor neighbours' children, with whom he played, for whom he devised games, and on whom he lavished hours of careful attention, even to the point of running-up dolls' dresses. 'Do I contradict myself? Very well then

I contradict myself.' Lawrence would have agreed with Whitman's wry acknowledgement that 'I contain multitudes'.

EXTRACT FROM THE NIGHTINGALE

This glorious piece of knockabout but spot-on criticism was first published in *Forum* and the *Spectator*, both journals carrying the essay in September 1927.

EXTRACT FROM CHAOS IN POETRY

In his note to this, Anthony Beal says that it was first written in 1928 as part of a preface to *Chariot of the Sun*, by Harry Crosby, but first published in *Exchanges*, 1929. Crosby was a very minor poet but a reckless liver, who took part in a suicide pact with a woman friend in a hotel in New York, 1929. He had been editor and publisher of the Black Sun Press, had read and been much impressed by *The Plumed Serpent* (never a good sign), and offered Lawrence large sums of money for some of his stories, to be published by the press. The planned introduction to Crosby's poems is masterful in saying nothing about them, but concentrating instead on Lawrence's familiar theme: the need to break out of the familiar, to find new worlds. This concern to 'de-familiarize' the world is a central tenet of modernism, but in Lawrence it has a unique unfakable verve. For the relations between Lawrence and Crosby see Caresse Crosby: *The Passionate Years* (London, Alvin Redman, 1955).

INTRODUCTION TO THE PRIVATELY PRINTED EDITION OF *PANSIES*, PUBLISHED 1929

This was written after and in the light of both the banning of *Lady Chatterley's Lover* and the police intervention over the exhibition of Lawrence's paintings at the Warren Gallery, 1929. (For more on these events, see the note to 'Innocent England' below.) Lawrence's introduction to *Pansies* rehearses arguments that he also puts forward in his essay, 'Pornography and Obscenity', first published in the July–September 1929 issue of the magazine *This Quarter* (it is reprinted in Anthony Beal's *D. H. Lawrence: Selected Literary Criticism*). In calling his poems *Pansies* Lawrence is making a double pun. As he points out, the French verb *panser*, which literally means 'to dress' or 'to groom', can be used in the sense of dressing or soothing a wound. He offers his little poems, he says, to soothe the emotional and psychic wounds of English sensibilities. But *Pansies* also recalls Pascal's *Pensées*, to which indeed Lawrence refers, as he does to La Bruyère's *Les Caractères*. Pascal (1623–62) wrote the *Pensées* between 1657 and 1658, although they were not collected together and published until after his death. They are about the nature and problems of religious understanding, and Pascal repeatedly asserts his doubts as to the worth of rational argument in trying to arrive at proof of Christian truth. Intuition might be more important than reason. 'The heart has its reasons, which the reason cannot understand', is perhaps the most famous of his *pensées*, and one likely to appeal to Lawrence, for all his rejection of orthodox Christianity. For, as he himself said, he was a deeply religious man; and this introduction everywhere reveals his contempt for mere 'mind'. To promote intellect at the expense of all else is most dangerously to divide the self against itself.

The *Pansies* also reveal Lawrence's contempt for worldly vanity. Given this, it is obvious that he would have seen much to admire in La Bruyère's *Caractères*. La Bruyère (1645–96) published this collection of epigrams and *aperçus* in 1688. They are brutal in their moral and social revelations, their dismissal of all appeals to worldly values. In their pages we meet Philémon, who prides himself on his clothes and jewels. As a result, so La Bruyère is told, the man is well worth seeing. 'Send me his clothes, then, and keep the man,' he replies. Lawrence would have liked that.

As would Jonathan Swift (1667–1745). There has been much discussion as to where Swift stands in relation to the subject of 'The Lady's Dressing-Room' (1730), from which Lawrence quotes in order to show that Swift was himself horrified by Celia's natural functions. The orthodox view is that Swift was not shocked, but wanted to shock his readers into an acceptance of fallen humanity and to deny them the dream of perfection which human vanity, in whatever guise, tries to flesh out. Under the appearance of flawless beauty is the flawed woman. Under the handsome beau is the diseased rake. Still, it is difficult not to feel that here and in other poems there is more than the satiric moralist at work in Swift's savage indignation at human pride and folly.

It is worth noting that towards the end of this introduction Lawrence warns that 'If the young do not watch out, they will find themselves, before so many years are past, engulfed in a howling manifestation of mob-insanity, truly terrifying to think of.' Four years after he wrote those words Hitler's storm-troopers were in power, rooting out 'decadent filth', and busy promoting, among much else that was terrifying, the concept of 'pure' aryanism.

LIZARD . . . TWO PERFORMING ELEPHANTS

From *Pansies* and *More Pansies*. These are among the better fragmentary pieces on which Lawrence worked during his last years. Charles Davey's pamphlet, *D. H. Lawrence, A Living Poet* (London, Brentham Press, 1985), provides a generous, enthusiastic account of these late works.

NOTTINGHAM'S NEW UNIVERSITY

The Lawrences were back in England from December 1923 until the end of January 1924. Sir Jesse Boot, the chemist, had given money and land on which to construct new university buildings (finished in 1928). They replaced the handsome Gothic structure which had been the original university college and which Lawrence had attended from 1906–8. Before then he had started adult life by working with a firm of manufacturers of surgical goods, called Hayward's. Auden calls this and a number of other, rhyming poems of the late period (they include 'Red-Herring', 'The Little Wowser', and 'Innocent England') satiric doggerel. Satiric doggerel is, Auden argues, 'the weapon of the outsider, the anarchist rebel, who refuses to accept conventional laws and pieties as binding or worthy of respect. Hence its childish technique, for the child represents the naive and personal, as yet uncorrupted by education and convention. . . . At this kind of satiric doggerel, Lawrence turned out to be a master' (*The Dyer's Hand*, p. 295).

INNOCENT ENGLAND

In 1928 *Lady Chatterley's Lover* had been privately printed in Italy. The fact that it was known to have been written and published caused a scandal in England, where Lawrence was considered by the authorities to be virtually a proscribed author. The following spring, the Warren Gallery in London mounted an exhibition of twenty-nine of his paintings. The police raided the exhibition, closed it, and bore off thirteen of the paintings. They also wanted to take some works by Blake, but allowed these to remain when told that the artist had been dead for a hundred years. George Grosz was not so lucky. A copy of his *Ecce Homo* was seized. At first, the pictures were under orders to be burned, but Lawrence persuaded Dorothy Warren to compromise with the police, and the worst was avoided. Lawrence's poem comes out of the episode. It should be noted that Lawrence had always taken painting seriously.

BAVARIAN GENTIANS

The poem exists in more than one version. The Lawrences moved from Italy to Germany in the summer of 1929. According to Harry T. Moore, Lawrence's first title for the poem was 'Glory of Darkness', and he worked on it at Rottach, a hillside village in Bavaria. Lawrence was by then terminally ill with tuberculosis and Frieda feared he might die at any moment (*The Intelligent Heart*, pp. 505–8). The subject-matter of the poem marks a return to 'Medlars and Sorb-Apples', although the tone is very different. As the reference to 'September' sufficiently indicates, this is the season of fast-waning strength, an ode to late autumn, to 'slow, sad Michaelmas'. The feast of Michaelmas, which Lawrence's family probably upheld, falls on 29 September. It is the time of year when the evenings begin to close in, and this sense of encroaching dark – of night, death – is picked up in the first reference to the 'tall and dark' Bavarian gentians. It is as though the flowers have thrust up from Pluto/Dis's underworld, to guide Demeter's daughter Persephone back underground. The rapt movement of the poem, the long, steadily cadenced lines, enact a kind of ritualistic event, one that moves ineluctably from the first announcement of 'soft September' through 'the white-cast day' and 'first-frosted September' – with their suggestions of a coming, final cold – to 'the marriage of the living dark'. There is no protest about this. 'Reach me a gentian, give me a torch!' And later, 'Give me a flower on a tall stem.' Lawrence is entirely conscious of confronting, of going into, the dark, and although one cannot say he desires it, he does not shrink from it. Of course, he is only 'wedding-guest / at the marriage of the living dark', not the bride or groom of darkness. But this is to say no more than that he is fully and tactfully aware that in some sense he will be a faithful witness. Consciousness is all, and living into the moment of death, retaining an avid curiosity to the very last, is something for which other writers have prayed, Henry James and W. B. Yeats among them. Curiosity is not the key-note here, nor even avidity. Wholeness of purpose, however, *is* present in this very remarkable poem. For the variant version, see the appendix.

THE SHIP OF DEATH, SHADOWS

As with 'Bavarian Gentians', 'The Ship of Death' exists in more than one version. And as with 'Bavarian Gentians', I print the version that it seems Lawrence intended as the final one. In an essay called 'D. H. Lawrence's Self-Consciousness', Barbara Hardy remarks that 'in many of the death-poems, repeated images of diminution are touching, slimming down the self, "the little, slender soul", "the fragile soul", and "small frail sail" and "little ark" with "little cakes" ' (*D.H. Lawrence in the Modern World*, p. 44). 'The Ship of Death' refers at least in part to the ancient Egyptian belief that you needed a ship to ferry you across to the land of the dead. In Egyptian tombs, therefore, the dead, mummified body was left with oars and with votive offerings including models of ships and cakes and wine for the voyage. But for Lawrence there is no land of the dead. There is instead oblivion, an entire lapsing out from consciousness. This is a poem of graceful lyricism, and its measured calm can absorb the occasional echo of Tennyson ('dim, calm thoughts and quiet hands') without damage to its originality. As to 'Shadows', it clearly links back through 'Tabernacle' to 'The Ship of Death', and as Holly Laird says, 'such poems acted as the vehicle for Lawrence's strange urge to wrestle through his thoughts in a journey larger than any single poem could encompass' (*Self and Sequence: The Poetry of D.H. Lawrence*, p. 228). I don't myself see anything strange about this urge, though it is certainly a deep, persistent one. She is, however, right to draw attention to *Apocalypse*, where Lawrence insists that 'Today, it is almost impossible for us to realise what the old Greeks meant by god, or *theos*. Everything was *theos*.' This in its turn reminds us of *Birds, Beasts and Flowers*. Lawrence worked on the Apocalypse essay during 1928, though he seems not to have finished it. It was published in 1931. *Apocalypse* is profoundly anti-Christian. Lawrence argues passionately against Christian morality and humility – hate masquerading as love – and on behalf of what he sees as pagan wholeness, acceptance of the entire cosmos. (It is obvious how this can connect to his love of Whitman.) He also announces that 'We are unnaturally resisting our connection with the cosmos', and I assume that here cosmos and God are one: theos. This cosmos may be the 'unknown God' of 'Shadows'. Yet again, the unknown connects to the unfamiliar to make possible a vision of cohesion and completeness. In contrast, the Christian scheme makes for separation rather than 'proper unison'. 'What man most passionately wants,' Lawrence insists, 'is his living wholeness and his living unison, not his own isolate salvation of his "soul". . . . We ought to dance with rapture that we should be alive and in the flesh and part of the living, incarnate cosmos' (*Apocalypse*, New York, Viking Press, 1960, pp. 197–9). The essay deserves to be read against the last poems, for it does much to explain them, in particular the hopes of the ending of 'Shadows': the acceptance of being broken down to the unknown God's oblivion, 'to send me forth on a new morning, a new man'. For the variant versions, see the appendix.